INSIGHT GUIDES **EATING IN**

PARIS

Restaurants
Bars, Pubs
and Cafés

About This Book

In the face of such fierce competition from London and New York, Paris has its work cut out to maintain its reputation as one of the world's culinary capitals. But the new wave of successful contemporary restaurants, and the new generation of innovative young chefs keen to modernise French cuisine, are keeping it firmly on top. That's not to say that the classic red banquette, chalkboard menu and surly waiter experience most visitors to Paris look forward to is in danger of extinction. Traditional bistros and brasseries remain an integral part of the city fabric and the life of its inhabitants who hold their culinary heritage very dear. You only have to look at the concentration of restaurants in each *quartier* to realise that eating out remains a fundamental part of Parisian daily life.

With such an abundance of eateries, however, the choice can be overwhelming. To help you make an informed decision, we assembled a team of writers with a passion for food and asked them to give us a rundown of recommended restaurants for the neighbourhoods they live in, work in, relax in, and love to eat in. We have divided the city up into 8 central districts, with an additional chapter covering the outer *arrondissements*. Each chapter begins with an overview of the area and the type of restaurants you might find there, pinpointing any markets, food shops or other gastronomic landmarks worth a special mention. To help narrow down your choice, we also give our top five recommendations for each area.

The Listings

The listings are organised by type of cuisine or establishment. The Haute Cuisine restaurants for each area are listed first. These are the most expensive Parisian establishments and all need to be booked, in most cases weeks in advance. The places listed under the Bistro and Brasserie headings are, broadly speaking, traditional, though many adopt a more modern approach to traditional bistro or brasserie fare. Those restaurants which fall under the Contemporary category are truly innovative, and in many cases as notable for their designer décor as their ground-breaking cuisine. The cuisine of Southwestern France and Provence are at the forefront in the Regional category, but there are opportunities to sample the cuisine of most of France from Brittany to the Basque country. The International category encompasses everything else, though Italian, Japanese, North-African and Southeast Asian restaurants predominate.

Each restaurant is given a price code *(see below)* for an idea of how much you can expect to spend. The reviews are kept short and to the point; they aim to give an overall impression of the restaurant's food, style and ambience, and the level of service. On the whole they are positive recommendations, but any negative aspects, such as slow service or high noise levels, are pointed out. The information is based on the experience of one person and should only be used as a guide. The restaurant reviews are supplemented by a short-list of recommended bars and pubs for each area.

The Contributors

The guide was compiled by Insight editor Cathy Muscat, with the help of chef and cookery writer Laura Calder. Chapters and features were written by: Laura Calder *(The Islands, Marais and Beaubourg; Bastille, République and Canal St-Martin; Tearooms, Le Fooding, Markets, Wine, Eating Alfresco)*, Gina Doubleday *(Butte-aux-Cailles and Chinatown; Belleville and Ménilmontant)*, Tina Isaac *(Invalides and the 7th)*, Camille Labro *(Montmartre, Pigalle and Batignolles, After Hours)*, Alec Lobrano *(Champs-Elysées)*, Stephen Mudge *(Les Halles, Louvre and Palais Royal; The Latin Quarter and Saint-Germain)*, Adam Sage *(Opéra, Bourse and the Grands Boulevards; Celebrity Chefs)*, Olivia Snaije (*the 14th, 15th, 16th and 17th arrondissements*). Editorial back-up was provided by Clare Peel and Siân Lezard, and the book was proofread by Sylvia Suddes.

How to use this guide

Each restaurant review contains the following information:

Address and grid reference: Each address is given with its *arrondissement* (1st to 20th) and a corresponding grid reference. This refers to the map in the introduction to each area chapter, on which each restaurant is plotted. Metro stations are also clearly marked.

Opening times: B=breakfast, Br=brunch, L=lunch, T=tea, D=dinner. Specific opening times are not given, except where they are exceptional. For more about opening times see page 154.

Price codes: **€** = under **€**25 **€€** = **€**25–40 **€€€** = **€**40–60 **€€€€** = 60+
These prices are based on the cost of an average 3-course dinner per person including half a bottle of house wine, or the cheapest wine available, and any cover or service charge. Lunch is often cheaper.

Website: where the restaurant has its own website with up-to-date information on menus and prices, this has been given.

Editorial

Series Editor **Cathy Muscat**
Editorial Director **Brian Bell**
Art Director **Klaus Geisler**
Picture Manager **Hilary Genin**
Photography **Britta Jaschinski**
Production **Linton Donaldson, Sylvia George**
Cartography **Zoë Goodwin, Laura Morris**

Distribution

UK & Ireland
GeoCenter International Ltd
The Viables Centre, Harrow Way
Basingstoke, Hants RG22 4BJ
Fax: (44) 1256-817988

United States
Langenscheidt Publishers, Inc.
46–35 54th Road,
Maspeth, NY 11378
Fax: (718) 784-0640

Canada
Thomas Allen & Son Ltd
390 Steelcase Road East
Markham, Ontario L3R 1G2
Fax: (1) 905 475-6747

Worldwide
Apa Publications GmbH & Co. Verlag KG (Singapore branch)
38 Joo Koon Road, Singapore 628990
Tel: (65) 6865-1600.
Fax: (65) 6861-6438

Printing

Insight Print Services (Pte) Ltd
38 Joo Koon Road, Singapore 628990
Tel: (65) 6865-1600.
Fax: (65) 6861-6438

First Edition 2004

CONTACTING THE EDITORS
Although every effort is made to provide accurate information, we live in a fast-changing world and would appreciate it if readers would call our attention to any errors or outdated information that may occur by writing to:

Insight Guides, P.O. Box 7910, London SE1 1WE, England. Fax: (44) 20-7403 0290. insight@apaguide.co.uk

Introduction

Listings

Features

Directory

Maps

For individual zone maps, see area chapters

404

69 rue des Gravilliers, 3rd *[page 72]* For fluffy cous-cous and Moroccan mint tea in the Marais.

Fontaine de Mars

129 rue St-Dominique, 7th *[page 118]* For the pretty terrace, tinkling fountain and friendly waiters.

Aux Lyonnais

32 rue St-Marc, 2nd *[page 55]* For modernised Lyonnaise specialities in a low-key but stylish bistro.

Market

15 avenue Matignon, 8th *[page 28]* For East-meets-West cuisine and the trendy buzz.

Le Square Trousseau

1 rue Antoine-Vollon, 12th *[page 87]* For its glorious interior and innovative bistro food.

L'Atelier de Joël Robuchon
5 rue Montalambert, 7th [page 122] For fabulous, affordable food by one of France's top chefs.

Le Train Bleu
Gare de Lyon, 12th [page 83] For a romantic meal in a nostalgic setting.

Le Meurice
Hôtel Meurice, 228 rue de Rivoli, 1st [page 41] For the best of French haute cuisine and a palatial venue.

Café Marly

93 rue de Rivoli, 1st [page 44] For a leisurely lunch overlooking the Louvre.

Allard
41 rue St-André-des-Arts, 6th [page 101] For that Left Bank atmosphere and classic favourites.

Eating Out in Paris

French cuisine – haute or otherwise – has an unrivalled reputation across the globe. This guide brings the best of culinary Paris

There are bistros, brasseries and bakeries; glamorous starred restaurants with views across the Seine; sleek jet-set haunts open late into the night; sprawling markets; street kiosks selling crêpes in winter; exotic canteens with spicy brochettes and beignets; speciality food shops carrying teas, chocolates, caviar, truffles, etc; kitchen stores laden with copper pots and whisks; patisserie windows as colourful as crown jewels; benches for picnics in the parks; café tables tumbling into the streets; and – best of all – a widespread, deep-rooted passion for food that will convert even the most abstemious of souls into *bon vivants.*

From classic to contemporary

Paris has the reputation of being one of the best food cities in the world. However, over the past ten years gastronomic critics have been hard on the French capital, claiming that, unlike in London, New York and Sydney, the culinary scene has been stubbornly slow to evolve. 'Your three-star menus are like funeral processions,' cry the critics. 'Duck à l'orange, again? I had this last time!' There is some truth to these reproaches – France is conservative when it comes to food – but this attitude is not without benefits, especially for visitors, and, furthermore, in many ways it makes sense.

Opposite:* *style, culture and cuisine at the Louvre's Café Marly

The great cuisines of the world can be counted on one hand, and French cuisine is one of them. What the term implies is an established, coherent body of ingredients, techniques and dishes, which have all been studied and perfected by masters of the art over many years. So, if a chef doesn't immediately run out and hurl lemongrass into his coq au vin, it doesn't necessarily mean that he's unimaginative: it simply means that he respects tradition and has enough experience with flavour to know that it's a bad idea. In other words, it could be argued that French cuisine went through its culinary adolescence long ago, and that at this stage there are some taste thrills it considers not worth pursuing. Call it boring if you want to.

This is not to say that French food isn't evolving, because it is – even if cautiously. New flavours are integrated into the cooking all the time. But they are mindfully integrated. Curry, lime, peanut, hot peppers, coconut and lemongrass are all common on gastronomic menus. Most dishes remain French at the core, but exotic nuances are certainly part of the high-end experience. And in the middle ground, couscous is certainly eaten as often as boeuf bourguignon, while sushi now seems to be the city's favourite fast food.

Even in terms of technique, French cooking has modernised; sauces and pastries, for example, tend to be lighter than previously, and vegetables are more preva-

lent on menus. And, menus themselves have been simplified – better aligned to contemporary appetites. Still, it's a slow-and-steady-wins-the-race approach to moving cuisine forward.

The advantage of this from a visitor's perspective is that the classic dishes we dream about abroad can still be found in authentic form on French tables. If you want French onion soup, you can find it, and there'll be no scoop of curry sorbet floating around in it. If you order steak au poivre, out will come that desired slab of beef in a creamy, peppery sauce that spills across the plate towards your crispy pile of frites. No surprises – good, because you didn't want any. There are even a few bistros left where old-style service is still the norm, so when you order, say, rice pudding, you'll be given a family-sized dish from which you can serve yourself until you swear that you'll never want to see rice pudding again for as long as you live.

It can all sound very idyllic, but fear not, the dreadful French restaurant experience still abounds: the flowery wallpaper, those pink polyester napkins, the huffy waiter, the Côtes du Rhône as cold as the North Atlantic, fish cooked beyond recognition and accompanied by asparagus spears on crutches. There's plenty of mediocrity as far as restaurant food goes, but the French are so French about it all that sometimes even the most ghastly meals can have a certain charm.

Another thing that makes French food extraordinary (and the bad French food, on a gracious day, forgivable) is the degree to which it is social. Occasionally, you'll spot someone dashing along the *quai* nibbling at a falafel, but it's quite rare. Even with the increased pace of modern life, the French still believe in sitting down and sharing meals in good company over a bottle of wine. They take time to eat – they make time. In fact, food in France, more than just sustenance, is a lifestyle, and this, if nothing else, is something you'll wish you could pack in your bag and take home with you when you leave.

Top: chef at Le Grand Véfour; cosy dining in L'Apparement Café – popular with the hip Marais crowd

Where to eat

Eateries in Paris are still by and large French: bistros, brasseries, cafés and haute-cuisine establishments. Bistros are small and quaint, serving simple, traditional dishes. The food quality varies from one to the next, unlike the menus, which are practically carbon copies of each other: eggs poached in red wine, potato and herring salad, duck confit, beef daube, chocolate mousse and tarte Tatin – over and over and over again. Brasseries (the louder, brighter, *belle époque* option) offer a range of bistro options, but specialise in seafood – heaps of oysters being shucked by men in overalls outside, platters of mussels, langoustines, lobsters and clams spinning past on waiters' dexterous palms – and Alsatian specialities including choucroûte and plenty of beer. Cafés, in the traditional sense of the term, usually serve sandwiches, notably the ubiquitous Crôque Monsieur (grilled ham and cheese) and a variety of giant composed salads. However, modern 'cafés' – trendy, chic establishments that pack in fashionable crowds – serve full menus, typically of contemporary, cosmopolitan food with a Mediterranean bent.

At the high end, Michelin-starred restaurants range from being gloriously old-fashioned, with truffle-studded foie gras terrines and venison in grand old sauces, to being acrobatically cutting-edge with hot pepper sorbets to cleanse the palate between veal slow-cooked in orange juice and desserts that show off

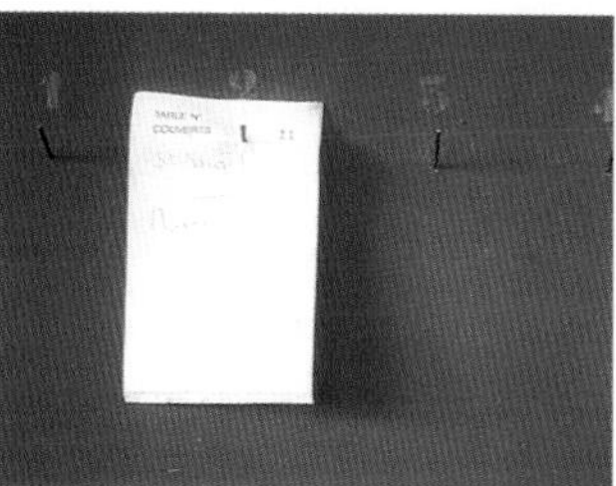

Clockwise from top: pavement terrace at Le 20 in the 7th; refreshments at Le Bistrot du Peintre, Bastille; orders at Chez Nathalie, in the 13th

milk or chocolate in five different ways. One of the best ways to enjoy the starred places is to opt for a tasting menu *(dégustation)*, which affords you hours at the table tasting a host of dishes (in smaller-than-usual portions, so that there's room for them all).

If you get to the point where you think you might burst if you have to look at another plate of French food, take a break by seeking out some of the city's international restaurants. Remember, the peripheral cuisines in any city are an important part of its character because they change from place to place. Vancouver is well known for Chinese, Los Angeles for Mexican, London for Indian, Melbourne for Greek and Italian, for example. And, Paris is especially good for food from Morocco, other parts of Africa, the Antilles, Thailand, Vietnam and, increasingly, Japan. The greatest concentration of Chinese and Vietnamese restaurants are in the 5th and 13th *arrondissements*, while Japanese eateries have all but taken over the 1st. The best Moroccan restaurants are peppered across the capital, but the 11th and 12th *arrondissements* are good places to start. There is excellent Lebanese food in the 8th and 16th, while good African food can be found in the 9th and 20th. And great, cheap Indian canteens are concentrated on the streets behind the Gare du Nord in the 10th.

What better way to experience the different *quartiers* of Paris than through the city's exceptional – and delicious – culinary scene.

Menu Reader

An A–Z of French vocabulary to help you understand the menu

Agneau	lamb
ail	garlic
à la bordelaise	beef with red wine, and shallots
amuse-bouche/ amuse-gueule	appetizer/ "amuse the mouth"
andouillette	offal sausage
anis	aniseed
artichaut	artichoke
assiette	plate
Bar	sea bass
basilic	basil
béarnaise	hollandaise sauce with shallots and tarragon
beurre	butter
beignet	fritter
bien cuit	well cooked
bifteck	steak
biologique	organic
blanc de poulet	chicken breast
bœuf	beef
bœuf bourgignon	beef stew with red wine
boudin blanc	veal, chicken or pork sausage
boudin noir	black pudding
bouillabaisse	seafood stew
brochet	pike
brochette	kebab
Caille	quail
calamar	squid
campagne	country-style
canard	duck
canette	duckling
cannelle	cinnamon
carbonnade	casserole of beef, beer and onions
carré d'agneau	rack or loin of lamb
carrelet	plaice
cassis	blackcurrant
cassoulet	stew of beans, sausage and duck
cerise	cherry
cervelle	brains
champignons	mushrooms
chantilly	whipped cream
charcuterie	cured meats
châtaigne	chestnut
châteaubriand	thick steak
chaud	hot
chausson	turnover
cheval	horse
chèvre	goat's cheese
chou	cabbage
choucroute	sauerkraut
citron	lemon
citron vert	lime
citronelle	lemongrass
cochon	pig
cœur	heart
coing	quince
concombre	cucumber
confiture	jam
contre-filet	sirloin
coq-au-vin	chicken cooked in red wine
coquillages	shellfish
coquille St-Jacques	scallop
cornichon	pickled gherkin
côte	rib/chop
coulis	thick sauce
crème anglaise	custard
crêpe	pancake
crêpe Suzette	pancake flambéed in orange liqueur
cresson	watercress
crevette	prawn (shrimp)
croque-madame	croque-monsieur topped with an egg
croque-monsieur	toasted ham-and-cheese sandwich
en croûte	in pastry
cuisse	leg
curcuma	turmeric

Daube meat braised in red wine
daurade sea bream
désossé(e) boned
dinde turkey
dorade sea bream

Echalotte shallot
écrevisse crayfish
entrée first course
épicé(e) spicy
épinards spinach
espadon swordfish
estragon tarragon

Faisan pheasant
farci stuffed
faux-filet sirloin steak
fenouil fennel
feuilleté puff pastry
fève broad bean
filet mignon tenderloin
fines herbes mixed herbs
flétan halibut
foie liver
foie gras duck or goose liver, fattened
fondue melted
fondue savoyarde cheese fondue
fondu bourguignonne beef fondue
forestière with mushrooms
frais/fraîche fresh
fraise strawberry
framboise raspberry
frit(e) fried
frites French fries
froid(e) cold
fromage cheese
fruits de mer seafood
fumé(e) smoked

Garni garnished
gésiers gizzards
gibier game
gingembre ginger
girolle wild mushroom
glace ice cream, ice
glacé frozen
gougère cheesy choux pastry
goujon breaded strip
gratin dauphinois sliced potatoes in milk and cheese
grenouille frog
grillé(e) grilled
groseille redcurrant

Hareng herring
haricot bean
hollandaise egg, butter, vinegar and lemon sauce
homard lobster
huile oil
huître oyster

Île flottante soft meringue in in vanilla custard

Jambon ham
jardinière with vegetables
jus juice

Lait milk
langue tongue
lapin rabbit
lardons bacon cubes
légume vegetable
lentille lentil
lièvre hare
lotte monkfish
loup sea bass
lyonnaise with onions

Mâche lamb's lettuce
magret de canard duck breast
maïs sweetcorn
maquereau mackerel
marjolaine marjoram
marron chestnut
menthe mint
merguez spicy sausage
merlan whiting
meunière fried fish with butter, lemon and parsley sauce
meurette poached in red wine/stock
miel honey

mignon	small fillet	**potage**	thick soup
minute	fried rapidly	**pot-au-feu**	boiled beef with vegetables
moelle	bone marrow	**poulet**	chicken
Mornay	Béarnaise sauce with cheese	**primeurs**	early fruit and vegetables
morue	cod, salt cod	**provençale**	with garlic, olive oil and tomatoes
moules	mussels		
moutarde	mustard	**Quenelle**	poached dumpling
mûre	blackberry	**queue de bœuf**	oxtail
myrtille	blue-/bilberry		
		Radis	radish
Nature	ungarnished	**raie**	skate
navarin	lamb stew	**à la reine**	with chicken
navet	turnip	**rémoulade**	mayonnaise with mustard, herbs, capers and gherkins
noix	nuts	**ris**	sweetbreads
nouilles	noodles	**riz**	rice
		rognon	kidney
Oeuf	egg	**roquette**	rocket
oie	goose	**rôti**	roast
oignon	onion	**rouget**	red mullet
		rouille	mayonnaise spiced with cayenne pepper
Pain	bread		
palombe	wood pigeon	**Sablé**	shortbread biscuit
en papillote	steamed in foil or paper packets	**saignant**	rare (meat)
pané(e)	breaded	**salé(e)**	salted
parmentier	with potato	**sandre**	pike-perch
pâte	pastry	**sanglier**	wild boar
pâtes	pasta	**saucisse**	fresh sausage
paysan	rustic style	**saucisson sec**	dried sausage
perdreau	partridge	**saumon**	salmon
persil	parsley	**sauvage**	wild
petit pois	pea	**sec/sèche**	dry
pied	foot (or trotter)	**sel**	salt
pignon	pine nut	**sirop**	syrup
pintade	guinea fowl	**soja**	soya
pissaladière	anchovy, tomato and onion tart	**sucre**	sugar
pistou	pesto	**sucré(e)**	sweet
poché(e)	poached		
poêlé(e)	pan-fried	**Tapenade**	Provençal paste with olives and capers; often with anchovies
poire	pear	**tartare**	raw minced steak
poireau	leek	**tarte Tatin**	caramelised upside-down apple cake
poisson	fish		
poivre	pepper		
poivron	green/red pepper		
pomme	apple		
pomme de terre	potato		
pommes frites	chips/French fries		
porc	pork		

tartine	buttered open sandwich
thon	tuna
tiède	warm
tourte	covered pie/tart
tranche	slice
truffe	truffle
truite	trout
Veau	veal
viande	meat
volaille	poultry

Ordering Drinks

coffee (black)	café
...with milk	...au lait
filter coffee	café filtre
iced coffee	café frappé
decaffeinated	déca/décaféiné
tea	thé
...with milk	...avec du lait
herbal tea	tisane
camomile	verveine
hot chocolate	chocolat chaud
mineral water	eau minérale
...sparkling	...gazeux
...still	...non-gazeux
orange juice (fresh)	orange pressée
lemon juice (fresh, served with sugar)	citron pressé
...with ice	avec des glaçons
beer	bière brune
lager	bière blonde
...draught	...pression
...bottle	...bouteille
a glass of...	un verre de...
...white wine	...vin blanc
...red wine	...vin rouge
house wine	vin de maison
sparkling wine	crémant
jug of water/wine	carafe d'eau/de vin

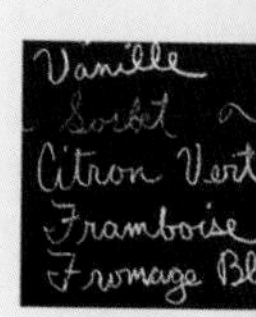

Useful Phrases

table d'hôte	set menu
prix fixe	fixed price menu
le menu	set menu
à la carte	dishes from the menu are charged separately
boisson comprise	drink included
service compris	service is included

If ordering steak:

rare	bleu
medium	à point
well done	bien cuit

I would like to reserve a table (for two/three/four)	Je voudrais réserver une table (pour deux/trois/quatre personnes)
Do you have a table?	Avez-vous une table?
I'd like to order	Je voudrais commander
Do you have...?	Avez-vous...?
I am a vegetarian	Je suis végétarien(ne)
What do you recommend?	Qu'est-ce que vous recommandez?
Do you have local specialities?	Avez-vous des spécialités locales?
What is the dish of the day?	Quel est le plat du jour?
That's not what I ordered	Ce n'est pas ce que j'ai commandé
May I have more wine please?	Encore du vin, s'il vous plaît?
Enjoy your meal	Bon appétit!
The bill please	L'addition s'il vous plaît

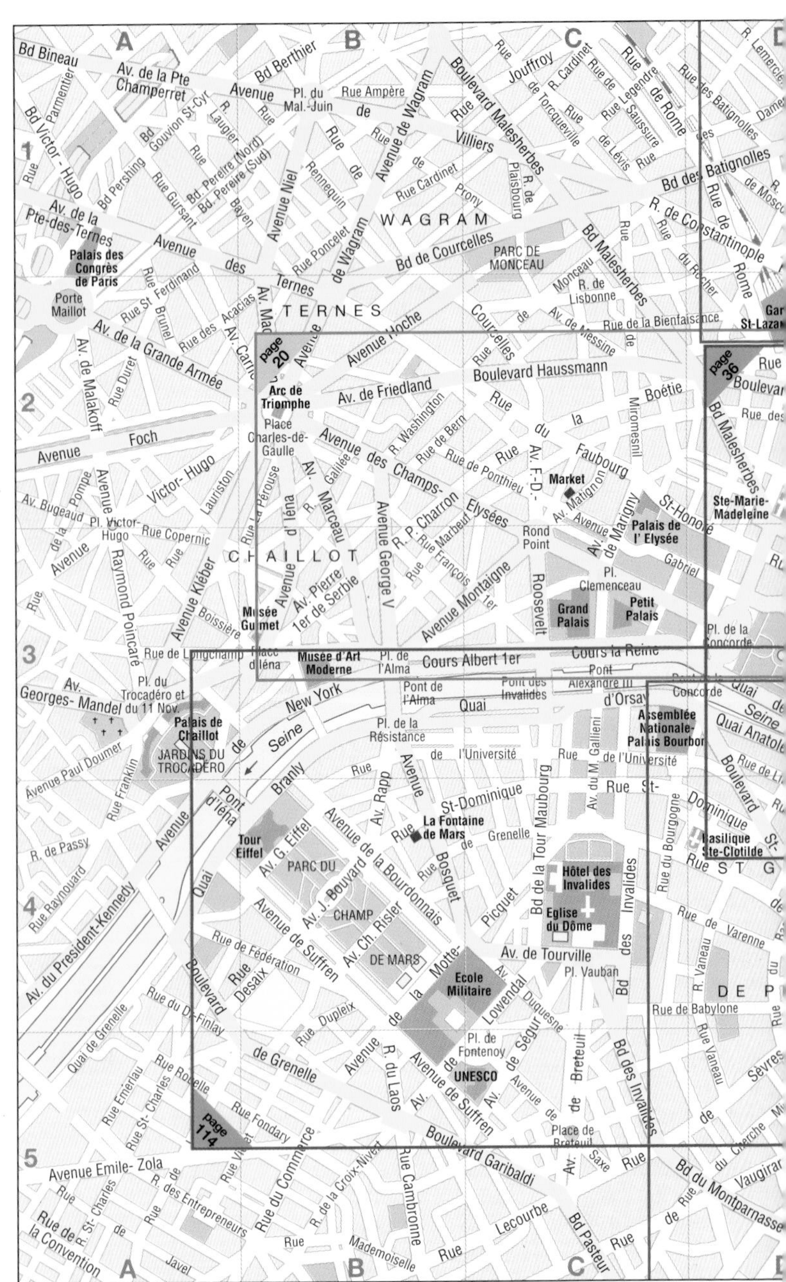
A
B
C
D
1
2
3
4
5
Bd Bineau
Av. de la Pte Champerret
Bd Berthier
Avenue de Villiers
Pl. du Mal.-Juin
Rue Ampère
Boulevard Malesherbes
Rue Jouffroy
R. Cardinet
Rue de Rome
Rue des Batignolles
Rue Parmentier
Bd Victor - Hugo
Bd Gouvion St-Cyr
R. Laugier
Rue de Rennequin
Avenue de Wagram
Rue de Torcqueville
Rue Legendre
Rue de Saussure
Rue de Lévis
Bd Pershing
Bd. Pereire (Nord)
Bd. Pereire (Sud)
Rue Bayen
Avenue Niel
Rue de Prony
Rue Cardinet
R. de Plaisbourg
Bd des Batignolles
Rue de Rome
R. de Constantinople
Av. de la Pte-des-Ternes
Rue Gursant
WAGRAM
Rue Poncelet
Bd de Courcelles
PARC DE MONCEAU
Bd Malesherbes
Rue du Rocher
Palais des Congrès de Paris
Avenue des Ternes
Rue St Ferdinand
Rue Brunel
Rue des Acacias
Av. Mac-Mahon
Monceau
R. de Lisbonne
Porte Maillot
TERNES
Avenue Hoche
Rue de Courcelles
Av. de Messine
Rue de la Bienfaisance
Av. de la Grande Armée
Av. de Malakoff
Rue Duret
Av. Carnot
page 20
Arc de Triomphe
Place Charles-de-Gaulle
Av. de Friedland
Boulevard Haussmann
Rue la Boétie
Miromesnil
page 36
Bd Malesherbes
Avenue Foch
R. Washington
Rue de Berri
Rue de Ponthieu
Rue du Faubourg St-Honoré
Av. F.-D.-Roosevelt
Market
Av. Matignon
Avenue de Marigny
Palais de l' Elysée
Ste-Marie-Madeleine
Avenue Victor- Hugo
Lauriston
Rue La Pérouse
Av. Marceau
R. Galilée
Avenue des Champs-Elysées
Avenue George V
R. P. Charron
Rue Marbeuf
Rue François 1er
Rond Point
Av. Bugeaud
Pl. Victor-Hugo
Rue Copernic
Rue de la Pompe
Avenue Raymond Poincaré
Avenue Kléber
CHAILLOT
Avenue d' Iéna
Av. Pierre 1er de Serbie
Avenue Montaigne
Gabriel
Pl. Clemenceau
Grand Palais
Petit Palais
Rue Boissière
Musée Guimet
Pl. de la Concorde
Rue de Longchamp
Place d'Iéna
Musée d'Art Moderne
Pl. de l'Alma
Cours Albert 1er
Cours la Reine
Pont Alexandre III
Pont des Invalides
Pont de l'Alma
Av. Georges- Mandel
Pl. du Trocadéro et du 11 Nov.
Av. de New York
Quai d'Orsay
Concorde
Quai Anatole
Palais de Chaillot
JARDINS DU TROCADERO
Quai de Seine
Pl. de la Résistance
Assemblée Nationale-Palais Bourbon
Avenue Paul Doumer
Rue Franklin
Quai Branly
Rue de l'Université
Rue de l'Université
Av. du M. Gallieni
Boulevard St-Germain
Pont d'Iéna
Av. Rapp
Avenue Bosquet
Rue St-Dominique
Rue St-Dominique
Rue du Bourgogne
Basilique Ste-Clotilde
Tour Eiffel
Av. G. Eiffel
Avenue de la Bourdonnais
La Fontaine de Mars
Rue de Grenelle
Bd de la Tour Maubourg
R. de Passy
PARC DU CHAMP DE MARS
Av. J. Bouyard
Rue Cler
Rue Picquet
Hôtel des Invalides
Bd des Invalides
Rue de Varenne
Rue Raynouard
Quai
Avenue de Suffren
Av. Ch. Risler
Eglise du Dôme
Av. du President-Kennedy
Rue de Fédération
Rue Desaix
Avenue de la Motte-Picquet
Ecole Militaire
Av. de Tourville
Pl. Vauban
Boulevard de Grenelle
Av. Lowendal
Av. Duquesne
R. Vaneau
Rue de Babylone
Rue du Dr-Finlay
Rue Dupleix
Pl. de Fontenoy
Avenue de Ségur
Av. de Breteuil
Bd des Invalides
Rue Vaneau
Quai de Grenelle
Rue Emeriau
Rue St- Charles
Rue Robelle
Avenue de Suffren
R. du Laos
Av. de Lowendal
UNESCO
Av. de Saxe
Rue de Sèvres
page 114
Rue Fondary
Rue Violet
Rue du Commerce
Boulevard Garibaldi
Place de Breteuil
Rue du Cherche Midi
Avenue Emile- Zola
R. des Entrepreneurs
R. de la Croix-Nivert
Rue Cambronne
Rue Lecourbe
Bd Pasteur
Bd du Montparnasse
Rue de Vaugirard
Rue de la Convention
R. St- Charles
Rue de Javel
Rue Mademoiselle

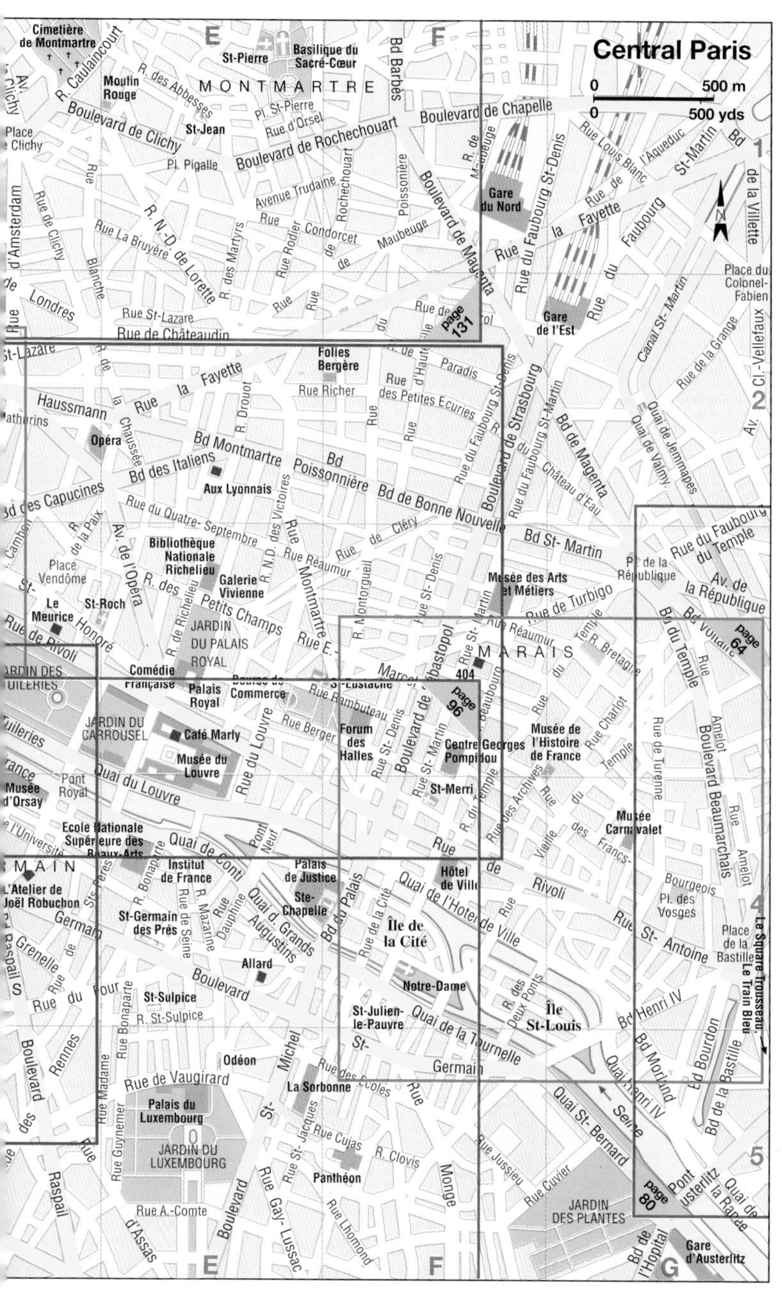

Central Paris
0 500 m
0 500 yds
MONTMARTRE
Cimetière de Montmartre
Basilique du Sacré-Cœur
St-Pierre
Moulin Rouge
St-Jean
Pl. Pigalle
Boulevard de Clichy
Boulevard de Rochechouart
Boulevard de Chapelle
Gare du Nord
Gare de l'Est
Rue du Faubourg St-Denis
Rue La Fayette
Boulevard de Magenta
Canal St-Martin
Place du Colonel-Fabien
Folies Bergère
Rue Richer
Opéra
Bd Haussmann
Bd des Italiens
Bd Montmartre
Bd Poissonnière
Bd de Bonne Nouvelle
Bd des Capucines
Aux Lyonnais
Bibliothèque Nationale Richelieu
Galerie Vivienne
Place Vendôme
Le Meurice
St-Roch
Rue de Rivoli
JARDIN DU PALAIS ROYAL
Comédie Française
Palais Royal
Bourse du Commerce
St-Eustache
Bd St-Martin
Pl. de la République
Musée des Arts et Métiers
Rue de Turbigo
MARAIS
404
Forum des Halles
Centre Georges Pompidou
St-Merri
Musée de l'Histoire de France
Musée Carnavalet
Boulevard Beaumarchais
Pl. des Vosges
Place de la Bastille
Le Square Trousseau, Le Train Bleu
JARDIN DES TUILERIES
JARDIN DU CARROUSEL
Café Marly
Musée du Louvre
Quai du Louvre
Musée d'Orsay
Pont Royal
Ecole Nationale Supérieure des Beaux-Arts
Quai de Conti
Institut de France
Pont Neuf
Palais de Justice
Ste-Chapelle
Hôtel de Ville
Quai de l'Hotel de Ville
L'Atelier de Joël Robuchon
St-Germain des Prés
Île de la Cité
Notre-Dame
Île St-Louis
Allard
St-Sulpice
St-Julien-le-Pauvre
Quai de la Tournelle
Boulevard St-Germain
Odéon
Rue de Vaugirard
La Sorbonne
Palais du Luxembourg
JARDIN DU LUXEMBOURG
Panthéon
Rue Gay-Lussac
Rue Monge
Boulevard St-Michel
Boulevard Raspail
Quai St-Bernard
Seine
JARDIN DES PLANTES
Gare d'Austerlitz
Pont d'Austerlitz
page 131
page 96
page 64
page 80
E F G
1 2 4 5

Champs-Elysées

After over a decade of regeneration, this great avenue and its environs are flourishing. Haute cuisine and haute couture reign supreme

The dramatic and ongoing revival of the Champs-Elysées was launched with a daring urban redesign project by the city of Paris in 1992, and it's still going strong, as growing numbers of restaurants and cafés, along with bars and stylish nightclubs, join the fashion and luxury goods boutiques that heralded the early success of the monumental thoroughfare's comeback as one of the world's premier leisure destinations. Today, 'Les Champs', as Parisians call it, is the spine of a thriving and decidedly glamorous district of Paris, mostly in the city's 8th *arrondissement* and roughly bound by the Seine on the south and boulevard de Courcelles on the north, with rue Royale and avenue Marceau serving as the eastern and western boundaries respectively. In the ten or so years that the Champs and its environs have been gaining new lustre, it has become the location for many of the avant-garde, fashionable and spectacular restaurants in Paris – an area with a distinctive gastronomic vocation.

Reversal of fortune

First initiated by Louis XVI in 1667, the Champs-Elysées, or 'Elysian Fields' (burial grounds of the blessed and most beloved after death in Greek mythology) was originally laid out by landscape architect André Le Nôtre to create a visual prolongation of the Tuileries gardens running west from the Louvre palace. The wide street lined with elegant gardens and rows of trees later continued its development after the completion of the Arc de Triomphe, celebrating Napoléon Bonaparte's military triumphs, in 1836.

By the turn of the 20th century the Champs, in contrast to the rather common Grands Boulevards (Poissonnière, Bonne-Nouvelle, etc) had reached a zenith of popularity and elegance, attracting stylish and monied types from all over the world to linger on its animated café terraces. The sophisticated spectacle on the avenue evaporated during World War I, but made a brief but giddy comeback during the 1920s. This was followed by the Depression, World War II and, with the post-war popularity of the automobile, growing traffic problems, as the Champs shifted from a luxury address to a commercial one distinguished by numerous cinemas and airline offices during the 1950s, '60s and '70s. The opening of the RER (an express rail service connecting the working-class suburbs with central Paris) further changed the avenue, and by the 1980s it had become quite dumpy, with an atmosphere comparable to a tatty shopping mall.

***Opposite:** minimalism at Café Lenôtre. **Below:** decorative chillis at Copenhague*

Determined to resurrect the area, Jacques Chirac, then mayor of Paris, budgeted 75 million euro to renovate, modernise and beautify the Champs: street parking was replaced by underground car parks; new street furniture was added, including architect Jean-Michel Wilmotte's handsome teak benches and retro Art Nouveau newspaper kiosks; new signage was installed; pavement was replaced with dove-grey granite paving stones; and the number of trees doubled. Not surprisingly, Parisians gave the avenue a second look. A turning point occurred in 1999, when Ladurée, the venerable Parisian tearoom in rue Royale, opened a second branch at No. 75, while Louis Vuitton banked on the return of the carriage trade the same year with a glamorous new boutique at No. 101.

Place de la Concorde to the Rond-Point

Starting at place de la Concorde (site of the Hôtel de Crillon and Les Ambassadeurs, one of the most beautiful restaurants in the world, *see page 22*), it is today a treat to stroll up the Champs to the Arc de Triomphe, especially if you've booked at one of the many outstanding tables in the area. The recently opened Café Lenôtre *(see page 26)*, in the Napoléon III pavilion at No. 10, has a restaurant, café, shop and cooking school; pop in for an éclair and a coffee, or, in good weather, for a salad on the garden terrace. Another fine spring or summer day, when you're feeling flush, splurge on a classic French meal at Laurent, in a similarly pretty pavilion nearby. Lasserre *(see page 22)*, with its electrically opening roof and delicious 1950s' atmosphere (Audrey Hepburn loved the place) offers contemporary French cooking, and further down, when you reach avenue Montaigne, you'll be hopelessly spoilt for choice.

For a peek at life among the beautiful people and some excellent modern French cooking, head down avenue Matignon to Market *(see page 28)*, French-born, New York-based Jean-Georges Vongerichten's popular new place. Alternatively, avenue Montaigne promises everything from a salad or grilled fish at L'Avenue *(see page 26)* to wonderful steak tartare at the lovely old-

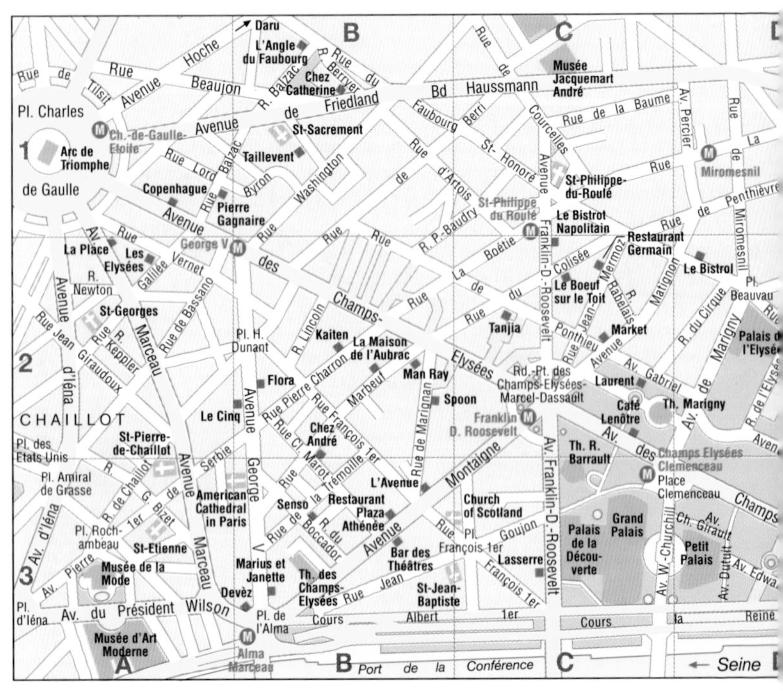

fashioned Bar des Théâtres *(see page 25)*, spectacular haute cuisine food by Alain Ducasse at the Restaurant Plaza Athénée *(see page 23)*, and, on place de l'Alma at the end of the avenue, Devèz *(see page 24)*, a brilliant address for carnivores. Also here is Marius et Janette *(see page 28)*, one for fish fiends; it's pricey and the service can be frosty, but it's worth it for a superb catch-of-the-day menu and a chance to spot stars such as Jean-Paul Belmondo, a regular here.

Five of the Best

Market: a slick restaurant with a chic crowd and inventive modern cooking
Pierre Gagnaire: Gagnaire stops conversation with his subtle, nuanced dishes
Restaurant Plaza Athénée: truly sumptuous food from globe-trotting chef Alain Ducasse and team
Spoon: this 'world food' bistro (also by Ducasse) attracts a trendy young crowd
Taillevent: an elegant restaurant serving some of the best haute cuisine in town

The Golden Triangle and l'Etoile

The core of the Champs-Elysées neighbourhood is the 'Golden Triangle', named after its elegant fashion boutiques and monied clientele, and bound by the Champs and avenues Montaigne and George V. Since the early 1990s it has emerged as a thriving restaurant district, with popular new places including: Senso *(see page 29)*, Sir Terence Conran's second Parisian brasserie; neo-oriental Le Man Ray *(see page 27)*; Spoon *(see page 29)*, Alain Ducasse's blueprint for the modern bistro; and Flora *(see page 27)*, headed by talented chef Flora Mikula. These venues have joined long-running establishments such as Chez André *(see page 25)*, a bistro popular with politicians, and La Maison de l'Aubrac *(see page 25)*, reputed for its hefty steaks.

Once you've reached place Charles de Gaulle (or l'Etoile, as the star-shaped space around the Arc de Triomphe is popularly known), explore the quieter upmarket business-and-residential side of this part of Paris by following avenue de Friedland through to boulevard Haussmann. Along the way, you'll be grazing the doorstep of such elegant eateries as Pierre Gagnaire *(see page 23)*, famed as the three-star magician of the French kitchen; Taillevent *(see page 24)*, where chef Alain Solivérès has gourmets joining the usual crowd of bankers and politicians; and two of the best-loved brasseries in Paris: the theatrical Art Deco Le Boeuf sur le Toit, named after a Cocteau ballet *(see page 24)*, and the reassuringly old-fashioned Mollard *(see page 25)* with its stunning Art Nouveau decor.

Majorelle's splendid Art Nouveau interior at Lucas-Carton

Haute Cuisine

Les Ambassadeurs

Hôtel de Crillon, 10 place de la Concorde, 8th [E3]. Tel: 01 44 71 16 16. Open: L and D daily. **€€€€** *www.crillon.com*

This marble dining room with Baccarat crystal chandeliers and friezes of cherubim building the 18th-century Hôtel Crillon is one of the most opulent in the world. Young chef Jean-François Piège, formerly at the Restaurant Plaza Athénée *(see opposite)*, offers sumptuous contemporary French cooking including roast lamb and lobster with morel mushrooms. Impeccable service and superb wine list. Booking essential.

Le Bristol

Hôtel Bristol, 112 rue du Faubourg St-Honoré, 8th [D2]. Tel: 01 53 43 43 40. Open: B, L and D daily. **€€€€** *www.lebristolparis.com*

Two-star chef Eric Frechon moves between two grand settings within this elegant hotel – an oak-panelled oval dining room for winter and a tented garden room for summer. Dishes, such as langoustines roasted in orange and coriander, and sea bass with shellfish, are earthy and elegant. Booking esssential.

Le Cinq

Hôtel Four Seasons George V, 31 avenue George V, 8th [B2]. Tel: 01 49 52 70 00. Open B, L and D daily. **€€€€** *www.fourseasons.com*

Formerly head chef at Taillevent *(see page 24)*, Philippe Legendre has made Le Cinq a leading table since he arrived in 2001 with the reopening of the renovated hotel. A plush Wedgwood-blue dining room accented by dramatic Zen-style bouquets is a striking setting in which to sample dishes such as a *tourte* (tart/pie) of oxtail, red mullet sautéed in fennel and Tuscan bacon, and cannelloni stuffed with mango and banana and sprinkled with strudel crumbs. Superb wine list and kid-glove service. Booking essential.

Lasserre

17 avenue Franklin-D.-Roosevelt, 8th [C3]. Tel: 01 43 59 53 43. Open: D Mon–Sat, L Thur–Fri; closed August. **€€€€**

This jewel-box dining room has a retracting roof, so that you can feast under the stars. Once a favourite of stars from Marlene Dietrich to Audrey Hepburn, Lasserre is enjoying new popularity since the arrival of chef Jean-Louis Nomicos, who creates wonderfully

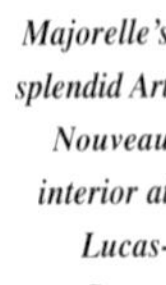

TIP

A wonderful place to start the shopping or sightseeing day is **Ladurée** (*16 rue Royale, tel: 01 42 60 21 79 or 75 ave des Champs-Elysées, tel: 01 40 75 08 75).* This oh-so-civilised tearoom is a Parisian institution, famous for its melt-in-the-mouth macaroons. The pain au chocolat et pistache is a rare treat.

extravagant dishes including dressed crab with a canapé of sea-urchin tongues, breaded foie gras with asparagus tips and morel mushrooms, and a sumptuous dessert of pineapple, coconut and lychees. Booking advisable.

Laurent

41 avenue Gabriel, 8th [C2]. Tel: 01 42 25 00 39. Open: L and D Mon–Fri, D only Sat. **€€€€** *www.le-laurent.com*
This 19th-century pavilion surrounded by chestnut trees in the gardens of the Champs-Elysées was formerly owned by expatriate British financier and *bon vivant* Sir James Goldsmith. It has since changed hands, but the overall experience is one of old-fashioned elegance, especially if you dine outside in summer. Expect classic French dishes such as fillet of beef with foie gras, roast lamb with olives and pine nuts, and crêpes suzette. Booking advisable.

Lucas-Carton

9 place de la Madeleine, 8th [E2]. Tel: 01 42 65 22 90. Open: L and D Tues–Fri, D only Mon and Sat, closed Sun. **€€€€** *www.lucascarton.com*
The gorgeous interior of this restaurant is as delicious as chef Alain Senderens's dishes.
The swirling wood panelling, glass lighting fixtures and partitions created in 1900 by leading exponent of the Art Nouveau style, Louis Majorelle, set a romantic scene. Senderens himself isn't in the kitchen much any more, but dishes such as roast duck Apicius (cooked with honey and spices), lobster served with a polenta incorporating its coral, and superb desserts including vanilla millefeuille or orange tart, delight an elegantly dressed and eminently cosmopolitan crowd. Booking essential.

Pierre Gagnaire 🍴

Hôtel Balzac, 6 rue Balzac, 8th [A1]. Tel: 01 58 36 12 50. Open: L and D Mon–Fri, D only Sat. **€€€€** *www.pierre-gagnaire.com*
Pierre Gagnaire is one of the most original and artistic chefs in the world today. The elaborate composition of his dishes verges on the Baroque – think suckling lamb rubbed in ewe's-milk curd and capers served with roasted rice, Chinese cabbage with toasted rice, and snails with fennel shoots.
A visit to this sedate grey dining room is essential for intrepid gastronomes. Book weeks ahead.

Restaurant Plaza Athénée 🍴

Hôtel Plaza Athénée, 25 avenue Montaigne, 8th [B3]. Tel: 01 53 67 65 00. Open: D only Mon–Wed, L and D Thur–Fri, closed Sat–Sun. **€€€€** *www.alain-ducasse.com*
Globe-trotting chef Alain Ducasse offers an appealingly modern take on French haute cuisine at the roomy, dove-grey dining room of this famous hotel. Service is precise and graceful, and the cooking sublime. Dishes such as poached Dublin Bay prawns with caviar, spider crab stuffed with its own meat, lamb roasted with peppers and Breton lobster with asparagus and morel mushrooms are unforgettable. Book one month in advance.

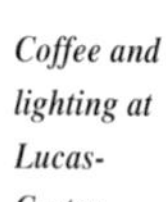

Coffee and lighting at Lucas-Carton

Art Deco brasserie Le Boeuf sur le Toit

TIP

Les Caves Taillevent *(199 rue du Faubourg St-Honoré, tel: 01 45 61 14 09)* stores some 30,000 bottles in its underground cellar, but this excellent *cave* is not just for connoisseurs. Prices range from stratospheric to downright cheap. Daily tastings in the Cave du Jour.

Taillevent

15 rue Lamennais, 8th [B1]. Tel: 01 44 95 15 01. Open: L and D Mon–Fri. **€€€€**
www.taillevent.com
This wood-panelled restaurant has held three Michelin stars for 30 years, and, with the arrival of a brilliant new chef, Alain Solivérès, the cooking has never been better. Solivérès respects such Taillevent classics as lobster boudin (sausage), but has also introduced dishes including grilled scallops with green olives and chorizo and a main course of tuna belly garnished with Espelette peppers, lemon, capers and Serrano ham. Fine oil paintings on the walls, extravagant floral arrangements, heavy silverware, hushed service and one of the world's greatest wine lists ensure this place its almost-mythical status. Book weeks in advance.

Brasseries

Le Boeuf sur le Toit

34 rue du Colisée, 8th [C2]. Tel: 01 53 93 65 55. Open: L and D daily. **€€**
Originally a cabaret, this brasserie, named after a ballet by Jean Cocteau and Darius Milhaud, is now part of the Flo chain but still pleasant for simple spur-of-the-moment meals. Huge Cubist-style chandeliers, acres of wood panelling and vast mirrors create a theatrical atmosphere. Begin with oysters (in season) or ravioli stuffed with ricotta and basil, then have steak, andouillette (tripe sausage) or grilled salmon. Booking is preferable but only necessary on weekends.

Devèz

5 place de l'Alma, 8th [B3]. Tel: 01 53 67 97 53. Open: L and D daily. **€€**
With a bar covered in polished cow's horn, this stylish brasserie is a carnivore's delight, serving excellent all-beef appetisers (steak tartare, smoked beef, carpaccio with asparagus, etc), Aubrac (ie from the Auvergne, like the owners) steaks, veal and other meaty treats, including the MacAubrac – a Gallic retort to the hamburger.

Mollard

115 rue Saint-Lazare, 8th [E1]. Tel: 01 43 87 50 22. Open: L and D daily. **€€** *www.mollard.fr*

The stunning Art Nouveau ceramic décor of this quiet, old-fashioned brasserie is as much of an attraction as its traditional menu, which runs to oysters, steaks, calf's liver with endives, and crêpes suzette. The service can be doddery, and the clientele is decidedly mature, but it's fine for a quiet meal and a glimpse of a Paris of yesteryear.

Bistros

Bar des Théâtres

6 avenue Montaigne, 8th [B3]. Tel: 01 47 23 34 63. Open: B, L and D daily, non-stop 6am–2am. **€€–€€€**

Popular with journalists and the showbiz crowd – the Théâtre des Champs-Elysées is just across the road – this much-loved hole-in-the-wall is one of the rare places to get a reasonably priced feed in an expensive part of town. It's smoky, crowded and noisy, but everyone's having a good time, in no small measure due to tasty classic cooking that runs to poached egg in port jelly, grilled sea bass and steak tartare. Booking recommended.

Chez André

12 rue Marbeuf, 8th [B2]. Tel: 01 47 20 59 57. Open: L and D daily, non-stop noon–1am. **€€**

Even members of the jet set love this old-fashioned bistro, long a favourite of politicians from the ministries near the Elysée Palace, home to the French president. Settle down on a banquette and enjoy the show, as waiters in white aprons serve hearty dishes such as foie gras, sea bass stuffed with wild mushrooms, and veal chop with gratin dauphinois. Other pulls include friendly service, a nice terrace and air conditioning. Booking recommended.

La Ferme des Mathurins

17 rue Vignon, 8th [E2]. Tel: 01 42 66 46 39. Open: L and D Mon–Sat. **€€–€€€**

One of the rare old-fashioned bistros in the heart of Paris, this place has a literary pedigree (it was often mentioned in the mystery novels of writer Georges Simenon). Come for hearty Gallic eats including chicken-liver terrine, sautéed trout, roast ham in a cream sauce and apple tart. Popular with the business crowd, so the evening clientele is distinctly international.

La Maison de l'Aubrac

37 rue Marbeuf, 8th [B2]. Tel: 01 43 59 05 14. Open: daily, 24 hours. **€€** *www.maison-aubrac.fr*

If you're hankering after a classic steak-frites at any hour, day or night, head for this Auvergnat outpost just off the Champs – a place that's been a hit with Paris clubgoers and night owls for over 40 years. A jolly atmosphere prevails – especially after midnight; the house wine is perfectly pleasant, and the meat, including the côte de boeuf for two, is excellent, especially for the price. Friendly service and an amusing and eclectic clientele.

Restaurant Germain

19 rue Jean-Mermoz, 8th [C2]. Tel: 01 43 59 29 24. Open: L and D Mon–Fri. **€€**

This small place off the busy Champs is more like a provincial bistro than a restaurant – one reason why it draws a loyal crowd of regulars. The combination of chef Frédérick Gauthier's bold modern bistro cooking – foie gras with a tarte Tatin of turnips, guinea hen pastilla with green cabbage, and Paris-Brest – and the friendly service make it popular, so book.

Did you know?

After two years under wraps, Champs-Elysées landmark and icon of 1960s' Paris, **Le Drugstore Publicis** *(No. 133)* has reopened. Famous as a place to pick up Gaulois and girls, it now sells cigarettes, magazines, pharmacy goods and beauty products till 2am. The brasserie and bar open until 1.15am, while the wine cellar and cigar cellar close at 11pm.

Wine list at La Maison d'Aubrac

TIP

End your shopping day or start your evening with a cocktail at the sleek **Atelier Renault** bar *(53, ave des Champs-Elysées, open daily, 10.30–1.30am)*. Happy hour is between 7pm and 8pm.

Cafés

Café Lenôtre

Pavillon Elysée, Carré Marigny, 10 avenue des Champs-Elysées, 8th [C2]. Tel: 01 42 65 85 10. Open: B, L and D daily. **€€–€€€** *www.lenotre.fr*

This pretty wedding-cake-style pavilion in the gardens of the Champs-Elysées is a useful address, since it serves non-stop and offers everything from breakfast to lunch, dinner, tea and snacks. The food is cosmopolitan, from salad with crabmeat and tiny prawns, to cod poached in spiced bouillon and plates of tapas. Note that Lenôtre is famous for its pastries. Booking advised.

Contemporary

L'Angle du Faubourg

195 rue du Faubourg St-Honoré, 8th [B1]. Tel: 01 40 74 20 20. Open: L and D Mon–Fri. **€€€**

The casual and lower-priced annexe of the venerable three Michelin-starred Taillevent has been a huge hit owing to its appetising, contemporary French food – try dishes such as the starter salad of mixed vegetables and the roast shoulder of lamb with black olives and garlic. The décor is minimalist – think Tuscan red walls, tan floors and black wooden tables with white-linen runners – while the crowd is well-heeled and stylish. Book in advance and wear your Prada, Gucci or Zegna to catch the vibe.

L'Avenue

41 avenue Montaigne, 8th [B3]. Tel: 01 40 70 14 91. Open: L and D daily. **€€–€€€**

This sleek brasserie on one of the world's most famous and exclusive fashion avenues is a mirror image of the neighbourhood, with fashion-house executives picking at salads alongside their international customers. The menu is a reflection of what stylish Parisians are eating nowadays – rocket salad with Parmesan, tuna steak with Balsamic vinegar reduction, and low-fat fromage blanc with fruit coulis. Look the part or you won't get in.

Chez Catherine

3 rue Berryer, 8th [B1]. Tel: 01 40 76 01 40. Open: L and D Mon–Fri. **€€€**

Originally cooking in an old-fashioned space in the 9th, Catherine Guerraz, one of the best female chefs in town, now holds forth in three dressy dining rooms in a decidedly silk-stocking part of town. Expect appealing, modern, market cooking, including a salad of girolles, frisée lettuce and sot-l'y-laisse, an especially tender chunk of chicken, pigeon with foie gras, sole meunière and pistachio-flavoured crème brûlée. Booking is essential.

Les Elysées

Hôtel Vernet, 25 rue Vernet, 8th [A2]. Tel: 01 44 31 98 98. Open: L and D Tues–Fri, D only Mon; closed August. **€€€€** *www.hotelvernet.com*

Bright and breezy Café Lenôtre

This elegant, old-fashioned dining room with a beautiful glass ceiling designed by Gustave Eiffel may initially strike you as the setting of an Agatha Christie novel, but once the pianist starts playing and chef Eric Briffard's cooking comes to the table, it all becomes *très Parisien*. Briffard, who previously cooked at the Hôtel Plaza Athénée *(see page 23)*, is a gifted traditionalist, as seen in dishes including his sublime salad of baby vegetables with pot-au-feu aspic or caviar-dotted scallops. Good-humoured formal service pleases a worldly international crowd. Booking essential.

L'Envue

39 rue Boissy d'Anglas, 8th [E2]. Tel: 01 42 65 10 49. Open: L and D Mon–Sat. ***€€–€€€***

With Hermès just down the road and the sleek new headquarters of Cartier next door, it's no surprise to find a fashionable modern restaurant showing clips from recent catwalk shows in this *quartier*. Unlike at so many fashion tables, however, service here is friendly and the food better than average, including sea-bass sashimi, Comté-cheese-and-chive soufflé and chicken in lemon-saffron sauce. Finish up with the roasted pineapple. Book ahead.

Flora

36 avenue George V, 8th [B2]. Tel: 01 40 70 10 49. Open: L and D Mon–Fri, L only Sat. ***€€–€€€***

Talented and hardworking chef Flora Mikula trained with Alain Passard of L'Arpège *(see page 116)*, but she's gone way beyond her master's style with a fascinating menu of contemporary French dishes inspired by the food of India, Morocco, Turkey and Vietnam. The pretty dining room, with floral wallpaper, 1940s-style glass wall sconces, mirrors, Wedgwood mouldings and a muted colour scheme, gives this place a quiet chic. Booking essential.

Le Man Ray

34 rue Marbeuf, 8th [B2]. Tel: 01 56 88 36 35. Restaurant open: D daily; bar open: every evening. ***€€–€€€*** *www.manray.info*

The Asian-inspired décor, with a long and very popular bar as its centrepiece, is the highlight of this well-established fashion restaurant with an East-meets-West menu and mood. Popular with thirtysomething professionals who are more inter-

Top and above: minimalism at L'Envue

Jean-Georges Vongerichten's fashionable Market

TIP

The **Virgin Megastore** *(52–60 ave des Champs-Elysées, tel: 01 49 53 50 00)* may be chaotic, but it has a great café on the top floor with a view of the Champs and you can sample the latest sounds until midnight.

ested in the music (mainly acid jazz, lounge mixes and house) and cocktails than the cooking. It's more of a scene than a restaurant, and rather amusing as such, but you can eat decently if you order very simply.

Marius et Janette

4 avenue George-V, 8th [B3]. Tel: 01 47 23 41 88. Open: L and D daily. **€€€**

Despite a somewhat cartoon-like maritime décor – think portholes and knotty pine – this fish house still draws one of the most elegant and powerful crowds in Paris. The food, by chef Bernard Pinaud, is superb and includes dishes such as gazpacho with crab, langoustine-stuffed ravioli, or John Dory in carrot sauce and a first-rate aïoli. Don't be surprised to spot the odd movie star here, although you should also come prepared to overlook the occasionally snippy service. Booking essential.

Market (🍴)

15 avenue Matignon, 8th [C2]. Tel: 01 56 43 40 90. Open: B and L Mon–Fri, D daily, Br Sat–Sun. **€€€** *www.jean-georges.com*

After a rocky debut, globe-trotting Alsatian-born, New York-based chef Jean-Georges Vongerichten has succeeded in creating a very popular contemporary table next to the glamorous new Parisian headquarters of Christie's auctioneers. The slick décor of polished grey stone and bleached wood accented by African art is signed by the Parisian decorator Christian Liagre, but the crowd is distinctly international, with a penchant for dishes such as a salad of mixed leaves, Japanese mushrooms, avocado and asparagus in a saké vinaigrette, scallops sautéed with citrus in sesame oil, and other East-meets-West-style preparations. Booking essential.

La Place

Hôtel Radisson SAS Champs-Elysées, 78 avenue Marceau, 8th [A2]. Tel: 01 53 23 43 63. Open: L and D Mon–Fri, closed for 3 weeks in August. **€€€**

With an intimate little garden for alfresco dining and a tiny dining room used throughout the rest of the year, this hotel restaurant is an insider's address among Paris gourmets. It's known for its provençal menu, created by consultant chef Jean-André Charial, of the famous Oustau de Baumanière in Provence. Dishes such as pasta with tomato-basil sauce to start, and a perfectly roasted rack of lamb for a main are typical. The excellent wine list highlights the south of France.

Senso

Hôtel Trémoille, 15 rue de la Trémoille, 8th [B3]. Tel: 01 56 52 14 14. Open: B, L and D daily. **€€€** *www.hotel-tremoille.com*

Occupying a handsome oblong dining room with dark parquet floors, pigeon-grey walls and a red-decorated niche at the end of the room, Sir Terence Conran's second Paris restaurant in the renovated Hôtel Trémoille is stylish in a low-key kind of way. A business crowd mixes with fashion and media types, plus occasional tourists, and everyone appreciates the satisfying contemporary cooking. Dishes include pumpkin soup with grilled pancetta, and smoked salmon and Niçoise-style stuffed tomatoes. There's a great wine list too. Booking advised.

Spoon (Ψ)

14 rue Marignan, 8th [B2]. Tel: 01 40 76 34 44. Open: L and D Mon–Fri. **€€€** *www.spoon.tm.fr*

Even after five years, Alain Ducasse's 'world food' bistro remains a hit with a mix of media, fashion and showbiz types. If the open kitchen is the major decorative element, the restaurant has two personalities, as white linen shades on the dining-room walls are raised in the evening to reveal purple upholstered walls. There's a multinational menu, adapted to the French palate, with dishes such as casserole of cod, aubergine and tomatoes in sesame cream, Thai soup with shellfish and lacquered tuna with wok-sautéed vegetables. Desserts are often of American inspiration, and the intriguing wine list comes from around the globe. Book ahead.

International

Le Bistrot Napolitain

18 avenue Franklin-D.-Roosevelt, 8th [C2]. Tel: 01 45 62 08 37. Open: L and D Mon–Fri, L only Sat. **€**

In an area dominated by fashion, it's a relief to find a friendly spot for a pizza and a salad after a film or a day out shopping. The pastas are good, too, and the house wines perfectly acceptable. Popular with a well-dressed crowd of regulars.

Copenhague

142 avenue des Champs-Elysées, 8th [A1]. Tel: 01 44 13 86 26. Open: L and D Mon–Fri, D only Sat. **€€€** *www.restaurantfloradanica.com*

What a surprise to step off the Champs into this peaceful Nordic bower, where a talented French

Copenhague for Scandinavian style and Danish cuisine

chef does a delicious riff on mostly Danish cooking. The dining room, dominated by a portrait of the Danish queen and tomato-red leather armchairs, overlooks the Champs; it's a fine place to sample dishes including a starter of marinated salmon stea, served with sweet mayonnaise and fresh dill, and mains such as veal sweetbreads caramelised in carrot juice and served with a mousseline of fresh peas. Note that Flora Danica is the less-expensive part of this restaurant at the same address, and both sections spill into the same, lovely garden (although into different areas). Booking essential.

Daru

19 rue Daru, 8th [B1]. Tel: 01 42 27 23 60. Open: L and D Mon–Sat. **€€** *www.daru.fr*

Just steps from the city's gilt-domed Russian cathedral, this is one of the city's oldest Russian restaurants, dating to 1918 and the arrival en masse of the White Russians in Paris. Start with the bortsch or one of the assiettes de Zakouski, several platters of assorted cold appetisers including aubergine caviar, potted salmon, herring pâté, stuffed vine leaves, salmon eggs, taramasalata and blinis (a lovely meal on its own), and then try the delicious filet royal of salmon. Cosy setting, charming service, fair prices and delicious menu. Booking recommended.

Kaiten

63 rue Pierre-Charron, 8th [B2]. Tel: 01 43 59 78 78. Open: L and D Mon–Sat. **€€**

Conveyor-belt sushi places are no longer novelties in New York or London, but they're scarce in Paris, which is why this place has been a hit in an expensive neighbourhood

Modish Moroccan, Tanjia

where quick, tasty, reasonably priced eats aren't easy to find. You serve yourself from the titbits that trundle by, choosing from tuna shashimi to California rolls, Nori (seaweed) cornets filled with salmon eggs and rice, and cuttle-fish sushi, etc, all of which are priced according to the colour of plate upon which they're served.

Tanjia

23 rue de Ponthieu, 8th [C2]. Tel: 01 42 25 95 00. Open: L and D daily. ***€€–€€€***

Nightclub impresarios Cathy and David Guetta have turned this Moroccan restaurant into a major fashion venue, where famous faces such as Isabelle Adjani are often spotted. Resembling a *riad*, or walled courtyard house, typical of Marrakesh, the restaurant is set around an atrium decorated with wooden fretwork. Signature dishes include assorted Moroccan hors d'oeuvres, tagine of lamb cooked for 10 hours with 25 spices or pigeon pastilla (crispy pastry leaves with spiced ground pigeon). Join the hipsters in the lounge bar downstairs for an after-dinner drink. Booking essential.

Cocktails at the Pershing Lounge

Bars and Pubs

As the Champs-Elysées and environs have morphed into the trendiest night-life zone for young high-flyers in Paris, a once buttoned-down *quartier* has seen a flowering of bars, cafés, bar-restaurants and clubs. The hottest bar at the moment is the **Bar du Plaza** *(Hôtel Plaza Athénée, 25 ave Montaigne, tel: 01 53 67 66 65)*, with décor by Patrick Jouin, the favourite interior designer of chef Alain Ducasse; it even has a sculpted glass bar that looks like it's made of giant ice-cubes. Come here for off-the-wall cocktails (vodka-water-melon juice-jelly shots), and mix with the Gucci-and-Prada-clad crowd.

Rather better established and *très showbiz* is **Le Doobie's** *(2 rue Robert-Etienne, tel: 01 53 76 10 76)*, frequented by a mix of famous faces from film and television, models, celebrity ath-letes, hard-partying bankers, and foreigners of all stripes; fun, lively and slightly pretentious, this place offers a spot-on snapshot of the night scene in and around the Champs.

Those in search of fellow Anglophones and a familiar pint, should head for **Poloroom** *(1 rue Lord Byron, tel: 01 40 74 07 78*, home to a pub with a long wooden bar, Chesterfields to sink into and a dramatically diverse crowd.

If you're looking for a classy place to meet for drinks – perhaps with some business motive – try **Le Baretto** (Hôtel de Vigny, 9–11 rue Balzac, tel: 01 42 99 80 00), a posh hotel bar with an Italian accent and a sophisticated atmosphere created by large, overstuffed, brown-leather easy chairs and low lighting. Similarly chic is the opulent Andrée Putman-designed Pershing Lounge *(Pershing Hall, 49 rue Pierre-Charon, tel: 01 58 36 58 00)*, a big pull for the designer crowd, who come to sip cocktails in style.

Finally, if you've been out late and crave that ill-advised last-one-for-the-road, head for the camp and frisky **Mathis Bar** *(3 rue de Pon-thieu, 8th)*, where a good time is guaranteed. It's open until 5.30am daily, except Sundays.

Celebrity Chefs

In a country where gastronomy is one of the highest art forms, the rise of certain celebrity chefs has been meteoric. But is it all for the good?

They are amongst France's greatest stars, featuring in the pages of glossy magazines and on prime-time television slots, writing books, appearing in advertisements, and signing up to lucrative sponsorship deals. So when do celebrity chefs find time to cook?

Hands-off versus hands-on

The truth is that many do not. Take Alain Ducasse, whose restaurant at the Plaza Athénée Hotel is the flagship of a culinary empire that includes two more haute cuisine establishments (the Louis XV in Monte-Carlo, and Alain Ducasse at Essex House in New York), and 11 other restaurants, bars, bistros and hotels. Since he can't be in all of them at once, Ducasse has had to develop a managerial role for himself, becoming a sort of gastronomic Bill Gates. He hasn't been without his critics for taking this approach. In 1998, when he was awarded the maximum three-star rating by Michelin for both the Plaza Athénée *(see page 23)* and the Louis XV, some accused him of being an impostor, stealing the plaudits from his assistants who did the real work. But the controversy died down when most observers agreed that it was the end result that counted, and the end result in Ducasse's restaurants is almost always exceptional.

Joël Robuchon, the man once described as the 20th century's greatest *cuisinier*, is another to have adopted a managerial style. He gave up cooking altogether in 1996 to write books, produce television programmes and act as a consultant to Japanese restaurants. Seven years later, however, he announced his return to the kitchens with the unveiling of the groundbreaking L'Atelier Joël Robuchon *(see page 122)*, Paris's hottest new restaurant.

There are, of course, still chefs who have their fingers on the spoon, such as Pierre Gagnaire, perhaps the most creative French contemporary cook, the inventor of recipes such as pigeon with chocolate. Although he became the joint owner of a brasserie in London in 2003, he can still be found most days in the

Too good to eat? Sea urchin and salmon at Le Meurice

kitchen of his restaurant at the Hôtel Balzac *(see page 23)*, standing among his staff, tasting sauces and arranging the dishes before they are taken out to diners.

At the Ambroisie restaurant *(see page 66)*, chef Alain Pacaud, is also ever present, and when he wants to relax, he takes a table there. 'I love dining with my wife in my own restaurant,' he says, 'It is a priceless pleasure.' Yet, chefs like Pacaud are exceptions, a handful of masters who buck the trend set by Ducasse.

Leading light Yannick Alléno at his craft

The latest name on everyone's lips is that of Yannick Alléno. His performances at Les Muses restaurant were praised by almost all the critics. Alléno's crab claws with citrus fruit jelly and herb-infused crab cream became one of most celebrated dishes in Paris. In 2003, he moved to the Hôtel Meurice, where he was asked to transform a restaurant that had lost its lustre. He rose to the challenge and turned its fortunes around swiftly. In just six months Le Meurice *(see page 41)* was awarded two Michelin stars assuring Alléno a place in the gastronomic hall of fame.

The price of fame

The celebrity chef scene can sound very glamorous, but privately, chefs admit that haute cuisine is a tense, unrewarding business. They point out that the cost of running a first-class restaurant in France is high – on average, about 60 euro per customer. As a result, even the best establishments have a small profit margin of only between 2 and 5 percent, and many famous culinary institutions lose money. It is little wonder that the most talented look for other ways to supplement their income, either by opening more restaurants or using their names to sell food products. And then there is the intense and unrelenting pressure from critics, ever ready to turn against restaurants if standards slip, even just a little.

In 1999, for example, Marc Meneau's restaurant in Vézelay, Burgundy, was downgraded from three to two stars, and he lost 30 percent of his customers and three of his five sponsorship deals. 'It was as though I had lost a child,' he said, adding that he had thought about killing himself at the time. In 2003, another famous chef, Bernard Loiseau, went through with his plan to commit suicide, after a critic said he had fallen slightly below his exceptionally high standards. Loiseau shot himself in his restaurant in Saulieu in Burgundy; his death was seen as a national tragedy and led to calls for the country's chefs to free themselves from the media's chains. Some chefs threatened to shun interviews and turn their backs on the star system, but these calls were unrealistic. Chefs who have worked their way to the top of their profession need the media to ensure that culinary glory leads to material benefits. And in a country where gastronomy remains one of the highest forms of art, the media also needs celebrity chefs. Realistically, neither side has any interest in breaking the relationship, however fragile and tense it may be. The star system may be criticised, but it is not about to end.

Les Halles, Louvre and Palais Royal

From open-all-hours market brasseries to upmarket glamour spots, these adjacent areas have something to suit all tastes and budgets

This chapter embraces two distinct faces of Paris. On the one hand is the central Halles area, once home to an historic city-centre market but now unfortunately characterised by an unsightly shopping mall; on the other, are some of the most exclusive streets in the capital, in the district around place Vendôme, the Louvre and Palais Royal.

Les Halles and rue Saint-Honoré

It was the novelist Emile Zola (1840–1902) who called les Halles the *ventre* (stomach) of Paris – a comment that seems curiously appropriate in a restaurant guide; however, what he was referring to was the extraordinary mix of prostitutes and ne'er-do-wells who gave the city's old market its distinctive character. It is a tragedy that this Covent Garden-style collection of covered markets was pulled down in 1969, without a clearly defined project of what do with the space. The so-called *trou des Halles* (market hole) dominated by the monumental Saint-Eustache church became a national joke, and was even used as a film set. The forum that fills the gap today was constructed in the 1980s; this underground shopping mall is architecturally devoid of charm and at best provides a functional set of popular shops. The immediate surroundings have been blighted by notoriously bad landscaping, and Zola's *ventre* has returned in a different form – late at night the area now feels distinctly seedy, peopled with drug dealers and disaffected suburban youth.

However, surrounding the market area there remain vestiges of the atmosphere of the old Halles, with brasseries such as Au Pied de Cochon *(see page 41)* staying open around the clock, as does the winning traditional bistro La Tour Montlhéry *(see page 42)*, known by everybody as Chez Denise, not forgetting the favourite lunchtime venue of portly businessmen, Chez la Vieille *(see page 42)*. The clientele of the all-night restaurants is no longer formed of hard-working market porters in the early hours of the morning, but exhausted partygoers or hungry insomniacs. Traditional, colourful sleaze is still present, as prostitutes offer their services on rue St-Denis, but what is lacking is the fruit-and-vegetable market that once formed the centrepiece to these nocturnal activities. The market has moved out of town to Rungis, but you can still see one of the old buildings at Nogent-sur-Marne. There remains one address to detain the serious cook in Les Halles, Dehillerin *(18–20 rue Coquillière)*, an Aladdin's cave of professional cooking materials.

Heading off towards the river from the Halles, you will find the imposing Théâtre du Châtelet standing across from the Théâtre de la

***Opposite:** the palatial dining room at Le Meurice. **Below:** dainty treats at Le Grand Véfour*

Ville. The Châtelet is home of one of the finest musical seasons in the capital, and the Théâtre de la Ville has an impressive dance season. A little further down the river is the Samaritaine, an Art Nouveau department store with a pleasant rooftop café offering a spectacular view of the capital.

Linking the twilight world of les Halles to the grandeur of place de la Concorde is rue Saint-Honoré, which runs from behind the Halles to rue Royale. This elegant street has a rich history, and during the Revolution was the official route between the Conciergerie on the Ile de la Cîté and the scaffold erected on place de la Concorde. The street formed the backdrop for David's famous picture of Marie-Antoinette on her final journey to decapitation, past her favourite pharmacy where she bought her beauty products (still in operation as the Pharmacie Machover, *115 rue Saint-Honoré*). Perhaps she reflected upon her infamous 'Let them eat brioche' comment en route; nowadays she would pass two of the best boulangeries in the city: both Gosselin at No. 123–5 and Julien at No. 75 sell some of the best baguettes in France.

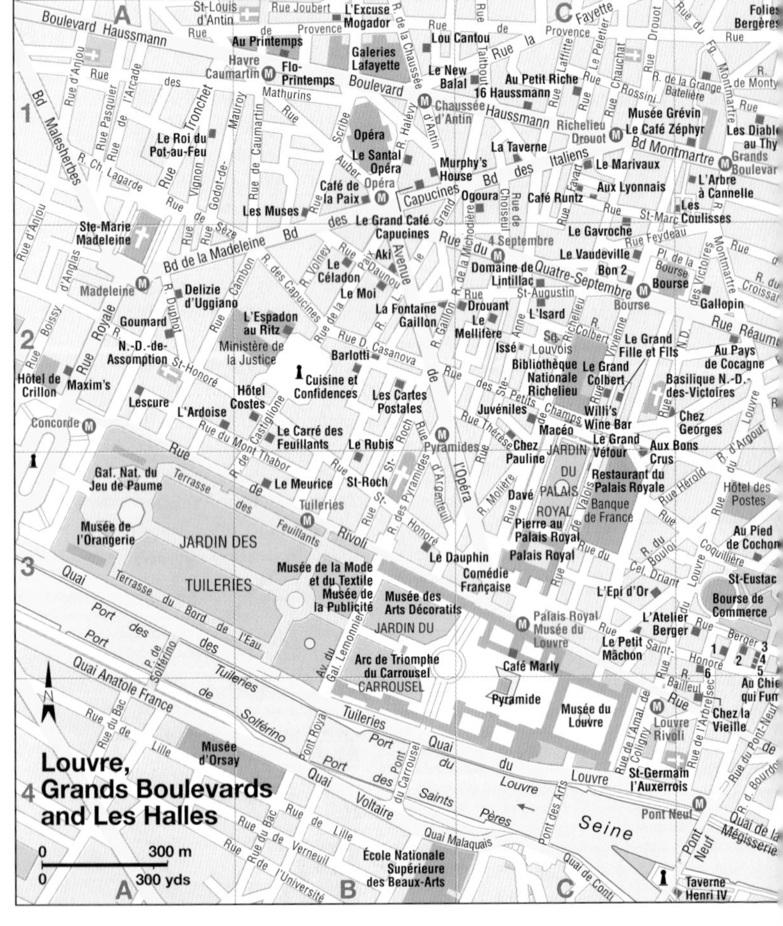

The Louvre and Palais Royal

And on the subject of the baguette, not only was Napoleon responsible for this slim loaf – he wanted one that would fit in a trouser pocket and be easy to march with – he also ordered the construction of the arcaded rue de Rivoli, which runs parallel with rue Saint-Honoré. Sadly, the arcades are now mostly filled with tourist tat, but a few grand hotels, such as the Meurice and the Régina, and the city's top tearoom Angelina, enliven a walk down the street.

Dominating the area is the Louvre, a monumental palace transformed into a museum, which fell under the late president Mitterrand's reforming hand. His *Grand Louvre* project involved the construction of the Sino-American architect I.M. Pei's pyramid, allowing easy access to the whole gallery, as well as an underground shopping mall and a careful display of the building's origins. Exhibitions aside, the museum's Café Marly *(see page 44)* has become a popular meeting place for Parisians and tourists alike, thanks to exemplary interior decoration and excellent food.

Les Halles
1 La Poule au Pot
2 Le Comptoir Paris-Marrakech
3 Chez Clovis
4 Chez Elle
5 Chez Denise
6 Midory

Stretching out in front of the Louvre, the Jardin des Tuileries extends to place de la Concorde, providing one of the main green lungs of the city. At the Concorde end of the garden you will find the Jeu de Paume and Orangerie museums, the former currently used for contemporary exhibitions and the latter housing Monet's *Water Lilies*.

At the same level as the Louvre, to the north of rue de Rivoli and rue Saint-Honoré, the gardens of the Palais Royal provide the ideal location for a moment of relaxation amid the austere splendour of Right Bank Paris. It is surrounded by exclusive boutiques and fine restaurants, including top restaurant Le Grand Véfour *(see page 40)*, which in the 18th century

FIVE OF THE BEST

Le Meurice: top cuisine from chef *du moment*, Yannick Alléno, in the opulent dining room of the Hôtel Meurice
Café Marly: a stylish museum restaurant overlooking the Louvre's pyramid
Chez Denise (La Tour Montlhéry): all-night bistro packing in hungry regulars
Chez la Vieille – Adrienne: gargantuan feast of French country cuisine
Le Grand Véfour: gastronomic temple within the serene Palais Royal confines

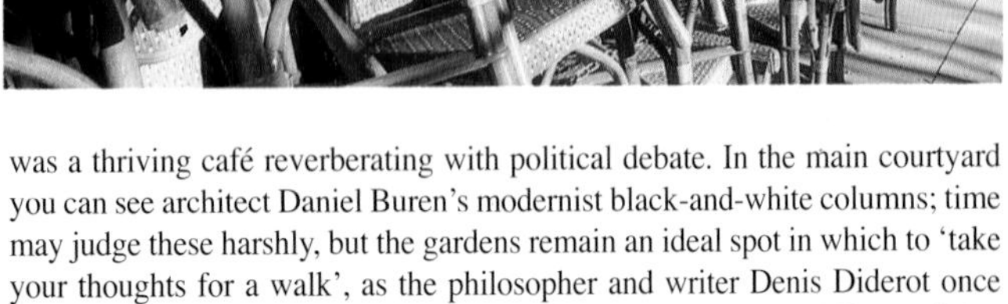

Above: slick service at Barlotti
Right: stacked chairs at the Palais Royal

was a thriving café reverberating with political debate. In the main courtyard you can see architect Daniel Buren's modernist black-and-white columns; time may judge these harshly, but the gardens remain an ideal spot in which to 'take your thoughts for a walk', as the philosopher and writer Denis Diderot once suggested. If a cigar helps in the process then La Civette *(157 rue Saint-Honoré, tel: 01 42 96 04 99)* opposite is the best tobacconist in Paris.

In one corner of the Palais Royal you will notice the Comédie Française theatre, which moved here at the end of the 18th century. If your French is up to a Racine tragedy, it makes for a great evening out, possibly combined with a meal at nearby luxury bistro Chez Pauline *(see page 42)*.

After crossing the junction with avenue de l'Opéra, rue Saint-Honoré becomes increasingly glamorous. Place du Marché-Saint-Honoré no longer houses a market, but an office block skilfully integrated into the old building by Ricardo Bofill. While Le Rubis wine bar *(see page 44)* is a vestige of former times, Italian restaurant and bar Barlotti *(see page 46)* and designer restaurant Cuisine et Confidences *(see page 45)* show the new face of this fashionable area, which rubs shoulders with the prestigious place Vendôme. This octagonal wonder of a square is home to the world's most expensive jewellers, and perfumeries, crowned by the Hôtel Ritz. The central column celebrating Napoléon's military exploits has had a chequered history, and during the Commune uprising in 1871 the painter Gustave Courbet instigated its destruction – he later gallantly paid for its restoration. Rue Saint-Honoré eventually ends its course on the aptly name rue Royale, where tea and cakes at chocolate-box tearoom Ladurée *(see page 126)* is an event not to be missed.

Eating Alfresco

Dining outdoors in one of the world's most beautiful cities is a luxury, and luckily it's one that most people can afford

Countless cafés and bistros in Paris have pavement terraces. The nicest ones spill into squares, such as bistros **La Fontaine de Mars** *(see page 118)*, with its restful fountain, **Chez Janou** *(see page 67)*, with ivy climbing its walls, and **L'Eté en Pente Douce** *(see page 135)*, half-way up a side stairway to the Sacré-Coeur. One of the city's most beautiful squares is place des Vosges, and **Ma Bourgogne** *(19 place des Vosges, 4th, tel: 01 42 78 44 64)* is a trustworthy bistro with excellent people-watching potential. The restaurant terraces in place Dauphine on the Ile de la Cité are magical on summer nights, while there are relaxing places to eat in the Jardin du Palais Royal – the best restaurant here is **Restaurant du Palais Royal** *(see page 46)*.

A (dining) room with a view

A table with a bird's-eye view is also enticing. The minimalist **Georges** *(see page 72)* on top of the Centre Pompidou has deliciously trendy eats for equally hip diners with deep wallets. For an upscale, discreet option, try the terrace at the **Hôtel Raphaël** *(17 avenue Kléber, 16th, tel: 01 53 64 32 00)*, with Paris spread out gloriously below. On ground level, leafy comfort is to be found at the **Café Lenôtre** in the Pavillon Elysée *(see page 26)*, while the sophisticated **L'Esplanade** *(52 rue Fabert, 7th, tel: 01 47 05 38 80)* has views over the floodlit Invalides. **Café Marly** *(see page 44)* has a gorgeous stone terrace within the Louvre, as well as good food and a typically chic clientele.

For an elegant two-star Michelin meal, head for the terrace of the **Pré Catelan** in the Bois de Boulogne *(see page 150)*. And if you like the idea of the great outdoors more than actually being there, **Lasserre** *(see page 22)* is an elegant dining room with a ceiling that opens towards the stars.

Parisian picnics

Half the fun of picnicking in Paris is shopping for supplies at the local markets *(see pages 92–93)*, boulangeries and delis. But for a one-stop shop **La Grande Epicerie de Paris** *(38 rue de Sèvres, 7th)* is filled with decadent goodies. Armed with the wherewithall for your picnic, just choose your spot. Though lacking in expanses of grass you can sprawl on, the city's manicured parks, squares and river banks are well equipped with benches. The lovely Jardin de Luxembourg in the 6th *arrondissement* has plenty of chairs scattered around, while the Jardin du Palais Royal is a haven of peace in the heart of the city, but the best daytime park for picnicking is the Buttes-Chaumont, in the 19th. It's a bit of a trek, but it's a pretty park to while away a sunny afternoon. Square du Vert-Galant on the tip of the Ile de la Cité is lovely in the evening, and favoured by a young and lively crowd. There aren't many places along the Seine where you can sit on the grass but in the 5th, below the Jardin des Plantes, is a romantic strip on quai Saint-Bernard. For a truly Parisian experience, head for the pedestrian Pont des Arts – take a bottle of chilled champagne and enjoy the sunlit or floodlit beauty of the banks of the Seine.

Eating alfresco at Ma Bourgogne, Place des Vosges

Haute Cuisine

Le Carré des Feuillants

14 rue de Castiglione, 1st [B2]. Tel: 01 42 86 82 82. Open: L and D Mon–Fri; closed Aug. **€€€€**

A stone's throw from place Vendôme, the wonderful Alain Dutournier prepares favourite dishes from his beloved southwest with a magician's hand. Grilled lobster, oysters with caviar from the Garonne, foie gras and more besides. Don't miss his pistachio macaroons for dessert. Dress appropriately for the formal dining room.

***Below and bottom:* Palais Royal's lavish Le Grand Véfour**

L'Espadon au Ritz

15 place Vendôme, 1st [B2]. Tel: 01 43 16 30 80. Open: B, L and D daily. **€€€€** *www.ritzparis.com*

The restaurant of the Ritz lives up to its image of polished culinary sophistication, even if for British tourists the hotel still carries poignant memories of the late Princess Diana, who had her final meal here. In season, sample asparagus with scallops and truffles, John Dory in seafood foam, and one of the house specialities: caramelised millefeuille.

Goumard

9 rue Duphot, 1st [A2]. Tel: 01 42 60 36 07. Open: L and D daily; closed early Aug. **€€€–€€€€** *www.goumard.fr*

One of the most elegant fish restaurants in Paris, with a spacious room awash with gorgeous Lalique crystal, and a discerning expense-account crowd. The chef is celebrated for his perfect, if pricey, fish dishes including scallops with artichokes and roasted turbot. Among the interesting, unusual desserts are saffron pears with cocoa sorbet and bergamot macaroons.

Le Grand Véfour 🍴

17 rue de Beaujolais, 1st [C2]. Tel: 01 42 96 56 27. Open: L and D Mon–Thur, L only Fri; closed Aug and Christmas. **€€€€**

This celebrated restaurant not only has stunning décor but also a fabulous view overlooking the Palais Royal. Classic cuisine – lobster salad, oxtail parmentier, and clever desserts involving confited vegetables – are the sorts of high-flying offerings prepared by Guy Martin, one of most imaginative and accomplished chefs in town.

Exquisite food from Yannick Alléno at Le Meurice

Maxim's

3 rue Royale, 8th [A2]. Tel: 01 42 65 27 94. Open: L and D Mon–Sat, Tues–Sat only July–Aug. **€€€€**
www.maxims-de-paris.com
Despite all the hype and tradition, Maxim's is no longer a popular evening out, but the food is pleasantly free of fashionable fripperies, and the 1900 decoration remains a gem. Service belongs to another more courteous age. A restaurant in a delightful time warp.

Le Meurice

Hôtel Meurice, 228 rue de Rivoli, 1st [B3]. Tel: 01 44 58 10 55. Open: L and D Mon–Fri, D only Sat. **€€€€**
The Meurice, overlooking the Tuileries gardens, has been gloriously restored to its glittering best, and the dining room offers a top dining experience after a lull of several years. Since September 2003 the restaurant has been the domain of rising star Yannick Alléno, the name on everyone's lips, recently awarded two Michelin stars. Ingredients are carefully sourced for dishes such as foie-gras terrine, veal shoulder in its own juice, and wild strawberries with crème-brûlée ice cream. In season, don't miss the bouillabaisse jelly served in a sea-urchin shell.

Brasseries

Au Chien qui Fume

33 rue du Pont-Neuf, 1st [D3]. Tel: 01 42 36 07 42. Open: L and D daily, non-stop noon–2am. **€€**
www.au-chien-qui-fume.com
The 'smoking dog' stays up until two in the morning and offers an extensive brasserie menu including shrimp and langoustine salad, or duck à l'orange. All the classic desserts are on offer, including iced nougat and chocolate mousse. Not a bad place to lap up the late-night atmosphere in Les Halles.

Au Pied de Cochon

6 rue Coquillière, 1st [D3]. Tel: 01 40 13 77 00. Open: B, L and D, non-stop 24 hours. **€€€**
www.pieddecochon.com
It's a tourist trap, but this brasserie never shuts, so if you've been revelling late into the night and are desperate for French onion soup, you'll find it here, just as market workers did in the early 20th century.

Bistros

L'Ardoise

28 rue du Mont-Thabor, 1st [A2]. Tel: 01 42 96 28 18. Open: L and D Wed–Sun. **€€**
A successful, modern bistro, which offers a good-value menu,

Did you know?

Place Vendôme, the smartest square in Paris, was originally laid out in 1699 to glorify Louis XIV. The king's equestrian statue was replaced by a copy of Trajan's Column in Rome, featuring Napoleon's military exploits. The square is now occupied by the Ritz, the Ministry of Justice, J.P. Morgan bank and luxury jewellers, which make it a big magnet for wishful window shoppers.

L'Escargot Montorgueil

written up on a blackboard – the *ardoise* in question. The typical bistro cooking is careful, even if the surroundings are rather utilitarian, but the position near the Tuileries gardens is convenient.

TIP

For a taste of what Les Halles used to be like, make for rue Montorgueil, a narrow, pedestrianised street packed with romantic cafés, friendly butchers and colourful fruit-and-veg stalls. This short strip of charm is one of the few places in Les Halles where it's easy to linger.

Aux Bons Crus

7 rue des Petits-Champs, 1st [C3]. Tel: 01 42 60 06 45. Open: B, L and D Mon–Sat. **€**

In an area with a high concentration of wine bars, this late-19th-century spot is perhaps the most humble of the lot. Traditional bistro dishes and plenty of unpretentious wines from which to choose.

Chez Clovis

33 rue Berger, 1st [D3]. Tel: 01 42 33 97 07. Open: L and D Mon–Sat. **€€**

Good hearty cuisine at the core of Les Halles in a simple terraced café. Generous helpings and convivial waiters provide an uncomplicated eating experience.

Chez Denise

5 rue des Prouvaires, 1st [D3]. Tel: 01 42 36 21 82. Open: B, L and D, 24 hours Mon–Fri; closed mid-July–mid-Aug. **€€**

In the old tradition of Les Halles, Chez Denise (aka La Tour Montlhéry) stays open 24 hours a day during the week. The home-cooking and massive portions also contribute to the popularity of this famed bistro, with its lively crowd of loyal locals.

Chez Pauline

5 rue Villedo, 1st [C2]. Tel: 01 42 96 20 70. Open: L and D Mon–Sat. **€€€**

This upmarket bistro attracts a well-heeled clientele who appreciate the comfortably chic atmosphere and lighter versions of old favourites, such as lentil soup with a poached egg, followed by a good steak. It's a great place for truffles in season – they're delivered right to the door from the South of France.

Chez la Vieille – Adrienne

1 rue Bailleul, 1st [D4]. Tel: 01 42 60 15 78. Open: L only Mon–Fri, D Thur. **€€€**

This classic bistro is ideal for a serious, homely feast, delivered in generous portions from which you can help yourself, by the delightful all-female staff. The Corsican owner will regale you with a cornucopian selection of starters, followed by a simple main course, such as tripe or pot-au-feu, then a vast choice of desserts. It's popular, so it's a good idea to book.

L'Epi d'Or

25 rue Jean-Jacques Rousseau, 1st [C3]. Tel: 01 42 36 38 12. Open: L and D Mon–Fri, D only Sat. **€€**

A lovely, old-world bistro with seriously well-prepared classics – a rare find in modern-day Paris. Foie gras made in-house, steak tartare served with salad or fries, excellent potato gratin and delicious clafoutis. The locals fill it up fast, so book ahead.

L'Escargot Montorgueil

38 rue Montorgueil, 1st [D3]. Tel: 01 42 36 83 51. Open: L and D Mon–Sat. **€€€**
www.escargot-montorgueil.com

Its hey-day has passed, but the 'snail of Montorgueil', its Second-Empire décor intact, remains a glamorous, tourist-friendly restaurant nonetheless. Sadly, the cooking is no match for the surroundings, but if you stick to a dozen plump garlicky snails, you can still get a feel for its past splendour.

Juvéniles

47 rue de Richelieu, 1st [C2]. Tel: 01 44 50 10 07. Open: L and D Mon–Sat. **€€**

Witty Tim Johnston's cramped but popular wine bar offers a truly special – and personal – selection of wines, as well as simple plats du jour, and a cheeseboard that celebrates the great British Stilton.

Lescure

7 rue Mondovi, 1st [A2]. Tel: 01 42 60 18 91. Open: L and D Mon–Fri; closed 3 weeks in August and last week of Dec. **€€**

Situated just off rue de Rivoli, this delightfully quaint restaurant has been in the same family for nearly 100 years. The menu is rigorously traditional – duck confit, beef bourguignon, rabbit with sorrel, etc – and provides excellent value for money.

Au Père Fouettard

9 rue Pierre-Lescot, 1st [E3]. Tel: 01 42 33 74 17. Open: L and D daily, till 1am. **€€**

A warm and cosy bistro, with cheerful service, a young clientele and its fair share of regulars. Cheap prices, and good food if you stick to the standards such as marrow tartines, roast suckling pig, chocolate tart or spice roasted apples. There's a lovely leafy terrace in summer.

Le Petit Mâchon

158 rue Saint-Honoré, 1st [C3]. Tel: 01 42 60 08 06. Open: L and D Tues–Sun. **€€€**

Mostly Lyonnais specialities in a high-end bistro with serious, but polite, proprietors. Dishes, served on tables decked with stiff, starched linens, include fish quenelles, beef jelly with coriander, and rhubarb-and-red fruit pudding.

The elegant colonnades of the Palais Royal

Did you know?
The word *clochard* (which means 'bum' or 'tramp' – depending on which side of the Atlantic you hail from) has its origins, according to some theories, in the word *cloche* (bell). A bell used to be rung at closing time at the market at Les Halles, indicating to the *clochards* that they could come to fetch the leftovers to eat.

Pierre au Palais Royal
10 rue de Richelieu, 1st [C3]. Tel: 01 42 96 09 17. Open: L and D Mon–Fri, D only Sat. **€€€**
A new team has taken over at this classic Paris restaurant. The interior is serious and reserved, and the food, previously as staid as the décor, is now taking a lighter, more fashionable approach to classics such as pigeon with figs and dates and iced orange soup.

Le Rubis
10 rue du Marché-Saint-Honoré, 1st [B3]. Tel: 01 42 61 03 34. Open: L only Mon–Sat. **€**
A one-of-a-kind local wine bar near the Marché Saint-Honoré, where the plats du jour – sausages with lentils, sautéed veal – are reliably delicious, and the wine flows freely. The nicotine-stained walls and half-barrel décor give the impression of being in the provinces.

Aux Tonneaux des Halles
28 rue Montorgueil, 1st [D3]. Tel: 01 42 33 36 19. Open: L and D Mon–Sat. **€**
Along with Aux Bons Crus *(see page 42)*, this is Patrick Fabre's second wine bar-cum-bistro with a busy, but easy-going atmosphere. Traditional comfort food is well prepared and perfect washed down with a smartly chosen Beaujolais. It's also good for a quick drink at the end of the day and for people-watching on the lower end of lively rue Montorgueil.

Cafés

Café Marly (🍴)
93 rue de Rivoli, 1st [C3]. Tel: 01 49 26 06 60. Open: L and D daily. **€€**
Alongside the pyramid of the Louvre, this designer museum café (another Costes brothers' hit) is perpetually abuzz with Parisian intelligentsia and tourists alike. The food, which is modern and light, is prepared to high standards, but sold for a steep price. You may have to wait for a seat, and it can take some arm waving to get served.

Taverne Henri IV
13 place du Pont-Neuf, 1st [D4]. Tel: 01 43 54 27 90. Open: B, L and D Mon–Sat, non-stop 9am–10pm. **€**
This historic wine bar on the Pont Neuf is still a quaint stop for a lunchtime tartine or cheese and charcuterie with a glass of wine. The service can be brusque, but the location on the Île de la Cité is compensation enough.

Regional

Le Béarn
8 rue des Halles, 1st [D4]. Tel: 01 42 36 93 35. Open: L and D Mon–Sat. **€**
This is a small and unpretentious bistro, near the Théâtre du Châtelet, where you can enjoy a

Mix art and cuisine at the Louvre's Café Marly

slice of pâté from the Béarn with a glass of wine. A memory of when Les Halles were filled with cramped bars just like this, before serious shopping became the order of the day here instead.

Le Dauphin

167 rue Saint-Honoré, 1st [B3]. Tel: 01 42 60 40 11. Open: L and D daily, noon–midnight. **€€–€€€**.
Located just opposite the Comédie Française, this bourgeois restaurant – all crisp linens and comfortable chairs – has been taken over by the management of the Café de Paris in Biarritz. They've brought a distinct Basque accent to the bistro cooking, although the rib of beef for two remains the classic choice. Not the cheapest option, however.

Contemporary

L'Atelier Berger

49 rue Berger, 1st [D3]. Tel: 01 40 28 00 00. Open: L and D Mon–Sat. **€**
The stylish contemporary cooking at this restaurant attracts a fashion-conscious crowd on the edge of Les Halles. Presentation and imagination are by turn impressive and delicious – crab nems, beef fricassée, baked apples – but it's best to go with a top model's slim appetite.

Les Cartes Postales

7 rue Gomboust, 1st [B2]. Tel: 01 42 61 23 40. Open: L and D Tues–Fri, L only Mon, D only Sat; closed 3 weeks July–Aug and last week in Dec. **€€€**
Located not far from the Marché Saint-Honoré, this restaurant has a Japanese chef, trained in the French tradition. The Oriental delicacy and occasional daring touches in his classical cuisine make this modern Zen-like restaurant a sophisticated place to eat. Older clientele and high prices.

Above: wine at Cuisine et Confidences. Left: the Zen-like Les Cartes Postales

Cuisine et Confidences

33 place du Marché-Saint-Honoré, 1st [B2]. Tel: 01 42 96 31 34. Open: L only daily. **€€**
Cuisine et Confidences has a lovely lunchtime terrace and an airy, clean décor that makes you feel like you're about to eat healthily before you even raise a fork to your lips. There's one hot plat du jour, otherwise the menu is comprised solely of salads, all of which are plentiful and tasty.

Hôtel Costes

239 rue Saint-Honoré, 1st [B2]. Tel: 01 42 44 50 25. Open: L and D daily. **€€–€€€**
www.hotelcostes.com

TIP

If you feel in need of a snack while wandering in the Tuileries, **Dame Tartine** *(tel: 01 42 77 32 22)*, no doubt a close relative of the Earl of Sandwich, and the **Chalet de Diane** *(tel: 01 42 96 81 12)* provide acceptable food at a reasonable price.

Hip design and international cuisine at Barlotti

TIP

Professional chefs have been coming to **E. Dehillerin** *(18 rue Coquillière)* since 1820. It is an Aladdin's cave for cooks, stocked with a huge range of knives, cooking utensils, pots and pans, plus heavy-duty kit from ham-slicers to ice-makers.

The ultimate designer hotel, the Costes plays host to stars and celebs from all over the world. Designer Jacques Garcia has created a riot of architectural styles from Napoleonic grandeur to Italian *palazzo*. The food is as precious and elaborate as you would expect in such surroundings – and just as expensive.

Macéo

15 rue des Petits-Champs, 1st [C2]. Tel: 01 42 97 53 85. Open: L and D Mon–Fri, D only Sat; closed 2 weeks Aug. **€€–€€€**

The modernised Second Empire dining room is cool, casual and elegant – a truly lovely setting noon or night. The restaurant is under the same management as Willi's Wine Bar next door, so the excellent wine list comes as no surprise; the food to go with it is underwhelming, however. Lots of American tourists. Bilingual service.

Restaurant du Palais Royal

43 rue de Valois, 1st [C3]. Tel: 01 40 20 00 27. Open: L Mon–Fri, D Mon–Sat. **€€€**

This is the most attractive terrace on the Palais Royal and the finest of the restaurants circling the inner gardens. The food, without being wildly imaginative, lives up to the view. Choose à la carte, or opt for the daily changing menu, which features dishes such as langoustine cappuccino, rouget with polenta, and a choice of sorbets.

International

Barlotti

35 place du Marché-Saint-Honoré, 1st [B2]. Tel: 01 44 86 97 97. Open: L and D daily. **€€**

The same management that masterminded the trendy (and over-hyped) Buddha Bar has now opened this high-fashion Italian spot, where a young and vibrant crowd enjoys top-class carpaccio and a long list of adventurous pasta dishes, as well as a cosmopolitan ambience.

Chez Vong

10 rue de la Grande-Truanderie, 1st [E3]. Tel: 01 40 39 99 89. Open: L and D Mon–Sat. **€€€**

Near the rather tawdry streets of the St-Denis area, this smart Chinese restaurant comes as something of a surprise. The menu features all the usual favourites, which are prepared to a standard rarely attained in Paris.

Le Comptoir Paris-Marrakech

37 rue Berger, 1st [D3]. Tel: 01 40 26 26 66. Open: L and D daily, non-stop noon–2am. **€€**

Right in the centre of Les Halles this spacious, clean-lined restaurant does a decent job of North African cuisine: tajines, brochettes, or fragrant lemon chicken until the small hours of the morning.

Davé

12 rue Richelieu, 1st [C3]. Tel: 01 42 61 49 48. Open: L and D Mon–Fri, D only Sat–Sun. **€€€**

Davé may look like an ordinary Chinese restaurant, but is, in fact, popular with a clientele of stars from fashion and showbiz. The owner knows how to flatter and cajole the celebrity palate with his classy Asian cookery. Great fun.

Delizie d'Uggiano

18 rue Duphot, 1st [A2]. Tel: 01 40 15 06 69. Open: L and D Mon–Fri, D only Sat. **€€€**

Authentic Tuscan cookery – top-quality charcuterie, pasta and rice, accompanied by the boss's own rich Chianti. An intimate and stylish celebration of Italian food.

Midory

49 rue de l'Arbre Sec, 1st [D3]. Tel: 01 42 97 47 30. Open: L and D Mon–Sat. **€€**

Word is getting out about this neighbourhood Japanese restaurant, where the chef prepares sushi before your very eyes and never forgets a face. Loyal regulars come in for a €10 Maki menu, including tasty miso soup, three different maki rolls, Japanese slaw, and sliced fresh fruit for dessert.

Bars and Pubs

For a classic apéritif, nothing can match the style and panache of the **Hemingway Bar** at the Ritz *(15 place Vendôme, tel: 01 43 16 30 30)*, named after the writer whose name is linked to bars across the world. Another comfortable hotel bar is to be found in the **Hôtel Régina** *(2 place des Pyramides, tel: 01 42 60 31 10)*. For a more fashion-conscious crowd a drink is a good way to explore the over-the-top decoration of the **Hôtel Costes** *(239 rue Saint-Honoré, tel: 01 42 44 50 00)*, where the rich and famous like to be seen. For a more laid-back experience **Le Fumoir** *(6 rue de l'Amiral-Coligny, tel: 01 42 92 00 24)* has proved one of the most popular spots in Paris. Just behind the Louvre, this bar and restaurant has one of the best happy hours in town, and the trendy book-lined space is always packed with bright young things from early evening. For a glass of wine in Les Halles **Le Cochon à l'Oreille** *(15 rue Montmartre, tel: 01 42 36 07 56)* is an unchanging café with bags of authentic atmosphere, or for a quick pre-concert drink the **Café Zimmer** *(1 place du Châtelet, tel: 01 42 36 74 03)*, just next door to the Châtelet, is a useful address. **Willi's Wine Bar** *(13 rue des Petits-Champs, tel: 01 42 61 05 09)* may not be an authentic Paris experience, but it remains enormously popular among Anglophones. And for great views with Art Nouveau touches, the top-floor café of the city's original department store, the **Samaritaine** *(23 quai du Louvre, tel: 01 40 41 20 20)* is unbeatable.

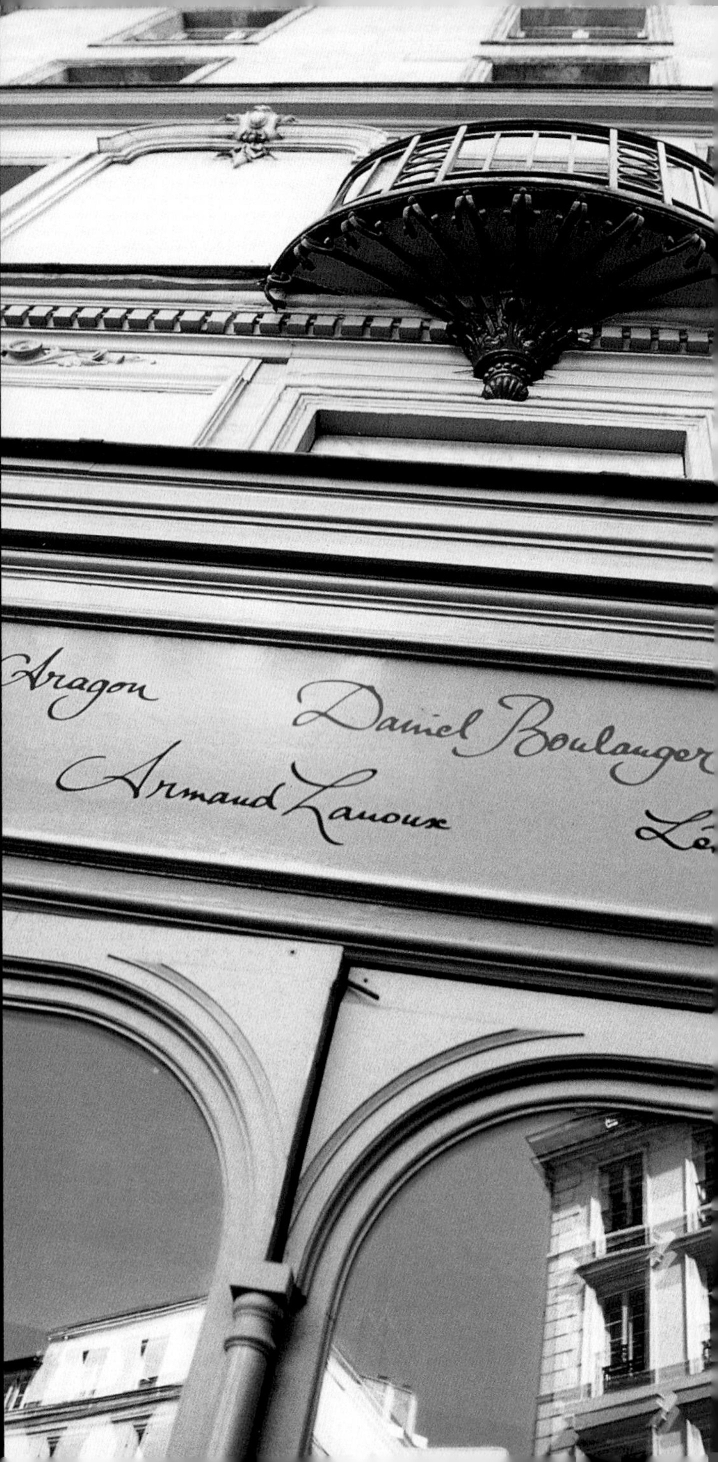
Aragon
Daniel Boulanger
Armand Lanoux

OPÉRA, BOURSE AND GRANDS BOULEVARDS

An area that combines the grandeur of the old city with the buzz of the new – and with restaurants and bars to match

There is the unmistakable stamp of Gallic grandeur in the area that runs from place de La Madeleine in the west to boulevard Sébastopol in the east. The monuments are imposing (often stunning, even), and the boulevards wide and busy, showing off Paris's striking ability to combine the historic with the present – to remain a city both lived in and living. Weaving through these loud and crowded streets are shoppers darting up to the Grands Magasins (department stores), bankers racing towards the Bourse (Stock Exchange), and tourists dipping in and out of multitudinous bistros and bars, not to mention numerous Japanese restaurants. There are many grand boulevards cutting through these neighbourhoods, so make a point of veering off on to the smaller streets, because this is where you'll discover some of the city's most enticing speciality food shops and restaurants, often hidden between an insurance broker and a travel agent. It is worth taking the time to explore.

The Madeleine and boulevard de la Madeleine

The Madeleine church was the fruit of anguished debate for 80 years in the 18th and 19th centuries, when it was mooted as a stock exhange, library and railway station, before Napoleon Bonaparte lost patience with the wrangling and ordered that it become a place of worship. It is a now a landmark, sitting in the centre of a square that is the setting for a flower market, as well as the biggest branches of France's best-known delicatessen chains, Hédiard *(21 place de la Madeleine, tel: 01 43 12 88 88)* and Fauchon *(26–30 place de la Madeleine, tel: 01 47 42 60 11)*. Both are well worth a visit, as are La Maison de la Truffe *(19 place de la Madeleine, tel: 01 42 65 53 22)*, the temple of truffles which also has a small restaurant, and the Maille mustard shop on the corner of the square where it meets boulevard de la Madeleine *(6 place de la Madeleine, tel: 01 40 15 06 00)*. Walk up this broad, straight Parisian avenue and at No. 8 is the Maison du Chocolat *(tel: 01 47 42 86 52)*, one of five elegant branches in the capital. Opposite, at Nos 3–5, is Lavinia *(see page 53)*, one of the best-stocked wine stores in Paris, with some of the most knowledgeable staff.

***Opposite:* Drouant. *Below:* licence to serve**

Opéra

Boulevard de la Madeleine leads into boulevard des Capucines, which opens into the wide expanse of place de l'Opéra. Stand in the middle of the square – or, better still, walk a little way down avenue de l'Opéra – to get a view of the Palais Garnier Opera House. A restoration programme began on this magnificent building, which dates from 1862 and was designed by the architect Charles Garnier, in the late 1990s, and it now gleams proudly on a sunny day. With its fabulously intricate façade and marbled halls, it has been described as the finest example of Second Empire architecture. Behind it, on one side of place de l'Opéra is rue Scribe, named after the prolific 19th-century playwright, Eugène Scribe. On this road is the Grand Hôtel *(2 rue Scribe, tel: 01 40 07 32 32)*, which is every bit as grand as its name, and the Musée de la Parfumerie Fragonard *(9 rue Scribe, tel: 01 47 42 93 40)*, which traces 3,000 years of perfume-making.

Les Grands Boulevards

The east side of place de l'Opéra is more buzzy and noisy than the west. Welcome to the Grands Boulevards (Great Boulevards), a popular place for shopping. Home to large, well-lit brasseries and a mix of pizza, sushi and hamburger joints, these boulevards are not necessarily the best place in which to eat, except in the early hours when everywhere else has shut. However, it is worth taking a walk down avenues that are invariably crowded with foreign holidaymakers, provincial French visitors and office-workers from the banks that have their headquarters there. It makes for a peculiarly Parisian combination of tourism and business. The boulevards date from the end of 17th century, when Louis XIV – le Roi Soleil (or Sun King) – felt secure enough on the French throne to demolish the city's medieval fortifications and turn them into what was soon a fashionable street. By the 19th century they were the centre of Parisian theatreland, but also of Parisian gangsterism. This earned them the nickname Criminal Boulevard. Happily, the gangsters have moved elsewhere over the past century, while the theatres have remained.

La Bourse

Between the boulevards and the Stock Exchange – La Bourse – lie the narrow streets that contain some of the finest bistros in Paris. Here, if the restaurants are full, it is a sure sign that they are good, for sub-standard establishments are swiftly deserted. Some of the city's most delightfully unexpected passageways and squares are situated off these streets. Take, for instance, place Gaillon, with its

The sumptuous Palais Garnier

FIVE OF THE BEST

Le Céladon: superb food by Christophe Moisand for lovers of high-class gastronomy
Chez Georges: an old-fashioned bistro, proclaimed by gourmets to be among the finest in Paris
Gallopin: inspired interpretations of classic French dishes in gorgeous, airy setting
Aux Lyonnais: bistro revamped by Alain Ducasse, specialising in cuisine from Lyon
Les Muses: refined French cooking at its very best and in elegant surroundings

fountain, or square Louvois, right by the Bibliothèque Nationale. And don't miss the small, ornate shopping arcades that date from the 19th century. There is the elegant Galerie Vivienne, where the designer Jean-Paul Gaultier has his *atelier*, or workshop; the Passage des Panoramas, with its philatelists; and, on the northern side of the Grands Boulevards, Passage Jouffroy, where the Paris waxworks museum, the Musée Grévin *(10 boulevard Montmartre, tel: 01 47 70 85 05)*, is situated. Bars and cafés flourish in these historic passages, and so do boutiques. For food and wine, try Legrand Filles et Fils in the Galerie Vivienne (between 4 rue des Petits-Champs, 6 rue Vivienne and 5 rue de la Banque), and for cakes, try La Tour des Délices in the Passage Jouffroy *(between 10 boulevard Montmartre and 9 rue de la Grange-Batalière)*. For chocolates, drop into Debauve & Gallais at 33 rue Vivienne *(tel: 01 40 39 05 50)*.

Above left:* *The window of L'Arbre à Cannelle

Sentier

East of the Stock Exchange, the atmosphere changes again, with the financiers giving way to the bustle of the Sentier. This Jewish district was – and to a large extent remains – the bastion of the French rag-trade, home to wholesale clothing merchants. It may not sound like much of a tourist attraction, but it should not be missed, for in the heart of the Sentier lies the most Parisian of streets, rue Montorgueil. It sometimes seems as though the whole of the city has converged upon this narrow pedestrian precinct, where you can have a coffee on a terrace, lunch in a bistro and then go shopping for fruit and vegetables in some of the most colourful greengrocers in the city. This crowded monument to the French culinary art is also home to the unmissable pâtissier, Stohrer, where the baba au rhum is said to have been invented in 1730.

Boulevard Haussmann

North of place de l'Opéra is the boulevard named after Baron Georges-Eugène Haussmann, the 19th-century town planner who gave Paris the long, wide, straight avenues that are its hallmark today. The Baron was famous for the symmetry that he imposed upon the city, but nowadays boulevard Haussmann is best known for its department stores, Le Printemps (No. 64) and Galeries Lafayette (No. 40), with their designer labels and luxury goods. Both are magnets for shoppers, although they also cater for gourmets and have well-stocked food halls.

Haute Cuisine

Le Céladon 🍴

Hôtel Westminster, 15 rue Daunou, 2nd [B2]. Tel: 01 47 03 40 42. Open: L and D Mon–Fri; closed Aug. **€€€–€€€€**
www.leceladon.com

Chef Christophe Moisand has established a reputation as one of the brightest young talents in Paris, bringing a delicate hint of Oriental spice to fundamentally Gallic recipes. Try wild escargots en ravioli with garlic and spinach, or milk-fed lamb braised with wild fennel seeds, and round off the meal with an exotic dessert such as banana tart with rum sabayon, spiced coulis and coconut sorbet, all served against an elegant Regency backdrop in the boutique Hôtel Westminster.

Drouant

18 place Gaillon, 2nd [C2]. Tel: 01 42 65 15 16. Open: L and D Mon–Fri; closed Aug. **€€€–€€€€**

Once frequented by Renoir, Rodin, and Pissarro, this thoroughly Art Deco restaurant, featuring a monumental staircase designed by Jacques-Emile Ruhlmann, is classically elegant. Chef Louis Grondard's dishes, such as langoustine tails with candied aubergine, saffron rouget with an artichoke tart or milk-fed lamb roasted in garlic, are equally refined. Every October, the prestigious Goncourt literary prize is hosted in the grand Louis XVI room here.

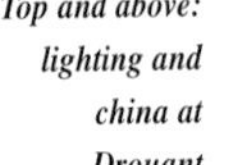

Top and above: lighting and china at Drouant

Les Muses 🍴

Hôtel Scribe, 1 rue Scribe, 9th [B1]. Tel: 01 44 71 24 26. Open: L and D Mon–Fri; closed 2 weeks in Aug. **€€€–€€€€**

Situated in the basement of the Hôtel Scribe, this elegant restaurant serves exquisite dishes such as oysters sautéed in a shallot bouillon and served with slices of foie gras; roasted duck with liquorice butter, mango chutney and crisp potatoes; and wild strawberries in saffron millefeuille pastry with vanilla ice cream and maple syrup – all the inventions of dynamic young chef Jean-François Rouquette.

Brasseries

Flo-Printemps

Le Printemps store (6th floor), 64 boulevard Haussmann, 9th [B1]. Tel: 01 42 82 58 84. Open: L only Mon–Sat, D Thur. **€€**

If you've been power shopping in this department store all morning and don't quite have the strength to leave the premises, enjoy a peaceful meal under its magnificent stained-glass dome. There's a complete menu, so you can choose a slice of quiche or copious salad, or more substantial fare such as steak tartare, tagliatelle with salmon, or roast fillet of duckling.

Gallopin 🍴

40 rue Notre-Dame-des-Victoires, 2nd [D2]. Tel: 01 42 36 45 38. Open: L and D Mon–Sat, non-stop noon–midnight. **€€€**
www.brasseriegallopin.com

This famous brasserie opposite the Stock Exchange opened in 1876 and is still decorated in the elegant belle époque style. Chef Georges Belondrade prepares refined versions of traditional dishes, including pâté 'maison', grilled meats and flambéed crêpes. The fish is a star attraction, with specialities such as haddock poached in milk with fresh spinach, and deliciously fresh seafood platters. Delightful.

Le Grand Café Capucines

4 boulevard des Capucines, 9th [B1]. Tel: 01 43 12 19 00. Open: B, L and D, 24 hours. **€€€**

Romantic dining at Gallopin

This sumptuous belle époque brasserie is a Parisian institution, open 24 hours a day, 365 days a year. Its opening in 1875 coincided with the inauguration of the nearby Palais Garnier, and the brasserie's velvet seats, fringed lamps and floral stained-glass ceilings are characteristic of the period. All the staples are here, from onion soup, snails and fresh seafood to crème brûlée. The terrace is ideal for a leisurely bite or drink and a spot of people-watching on the busy boulevard des Capucines.

Le Grand Colbert

4 rue Vivienne, 2nd [C2]. Tel: 01 42 86 87 88. Open: L and D daily, non-stop noon–1am. **€€**

This large, beautiful brasserie, which opened in 1830, offers the sort of traditional dishes that the French have always demanded from their brasseries. Choose from beef carpaccio, goat's cheese in pastry, sole meunière, Burgundian snails or frogs' legs in garlic, ripe cheeses, and rich and creamy chocolate mousse and îles flottantes.

Le Marivaux

11 boulevard des Italiens, 2nd [C1]. Tel: 01 42 96 40 66. Open: B, L and D daily, non-stop 6.30am–1am. **€**

This no-nonsense brasserie is a lively lunchtime venue offering a varied menu that changes daily. There is always a fresh fish of the day, such as sea bass, but there are unexpected choices too – couscous, for example. In the evenings, raclette (a substantial dish of potatoes, cold cuts and melted cheese) and fondue are the specialities.

La Taverne

24 boulevard des Italiens, 9th [C1]. Tel: 01 55 33 10 00. Open: non-stop daily 11am–1am. **€€**

This flash brasserie, with its heavy chandeliers and open, split stairways is geared mostly to tourists – the menu is available in seven languages – but it's still serious about its food. There are the usual seafood platters and steak dishes, along with healthy servings of sauerkraut. A piano player performs every night, just to keep things lively.

TIP

Lavinia *(3 boulevard de la Madeleine, 1st, tel: 01 42 97 20 20)* is a temple to French wine and spirits. Along with rows of bottles on two floors, it has a wide range of books on wine, including many in English. There's also a restaurant, where you can accompany *un verre de rouge* (a glass of red wine) with some decent food.

TIP

Paris is the world's best city for oyster lovers. In season, which is roughly from September–April, almost every brasserie in town has a big stand of oysters on ice out front, but one of the loveliest places to down a freshly shucked tray is the diminutive oyster bar at **Garnier** *(111 rue St-Lazare, 8th, tel: 01 43 87 50 40)*, situated just across the street from the Gare St-Lazare, Paris's busiest station.

Le Vaudeville

29 rue Vivienne, 2nd [C2]. Tel: 01 40 20 04 62. Open: B, L and D daily, non-stop 6am–2am. **€€**

This Art Deco brasserie, long a haunt for journalists, actors and financiers, has lost some of its lustre in recent years, but retains a lively Parisian atmosphere nonetheless. In addition to the usual seafood and grilled meat offerings are inventive daily specials, such as cod with potatoes in truffle juice. The speciality of the house is its foie gras escalope.

Bistros

Les Coulisses

20 galerie des Variétés, passage des Panoramas, 2nd [D1]. Tel: 01 44 82 09 52. Open: L and D Mon–Fri, D only Sat. **€€**

Appropriately named 'Backstage', this classy bistro is a second home to Parisian actors from the nearby Théâtre de Variétés. It offers authentic French dishes such as terrine de foie gras and beef bourguignon plus home-made pastries.

Chez Georges

1 rue du Mail, 2nd [C2]. Tel: 01 42 60 07 11. Open: L and D Mon–Sat; closed 3 weeks in Aug. **€€**

This monument to Gallic gastronomic history has glided effortlessly through the ages – its setting has changed little over the past 100 years – by offering traditional bistro food that is a cut above the norm. Try a fresh salad with bacon and a poached egg, duck with ceps and the classic desserts from crème de marrons to profiteroles.

Les Diables Au Thym

35 rue Bergère, 9th [D1]. Tel: 01 47 70 77 09. Open: L and D Mon–Fri, D only Sat; closed Aug. **€€**

This is a friendly, unassuming neighbourhood restaurant, with paintings by the restaurateur on the walls. The food is reliable without being dull, with selections including tarama mousseline, foie gras ravioli, lamb parmentier in marsala wine or duck roasted with cherries.

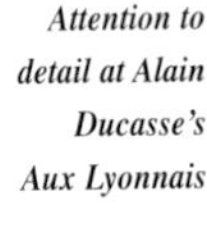

Attention to detail at Alain Ducasse's Aux Lyonnais

Traditional bistro, La Grille Montorgueil

L'Excuse Mogador

21 rue Joubert, 9th [B1]. Tel: 01 42 81 98 19. Open: L and D Mon–Fri; closed Aug and last week in Dec. **€€**

This small, authentic bistro hidden in the backstreets around the *grands magasins* serves simple dishes such as terrine de lapin (rabbit), grilled salmon, steak with shallots and fruit tarts. The wine list is tiny but chosen with care, and the staff are welcoming.

La Fontaine Gaillon

1 rue de la Michodière, place Gaillon, 2nd [B2]. Tel: 01 47 42 63 22. Open: L and D Mon–Fri; closed 3 weeks in Aug. **€€€**

This stunning restaurant, set in a 17th-century residence, complete with a tinkling fountain, was re-opened by celebrity couple Gérard Depardieu and Carole Bouquet in 2003. Depardieu, a dedicated gourmet, has chosen a menu that's traditional, unpretentious and affordable. Try the mussels, crab, or tuna carpaccio for starters, followed by duckling with figs, or sea bream in basil. Finish with pear millefeuille or dark chocolate fondant. The wine list features wines from Depardieu's own vineyard.

Le Gavroche

19 rue St-Marc, 2nd [C1]. Tel: 01 42 96 89 70. Open: L and D Mon–Sat 7am–2am; closed Aug. **€€**

The tone for this busy bistro is set by a menu adorned with the slogan *Gloire au vin* (Glory to wine) and by the row of empty bottles behind the tables. The atmosphere is convivial, the selection of Beaujolais is excellent, and the food is a simple but well-prepared selection of French staples including salads, steak and fries, and roasted lamb.

La Grille Montorgueil

50 rue Montorgueil, 2nd [D3]. Tel: 01 42 33 21 21. Open: L and D daily, non-stop until midnight. **€€**

A relatively calm, reliable bistro with simple charm – a rarity on rue Montorgueil. Try the mussel cassoulet or foie gras for starters, follow with steak tartare or magret de canard with raspberries, and end with a deliciously fresh fruit tart.

Lou Cantou

35 cité d'Antin, 9th [B1]. Tel: 01 48 74 75 15. Open: L only Mon–Sat; closed Aug. **€**

Located in a quiet street behind Galeries Lafayette, Lou Cantou has changed little since it opened in 1920, still serving hot lunches to shop workers and weary shoppers at simple wooden tables. Specials of the day include quiche, fresh ravioli in tomato sauce, confit de canard and rump steak with roquefort sauce. It's excellent value for money, as the menu starts at €12.

Aux Lyonnais

32 rue St-Marc, 2nd [C1]. Tel: 01 42 96 65 04. Open: L and D Tues–Fri, D only Sat. **€€**

Founded in 1892, this bistro still has its original décor, but was beautifully revamped by Alain Ducasse. The menu pays tribute to Lyonnaise specialities, with renditions of pikeperch and crayfish quenelles, Dombes frog's legs, charcuterie, excellent cuts of beef and regional wines. It is advisable to book ahead.

Au Petit Riche

25 rue Le Peletier, 9th [C1]. Tel: 01 47 70 68 68. Open: L and D Mon–Sat. **€€**

Opened in 1854, this restaurant is celebrating its 150th birthday in 2004, and dining here is indeed a trip to the past. The menu doesn't seem to have changed much in that time, with heavily traditional cuisine predominating: foie gras, fish soup, or oysters to start, then entrecôte, magret de canard or even blood sausage, tripe or tête de veau for those who are willing. Ease your digestion with prunes marinated in wine from the Loire, or baba au rhum, a house speciality.

Pierrot

18 rue Etienne-Marcel, 2nd [D3]. Tel: 01 45 08 00 10. Open L and D Mon–Sat. **€€€**

This bistro manages to be both traditional and trendy, with modern décor, food from the Aveyron region in the south of France and a clientele drawn largely from the Paris fashion industry. On the menu are various duck dishes and veal's liver as well as grilled tuna. Sit outside if the weather is good, and listen to the children in the school playground next door – it makes a nice change from the noise of traffic.

Le Roi du Pot-au-Feu

34 rue Vignon, 9th [A1]. Tel: 01 47 42 37 10. Open: L and D Mon–Sat; closed mid-July–mid-Aug. **€**

This traditional bistro with its red-and-white tablecloths specialises, as you might guess from the name, in pot-au-feu. Once a rural stew eaten by peasant farmers, it is now a fashionable dish among wealthy Parisian gourmets. The best part is the bone marrow. If you don't like pot-au-feu, however, go elsewhere, as it's just about the only thing on the menu.

Cafés

Café de la Paix

Place de l'Opéra, 9th [B1]. Tel: 01 40 07 36 36. Open: B, L and D daily, 7am–12.30am. **€€–€€€**

Rub shoulders with the chic, leisurely patrons of the beautifully restored Café de la Paix, while sampling an early morning crois-

Did you know?

Perhaps the most spectacular kitchen in Paris is in the turn-of-the-20th-century mansion, now the **Musée Nissim de Camondo** *(63 rue de Monceau, 8th, tel: 01 53 89 06 50)*. Recently renovated, the kitchen has massive ranges, a scullery full of copper pots and, elsewhere in the house, an impressive collection of porcelain.

Below and right: the king of pot-au-feu

sant and espresso, afternoon tea with pastries, or a glass of wine with oysters later in the day. A full menu offers temptations such as caviar, smoked salmon, sirloin steak, and a selection of cheeses and desserts. Fabulous location right by the Opéra.

Le Café Zéphyr

12 boulevard Montmartre, 9th [D1]. Tel: 01 47 70 80 14. Open: B, L and D daily, 8–2am. **€–€€**

A friendly café with an eclectic but very Parisian crowd. Fare is standard with light and carefully prepared dishes such as fish tagine or truffade (a delightful variation of mash). Specialises in products from the Auvergne, including an excellent selection of cheeses.

Le Grand Filles et Fils

12 Galerie Vivienne, 2nd [C2]. Tel: 01 42 60 07 12. Open: B, L and D Tues–Fri, non-stop 9am–7pm, 9am–1pm and 3–7pm Sat; closed Sun and Mon. **€€**

This fairy-tale *épicerie* now has a warm and wonderful wine bar opening on to the glorious Galerie Vivienne. Endive salad with Stilton, smoked mackerel, cheese platters, chocolate fondant and fruit tarts are examples of the light eats available to accompany exceptional wines. Be sure to explore the *épicerie* afterwards. Knowledgeable staff.

Regional

Café Runtz

16 rue Favart, 2nd [C1]. Tel: 01 42 96 69 86. Open: L and D Mon–Fri, D only Sat Sept–June; closed 1 week in May, 3 weeks in Aug. **€€€**

Here, amid wooden panels and green-and-white tablecloths, the speciality is cuisine from Alsace. The food is great, particularly the onion tart, the haddock in beurre blanc sauce, and the duck sausage in horseradish sauce. But why do they insist on playing those Cyndi Lauper records at lunchtime?

Domaine de Lintillac

10 rue St-Augin, 2nd [C2]. Tel: 01 40 20 96 27. Open: L and D, Mon–Sat, D only Sat. **€€**

This lovely little restaurant fills up quickly, as restaurateur Jean Guillot provides substantial southwestern dishes at reasonable prices – the foie gras, cassoulet, magret de canard and blood sausage with chestnuts are delicious. Each table has its own toaster, so you can warm your own bread. Many of the regional products are also available for purchase, including wines and foie gras.

L'Isard

15 rue St-Augin, 2nd [C2]. Tel: 01 42 96 00 26. Open: L and D Tues–Fri, D only Sat. **€€**

A simple but pleasant restaurant offering dishes made with traditional Pyrennean ingredients and

Opulent décor at the Café de la Paix

TIP

In-store eating options at the **Galeries Lafayette** department store *(40 bd Haussmann)* include a sushi bar, a smart restaurant and a champagne bar. Not to be outdone, nine restaurants and cafés inside **Printemps** *(64 bd Haussmann)* include a Ladurée tearoom and the Paul Smith-designed World Bar. On Rue St-Honoré, the Water Bar at **Colette** *(No. 213)* and Joe's Café at **Joseph** *(No. 277)* are hip lunchtime destinations.

given a touch of Parisian refinement. The tomato soup with roquefort is a favourite, along with the excellent jambon cru. Mains include cassoulet and magret de canard cooked in Madeira wine, but do not leave without trying the crema catalana, the Catalonian answer to crème brûlée.

Le Mellifère

8 rue Monsigny, 2nd [C2]. Tel: 01 42 61 21 71. Open: L and D daily. **€€**

This restaurant has a bistro feel, and a cuisine that brushes regional dishes with a modern stripe. Try the spicy pork boudin, red peppers stuffed with cod, or goat's cheese with black-cherry confiture. The house speciality, of which the chef is justifiably proud, is œufs cocottes with foie gras.

Au Pays de Cocagne

Espace Tarn, 111 rue de Réaumur, 2nd [D2]. Tel: 01 40 13 81 81. Open: L and D Mon–Fri, D only Sat; closed Aug and 24 Dec–2 Jan. **€€€**

Although the décor here is unimaginative, and the service a little slow, the rich southwestern food is authentic and served in large quantities. Try suckling pig with polenta galette or magret de canard, and wash it down with a glass or two of the regional wine, Gaillac. Regional products including wines, foie gras, biscuits, jellies and honey are available for purchase.

TIP

L'Arbre à Cannelle [D1] is an exquisite tearoom in the passage des Panoramas in the 2nd, and a pleasant place for either a swift lunch or a mid-afternoon break. Grab a seat on the terrace outside, and indulge yourself with one L'Arbre's sinfully rich chocolate cakes.

Contemporary

16 Haussmann

Hôtel Ambassador, 16 boulevard Haussmann, 9th [C1]. Tel: 01 48 00 06 38. Open: L and D Mon–Fri, D only Sat; closed 2 weeks in Aug. **€€€**

Philippe Starck designed this contemporary restaurant for the

buttoned-down set in bracing yellow-and-royal blue stripes. The food is just the conservative side of hip, with modern takes on traditional fare: pumpkin soup with pancetta and fried celery, asparagus risotto with truffle oil and parmesan, roasted tuna with soy piperade; and pear and chestnut macaroons to finish.

Bon 2

2 rue du Quatre-Septembre, 2nd [C2]. Tel: 01 44 55 51 55. Open: B, L and D daily, Br Sun; non-stop 8.30am–2am. **€€€**

This is the second Bon restaurant designed by Philippe Starck, and as it's located directly across from the Bourse, he's done a modern take on a men's club – even adding a running electric display which displays share prices throughout the day. Business lunchers can choose from oysters or pumpkin soup with chestnuts, grilled sole, roast chicken, or even a club sandwich, and finish with apple tart.

Stylish Japanese food and design at Aki

International

Aki

2 bis rue Daunou, 2nd [B2]. Tel: 01 42 61 48 38. Open: L and D Mon–Fri, D only Sat; closed Aug. **€€€**

This modern, spacious Japanese restaurant is a relief after the small, cramped ones that are popping up around the city. In addition to the standard sushi and sashimi, choose from interesting selections such as tuna with sesame avocado sauce, sea bream steamed with ginger and lime, or magret de canard with minced mango, ginger and teriyaki sauce.

I Golosi

6 rue de la Grange-Batelière, 9th [D1]. Tel: 01 48 24 18 63. Open: L and D Mon–Fri, L only Sat; closed Aug. **€€**

This modern Italian restaurant is situated above a café that also has an Italian food shop in the back room. It is home to a trendy Parisian crowd, drawn by the jovial atmosphere, the 500 Italian wines on offer and the cuisine, which can be excellent. The menu changes constantly, as it is based on market produce, but sample dishes include ricotta ravioli, risotto with white truffles, and fresh tomato pasta with artichoke hearts.

Issé

56 rue Ste-Anne, 2nd [C2]. Tel: 01 42 96 67 76. Open: L and D Tues–Fri, L only Sat, D only Mon; closed 3 weeks in early Aug. **€€–€€€**

One of the oldest and best-known Japanese restaurants in Paris, this place enjoys a well-justified reputation for its fine food. The cuisine is simple, and although some criticise the portions for being too small, the sushi is excellent, as is Issé's most celebrated dish – grilled crab.

Mi Cayito

10 rue Marie-Stuart, 2nd [D3]. Tel: 01 42 21 98 86. Open: L and D Mon–Fri, D only Sat. **€€**

Offering Cuban cuisine amid exotic décor and a convivial atmosphere,

Did you know

The first Paris stock exchange was opened in the street by a Scotsman, John Law, in 1719. It provoked such a speculative frenzy that a hunchback was said to have earned 150,000 livres from offering his back as a desk.

The ballroom at Café de la Paix can be hired for special occasions – and viewed on request

this restaurant has been an instant success since its recent opening. The cod croquettes with malanga (a type of elongated potato) are popular, as is the squid stuffed with mint and prawns.

Le Moi

5 rue Daunou, 2nd [B2]. Tel: 01 47 03 92 05. Open: L and D Mon–Sat, non-stop noon–11pm. **€**

With its bamboo bark and dark wood floor, this Vietnamese restaurant echoes colonial villas built by the French in Indochina. Try the spicy grilled sole, caramel pork, or prawns grilled in garlic, and finish off with ginger ice cream. Good for vegetarians.

Le New Balal

25 rue Taitbout, 9th [C1]. Tel: 01 42 46 53 67. Open: L and D daily. **€**

This comfortable, unpretentious restaurant serves Indian and Pakistani dishes at very reasonable prices: lunch menus start at €11. Choose from fish tikka, chicken korma, shrimp massala, lassis and traditional desserts.

Ogoura

20 rue de la Michodière, 2nd [C1]. Tel: 01 47 42 77 79. Open: L and D Mon–Sat, D only Sun. **€**

This small, quiet restaurant, doing simple, competitively priced food, is the kind of place that only the locals seem to know about – it's very popular with members of the local Japanese community. Try the tempuras and yakitoris, as well as the grilled prawns and tofu.

Le Santal Opéra

8 rue Halévy, 9th [B1]. Tel: 01 47 42 24 69. Open: L and D Mon–Sat **€–€€**

Tucked away in a passage just a stone's throw from the opera house, Le Santal was one of the first Vietnamese restaurants in Paris and offers an extensive menu of specialities in a discreetly lit, subdued atmosphere. Start with papaya salad or steamed ravioli, and move on to delicacies such as grilled chicken with lemongrass or grilled monkfish with saffron. Also offers a wide selection of French wines.

Bars and Pubs

Home to the US community in Paris, local institution **Harry's Bar** *(5 rue Daunou, 2nd, tel: 01 42 61 71 14)* also draws numerous locals attracted by its 270 or so different cocktails. Opposite is **Le Manneken-Pis** *(4 rue Daunou, tel: 01 47 42 85 03)*, a Belgian bar that is popular for its vast range of beers and its lively atmosphere.

A number of Irish pubs have also sprung up in this area since the mid-1990s; the most popular are **Kitty O'Shea's** *(10 rue des Capucines, 2nd, tel: 01 40 15 08 08)* and the **Kildare** *(6 bis rue du Quatre-Septembre, 2nd, tel: 01 47 03 91 91)*.

If you prefer a typically French bar, try **Au Vide Gousset** *(1 rue Vide-Gousset, 2nd, tel: 01 42 60 02 78)*, **Les Petits Carreaux** *(17 rue des Petits-Carreaux, 2nd, tel: 01 42 33 37 32)* or the delightfully old-fashioned **Le Petit Choiseul** *(23 rue Saint-Augustin, 2nd, tel: 01 42 96 02 47)*.

For a drink in a setting that is altogether more chic, drop into **Le Café de la Paix** *(see page 56)* on place de l'Opéra in the 9th or **Les Chenets** at the Hôtel Westminster *(15 rue Daunou, 2nd, tel: 01 42 61 57 46)*; both are steeped in Parisian elegance.

Among the more modern establishments are **L'Etienne Marcel** *(34 rue Etienne-Marcel, 2nd, tel: 01 45 08 01 03)* and **Footsie** *(10 rue Daunou, 2nd, tel: 01 42 60 07 20)*. Here, the prices of drinks rise and fall in proportion to the number of times they are ordered, mirroring the share prices at the Stock Exchange around the corner.

Le Fooding

This uniquely Parisian phenomenon was initially denigrated as nothing but the latest fad. Over five years on, it has proved its critics wrong

The term 'Le Fooding', coined in 1999 by Alexandre Cammas, a journalist at the French culture magazine *Nova*, joins the two English words 'food' and 'feeling' to express an attitude towards dining that craves motion, atmosphere, alluring food presentation, good vibrations, imagination, ntertainment, and time, as much as high-quality food on the plate. Says 'ammas, 'People need a lot more than just good food to feel well fed.' It's all bout approaching the table with the mind and all the senses, not just an empty elly and a greedy tongue. In a way, this is what France has always been amous for: *l'art de vivre*. Indeed, some have criticised the movement for reinenting the wheel. The rebuttal, however, is that the wheel *needed* reinventing: was stuck in a stuffy, conventional rut and had forgotten how to turn.

The creators of the Fooding movement, which was soon embraced by the ountry's press and top chefs as a much-needed injection of energy into the rench culinary scene, were, among other things, tired of the traditional sysems of evaluating restaurants. Says Cammas, 'When we judge a restaurant, ur criteria is: do we want to go back?' In this way, the movement places canens and bistros on a level with starred restaurants, understanding that various istes and contexts suit our moods at different times and that it is hard to claim at one is 'better' than another. One consequence of the movement's efforts is new-found openness in Paris towards world food and fusion food and all that ares to make modern with traditional French. In a country with such a deepoted culinary history – and, at times arrogance – le Fooding has inspired oticeable leaps forward. After a period of stagnancy, French food is once gain on the move.

Fooding hotspots Market and Senso

ooding for the masses

very year, 'La Semaine du Fooding' held in December in Paris, gains omentum. During this mouth-watering week, top chefs take their soups to utdoor markets and serve the public, classes are taught at the Grande Epicerie Paris, restaurants give two-for-one deals, debates are held on topics of gasonomic interest, and, at the closing celebration, prizes are awarded to restaunts and food shops for everything from 'best sweet food' to 'best bathroom'.

By all appearances, le Fooding shows no sign of fading. To get a taste of it r yourself, head for the truly good Parisian restaurants – at all levels of the erarchy – and feed yourself with feeling. That's what Fooding is all about.

SEFUL ADDRESSES

smattering of restaurants where *le Fooding* is fabulous:

strance *(see page 149)*
'Avant-Goût (take-away) *ee page 141)*
ellota-Bellota *(see page 124)*
e Chamarré *(see page 123)*
ux Lyonnais *(see page 55)*
Market *(see page 28)*
Sale e Pepe *(see page 139)*
Senso *(see page 29)*
Twinz (canteen), 101 rue St-Maur, 11th, tel: 01 40 21 03 37
404 *(see page 72)*

The Islands, Marais and Beaubourg

From ancient establishments in the oldest part of Paris to corner cafés, boho-chic restaurants and hip bars in two more recently modish areas

The islands, Marais and Beaubourg are among the most attractive areas of the city, home to an eclectic mix of buildings, both grandiose and bijou, quaint shops, casual cafés, bars and bistros, and, generally speaking, a free-spirited, easy-going ambience, day in, day out. To name every worthwhile eatery and shop is impossible; these areas, with their narrow, winding streets, are like a maze, and the best way to explore them is simply to wander and let yourself fall haphazardly upon hidden gems. In addition to numerous corner cafés, shaded restaurants and trendy bars, these include the magical charcuterie A la Ville de Rodez *(22 rue Vieille-du-Temple, 4th)* or Cuisineopilie *(28 rue du Bourg-Tibourg, 4th)*, sellers of antique kitchenware. Even the major department store in the neighbourhood BHV *(52 rue de Rivoli, 4th)*, with its vast kitchen department, has a secret: in the basement hardware section there's Bricolocafé, a café with wooden floors (you almost expect sawdust) and walls covered in tools. Although the hot chocolate is nothing to write home about, the café is a prime example of the kind of surprises to be found in the hidden nooks and crannies of these colourful neighbourhoods.

Ile de la Cité and Ile St-Louis

The islands are the most bourgeois and serious of the three neighbourhoods – and indeed the oldest: l'Ile de la Cité is where Paris began, before spreading to the mainland after the Roman invasion. Today, with the Palais de Justice, Hôtel Dieu and the Préfecture de Police holding fort, there is something of a mood of authority here, plus it's busy and boisterous with crowds swarming around Notre-Dame Cathedral and the Sainte-Chapelle. The nearest retreat from the madness is the broad and shaded place Dauphine, which is fringed with small, terraced restaurants. The trouble is that the food here can be mediocre and overpriced; in the heat of summer, however, that trade-off can be worthwhile. There's also the option of bringing a picnic to enjoy in the tiny green park at the nose of the island, square du Vert Galant.

***Opposite:** fun venue Chez Janou. **Below:** one of the many popular bistros on the rue des Francs-Bourgeois*

More stroll-worthy is l'Ile St-Louis, peaceful and picturesque, with some of the most expensive and admirable real estate in the city. Its main artery, rue St-Louis-en-l'Ile, has a couple of tearooms, notable butcher, cheese and pastry shops, and is home to legendary ice-cream makers, Berthillon *(31 rue St-Louis-en-l'Île, 4th, tel: 01 43 54 31 61)*.

The Marais and Beaubourg

Exit the island for the Marais via the Pont Louis-Philippe and carry on up the street sprinkled with exquisite paper shops as well as a few carrying original tableware such as Monastica and Sentou. Around the corner is rue François-Miron, where at No. 30 is Izraël, a storybook grocer crammed with oils, liqueurs, preserved lemons, blocks of nougat, pickles, teapots and a vast collection of old-fashioned foodie postcards. Now, you're right in the heart of the lower Marais.

The Marais is a mixed bag, and historically so. It began life as a swamp *(marécage)* on the city's outskirts, was later transformed into agricultural land, and eventually became inhabited. The golden age of the *quartier* began during the reign of Henri IV, who built the glorious place des Vosges for his court. At the same time, numerous *hôtels particuliers* (private mansions) were erected in the area, their owners all competing with one another for the greatest architectural beauty and lavish décor. Later, when Louis XIV moved the court to Versailles, the money followed, and the abandoned Marais was taken up by artisanal industry, notably furniture-makers, instrument makers and masons. It wasn't until the 1960s that the *quartier* began to regain its prestige thanks to a regeneration programme. Today, although it retains an arty-intellectual character (plus remnants of industry in the form of tacky wholesale accessories shops), the bohemian Marais is nonetheless one of the most expensive and sought-after neighbourhoods in all Paris.

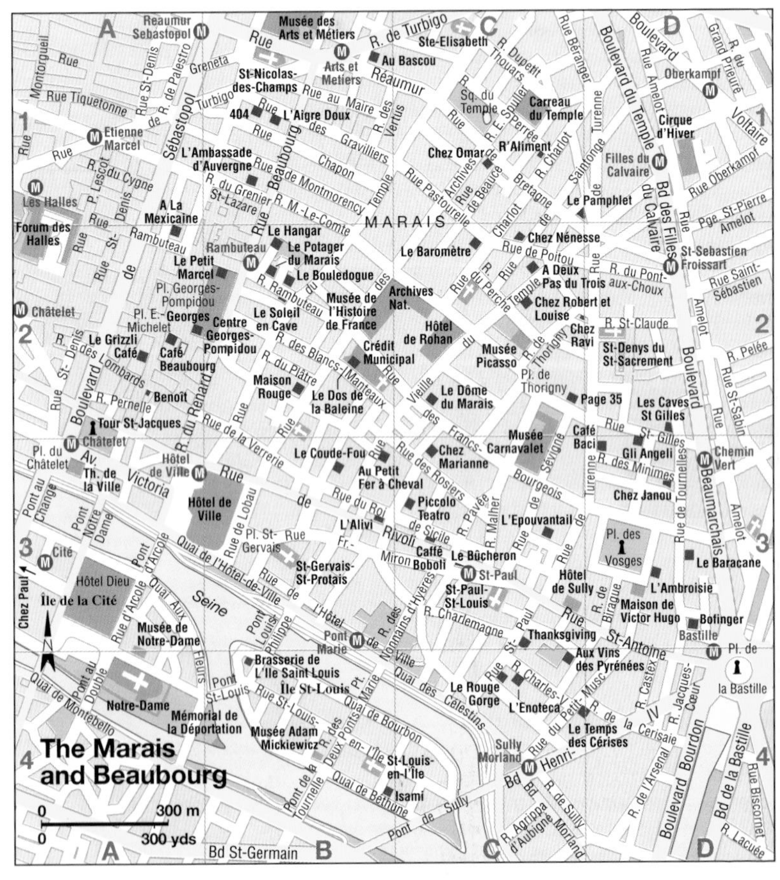

The food scene is entirely in sync with this eccentricity – with very few exceptions, this is not the place for grand dining. In the Marais, small (and casual) is beautiful: ideal if you're shopping along the crowded rue des Francs-Bourgeois, poking through the antique shops and galleries around the Village Saint-Paul, or visiting the Centre Pompidou (near to which are numerous outdoor eateries around the Nikki de Saint Phalle sculptures on place Igor-Stravinsky).

FIVE OF THE BEST

404: Moroccan food and magical ambience
Au Bascou: the best of the Basque country – imaginative cuisine, delightful service and an intimate environment
Benoît: upscale, old-world bistro – the classiest of the classics
Café Baci: ultra-fashionable venue, with light and delicious Italian food
Le Pamplet: delicious French food without the Michelin-starred prices

Gay culture is predominant, notably around rue des Archives and rue Vieille-du-Temple, and many of the bars and restaurants are especially gay-friendly *(see bars, page 75)*. A good deal of English can be heard in the streets, and catering to that market is the American grocery store Thanksgiving *(13 rue Charles-V, 4th)*, which sells everything from measuring cups to mini marshmallows, and the lovely English-language bookstore The Red Wheelbarrow *(22 rue Saint-Paul, 4th)*.

The bustling Jewish quarter is an attraction in and around rue des Rosiers. You'll find a whole strip of Jewish grocers and restaurants, selling falafels, poppy-seed cakes, halva, apple strudels and rye bread. Especially interesting are Sacha Finkelsztajn *(27 rue des Rosiers, 4th)* and Florence Finkelsztajn *(24 rue des Ecouffes)*. Further up, in the third *arrondissement*, rue Elzévir is becoming something of a Little Senegal. Le Petit Dakar *(6 rue Elzévir, 3rd, tel: 01 44 59 34 74)* is a restaurant with inexpensive North African specialities. Across the street, Youssou N'Dour's Senegalese club Jokko *(5 rue Elzévir, 3rd, tel: 01 42 74 35 96)* plays African music and serves African drinks to match the ambience.

Le Haut Marais

In recent years, people talk about the Marais having moved north into the third *arrondissement*. In fact, it is increasingly referred to as 'Le Haut Marais' (Upper Marais), an exciting area in the midst of transition and one well worth exploring. There are a number of interesting restaurants, a marvellous market street (rue de Bretagne), a small covered market, cafés and a smattering of shops of appeal to the gastronomically minded. Above all, don't miss the part-chic, part-delapitated rue Charlot, home to Food *(58 rue Charlot, 3rd)*, a food bookstore and food photography gallery. Also here is the plush tearoom, Apar'Thé *(7 rue Charlot)*, as well as AlTea *(41 rue Charlot)*, specialising in organic teas and a line of 'iced' teas *(see tearooms, page 127)*. Nearby there's Goumanyat *(3 rue Dupuis, 3rd)*, an upscale spice shop specialising in saffron. Rue de Poitou has an increasing number of handbag and clothing shops by small designers, as well as restaurants. And good small art galleries are dotted throughout the neighbourhood.

Wander back towards the 4th *arrondissement* down rue de Turenne, where there are two Italian delicatesssens: Frascati *(14 rue de Turenne, 4th)* and Pasta Linea *(9 rue de Turenne)*, as well as L'Argenterie de Turenne *(19 rue de Turenne)* for sterling knives, forks and teapots.

Haute Cuisine

L'Ambroisie

9 place des Vosges, 4th [D3]. Tel: 01 42 78 51 45. Open L and D Tues–Sat; closed 3 weeks Aug and 2 weeks Feb. **€€€€**

This is the one restaurant in the Marais offering a truly royal dining experience. A discreet entrance on place des Vosges delivers you into an intimate, Italianate dining room, where chef Alain Pacaud seduces the finest palates with langoustine tails with sesame and curry, lamb with garlic nougatine, fine chocolate tart, and a wine list to make you weep.

La Brasserie de l'Ile Saint-Louis – for a choice location, albeit at a price

Brasseries

Bofinger

7 rue de la Bastille, 4th [D3]. Tel: 01 42 72 87 82. Open: L and D daily till 1am, weekends and holidays non-stop. **€€–€€€**

Yes, it's a tourist trap, but this grand and busy bistro (it seats 300) with its elaborate red-and-gold décor is nonetheless one of the city's institutions, offering a truly Parisian experience. Order choucroute or a vast platter of oysters and other seafood, and wash it down with a chilly Riesling.

Le Bouledogue

20 rue Rambuteau, 3rd [B2]. Tel: 01 40 27 90 90. Open: L and D Mon–Sat. **€€**

A small brasserie with linen-decked tables on a busy street, this is a lovely friendly place that is great for casual week-night dining. The well-prepared food is traditional – think steak au poivre and grilled skate.

Brasserie de l'Ile Saint-Louis

55 quai de Bourbon, 4th [B4]. Tel: 01 43 54 02 59. Open: noon–midnight Fri–Tues, D only Thur; closed Aug, 1 week Feb. **€€**

If you eat on the island, you pay for it. Here, at least, the terrace is marvellously placed for people-watching and admiring the Seine. The food is hefty Alsatian: tripe terrine with Riesling, pork with apple marmalade, choucroute and lots of cold beer. Afterwards, you're perfectly placed for sampling ice creams at Berthillon *(see page 63)*.

Chez Omar

47 rue de Bretagne, 3rd [C1]. Tel: 01 42 72 36 26. Open: L and D Mon–Sat, D only Sun. **€€** *No credit cards.*

This old-time brasserie is a 3rd *arrondissement* institution, with a menu featuring both traditional French fare and Moroccan specialities. Since you can't make reservations, show up early to beat the cool crowd for reliable couscous and spicy merguez sausages, deliciously sweet pastries and great people-watching.

Bistros

Le Baracane (L'Oulette)

38 rue des Tournelles, 4th [D3]. Tel: 01 42 71 43 33. Open: L and D Mon–Fri, D only Sat. **€–€€**

A classic southwestern French bistro, with food a cut above, and prices a cut below. There are only 30 seats in the narrow, carpeted cream-coloured dining room, and they are usually full of tourists. Still, the food is very decent, if occasionally on the ambitious side; dishes include asparagus flan with sorrel sauce, confit de canard and a very good cassoulet.

Le Baromètre

17 rue Charlot, 3rd [C2]. Tel: 01 48 87 04 54. Open: L and D Mon–Fri; closed Aug. **€–€€**

The archetypal wine bar/bistro: rustic, loud and reasonably priced.

Beaubourg bistro Chez Janou

Wines by the glass at the bar can be accompanied with tartines or charcuterie. For lunch, try a giant salad, croque monsieur or an omelette, with a jug of red, of course. And, at night, traditional dishes include potato gratin, confit de canard and bass in red-pepper sauce.

Benoît 🍴

20 rue Saint-Martin, 4th [A2]. Tel: 01 42 72 25 76. Open: L and D daily; closed Aug. **€€€–€€€€**

Benoît, open since 1912, is an institution for those who appreciate hearty eating, but with class. Old-style service reigns. Forget fussy individual dishes – waiters will bring a whole pâté to the table and cut you a slab, or dish up beef and carrot casserole, or cassoulet, then tempt you with a slice of the heavenly prune and Armagnac ice-cream bomb that's the size of an igloo. Book ahead.

Chez Janou

2 rue Roger-Verlomme, 3rd [D3]. Tel: 01 42 72 28 41. Open: L and D daily. **€€**

Reserve on the terrace if you can – it's one of the nicest in the city and spills out onto a quiet, tree-lined street. Inside, Chez Janou is big and boisterous, with old posters and photographs cluttering the walls. The menu's rustic Provençal dishes include ravioli with ricotta and basil, and giant prawns flambéed with Pastis. It's not the most amazing food on earth, but the venue is wonderfully fun.

Chez Nénesse

17 rue Saintonge, 3rd [C2]. Tel: 01 42 78 46 49. Open: L and D Mon–Fri; closed Aug and last week in Dec. **€€**

A tiny, family-run place that's cute enough for a postcard, with chatty chef Roger Leplu peeking out of the kitchen, a permanent grin on his face. Everything except the ice cream is made in-house, from foie gras, cassoulette of snail and mushrooms, and mustard-rubbed rabbit to profiteroles, tarte Tatin and iced soufflés. Quintessential Paris. Book ahead.

Chez Paul

15 place Dauphine, 1st [A3]. Tel: 01 43 54 21 48. Open: L and D Tues–Sun; closed 2 weeks in Aug. **€€**

From the entrance on place Dauphine, Paul is but a shoebox,

TIP

The Marais has more than its fair share of museums, most of which are housed in restored *hôtels particuliers.* The **Musée Carnavalet** *(23 rue de Sévigné)* traces the history of Paris; the **Musée Picasso** *(5 rue de Thorigny)* is the artist's personal collection; the **Musée du Judaïsme** *(71 rue du Temple)* covers the art and history of Jewish communities; and the **Maison Victor Hugo** *(6 place des Vosges)* is dedicated to the life and work of the literary genius.

the colour of worn leather. Inside the seating stretches across to the Seine side; outside, a few tables dot the terrace, and on a summer's night there's nothing better than a chilled white wine with a generous serving of blanquette de veau à l'ancienne and a light crème brûlée à la verveine (with verbena) to end. The food is fairly standard, and not necessarily the cheapest in Paris, but the outdoor setting is hard to beat.

Chez Robert et Louise

64 rue Vieille-du-Temple, 3rd [C2]. Tel: 01 42 78 55 89. Open: L and D Mon–Sat; closed Aug. **€€** *No credit cards.*

The curtains are always drawn on this atmospheric restaurant from another age. Louise bustles through the kitchen carrying an apronful of onions and chops them on a table near the bar. Potatoes sauté and beef stews bubble in cast-iron pots over an open hearth.

***Below:** for privacy, try Chez Robert et Louise. **Bottom:** Chef at Le Dôme du Marais*

Go for the time travel. Warm and friendly service is not guaranteed, but the regulars keep coming back.

Le Coude Fou

12 rue du Bourg-Tibourg, 4th [B3]. Tel: 01 42 77 15 16. Open: L and D daily. **€€**

There are countless bistros in the Marais that look quaint and authentic, but serve memorably bad food. This looks like all the rest, but the food, at least, is dependable, the service friendly, and, best of all, there's always room and they're open every day. Soup served in a bread bowl, spicy quails and crème caramel are the kind of dishes you can expect.

A Deux Pas du Trois

101 rue Vieille-du-Temple, 3rd [C2]. Tel: 01 42 77 10 52. Open: L and D Tues–Fri, D only Sat. **€€**

A small, candlelit restaurant with a top floor overlooking the Picasso Museum gardens. Not all dishes are perfect on the restrained menu, but they know how to cook fish and everything is presented simply but stylishly. An interesting feature is the separate menu for side dishes, ranging from macaroni cheese to light green cabbage fricassée – for every main dish, you can choose two accompaniments. Sweet service.

Le Dôme du Marais

53 bis rue des Francs-Bourgeois, 4th [C2]. Tel: 01 42 74 54 17. Open: L and D Tues–Sat; closed 3 weeks Aug, 1st week Jan **€€–€€€**

The quiet, airy, dome-topped dining room draws a well-dressed, cosmopolitan crowd seeking retreat in the bustling Marais. Fresh and interesting dishes served with class include nettle soup, turbot with white-pepper sabayon, duckling with black cherries, and rhubarb with fresh cheese and rose jelly.

Le Grizzli Café

7 rue Saint-Martin, 4th [A2]. Tel: 01 48 87 77 56. Open: D and L, daily 11am–11pm. **€€**

A classic bistro with a people-watching terrace smack in the centre of the city. Here the food is generous, fresh and interesting: beef cooked on slate, crab with chives and grapefruit, peaches fried in salty butter, and banana pie. The service is not quite up to the food.

Le Hangar

12 impasse Berthaud, 3rd [B2]. Tel: 01 42 74 55 44. Open: L and D Tues–Sat. **€€** *No credit cards.*

Parisians would like to keep this spartan place a secret, which, considering its location, isn't difficult. Off rue Beaubourg, around a crooked dead-end alley, is a small terrace with a view of a blank wall; inside, the décor is equally humdrum. That said, the food, from lentil salads, marinated sardines and asparagus risotto to beef stroganoff, is delicious and very well priced.

Le Pamphlet 🍴

38 rue Debelleyme, 3rd [C1]. Tel: 01 42 72 39 24. Open: L and D Tues–Fri, D only Sat and Mon; closed 2 weeks in Aug and 2 weeks in Jan. **€€–€€€**

Whereas most restaurants in this part of town are low-key, local affairs, chef Alain Carrère offers a much more exciting French experience – and flawless quality. Squid-ink risotto with escargot beignets, and baked banana with spice-bread ice cream are just two examples on a menu that changes daily. The tables are nicely spaced out, and the décor is warmly provincial. There's a superb-value dinner menu at €30.

Le Petit Marcel

65 rue Rambuteau, 4th [B2]. Tel: 01 48 87 10 20. Open: B, L and D daily, non-stop 8am–midnight; closed Aug. **€**

This formerly postage stamp-sized bistro – now expanded – near the Pompidou Centre is as quaint as it gets. The locals will grab the few terrace seats first, but inside, beneath the painted ceiling on a rickety chair, you're just as much part of the scene. Salads, omelettes, steak frites, crumbles and brownies: very basic food, but decent, cheap and delightful.

R'Aliment

57 rue Charlot, 3rd [C1]. Tel: 01 48 04 88 28. Open: L and D Tues–Fri, L only Mon; closed Aug. **€€** *www.resodesign.com*

This fresh, modern canteen and grocery – a favourite with the fashion crowd – has an open kitchen, high bench seating, bright green walls and healthy, imaginative food made from organic ingredients. Typical dishes include carrot gazpacho with coconut milk, three-spice pasta with spring vegetables, strawberry jelly with ginger confit, and organic bread.

Le Rouge-Gorge

8 rue Saint-Paul, 4th [C4]. Tel: 01 48 04 75 89. Open: L and D Mon–Sat, noon–11.30pm, D only Sun; closed 2 weeks in Aug. **€€€**

Menus (and wines) in this lovely family-style wine bar-cum-restaurant explore a different region of France every two weeks. During 'Corsica Week' expect superb charcuterie and a splash of interesting dishes such as cheese beignets and piglet with polenta. Food is of a high standard (the chef shelling her own peas behind the bar is a good sign), but meats tend to be slightly overcooked. Friendly service.

Le Soleil en Cave

21 rue Rambuteau, 4th [B2]. Tel: 01 42 72 26 25. Open: L and D Wed–Sun; closed 3 weeks in mid-July–early Aug. **€–€€**

Did you know?

One of the world's greatest cookery encyclopaedias, and perhaps the most valuable tome on French gastronomy is the *Larousse Gastronomique*, created by Prosper Montagné with the collaboration of one Dr Gottschalk, and first published in 1938. It has been periodically updated since 1977 and is available in English.

Colourful cuisine at Le Soleil en Cave

A cosy, warm-coloured restaurant and wine cellar await behind the bright yellow façade, with a friendly, wine-savvy owner to advise you on your bottle. Buy one to take home, or to drink (for a small fee) in-house. Savoury tartines make up the bulk of the menu, but these are meal size and come with gargantuan salads; a plat du jour (the quality of which can vary) is another good option. Best at lunchtime.

Le Temps des Cerises

31 rue de la Cerisaie, 4th [C4]. Tel: 01 42 72 08 63. Open: L only Mon–Fri; closed Aug and 1 week in Feb. **€** *No credit cards.*

If you want to feel as if you're a million miles away from the stresses of everyday city life, come here to lunch on plain but decent bistro food and – why not – order that extra carafe of wine. Beyond the lacy curtains, this is a timeless place that's authentic and welcoming, just like being in the provinces.

Aux Vins des Pyrénées

25 rue Beautreillis, 4th [C4]. Tel: 01 42 72 64 94. Open: L and D Sun–Fr, D only Sat, Br Sun. **€€**

Good food, good wine and a good time are to be had in this bistro-cum-wine bar. The impressive window displays (corks and liqueur bottles in the form of matadors, athletes, fiddlers, drunks, etc) let you know in advance that you're here to have fun. Dishes including marinated salmon with pistou, cream of pea soup with poached egg, chicken with tarragon, and wild boar in wine are representative of a menu that's classic (and fairly heavy) but never dull.

TIP

For some dedicated relaxation, spend a day in **Les Bains du Marais** *(31–3 rue des Blancs-Manteaux, 3rd; tel: 01 44 61 02 02)*, a modern take on the traditional hammam, complete with steam room, massage and facial treatments and a restaurant/café.

Cafés

Le Bûcheron

14 rue de Rivoli, 4th [C3]. Tel: 01 48 87 71 31. Open: L and D Mon–Sat, L only Sun; closed 1 week in Aug. **€€**

It's a surprise to find a good place to eat on commercial thoroughfare rue de Rivoli, but here you have it. The menu, which ingeniously slides up on a board out of the tables, is Italian, with pasta and salads, veal escalopes, chicken fricassée, ice cream and almond parfait with pistachios all standards. Unpretentious décor and the sweetest service.

Café Beaubourg

100 rue St-Merri, 4th [A2]. Tel: 01 48 87 63 96. Open: B, L and D daily, non-stop 8am–1am. **€€€**

With a terrace overlooking the Centre Pompidou, this landmark café, designed by Christian de Portzamparc, is a study in style over substance. Food is mediocre, considering what you pay, but it's fine for a light meal. Either gaze out from the terrace or turn your gaze inward to the café's chic clientele.

Au Petit Fer à Cheval

30 rue Vieille-du-Temple, 4th [B3]. Tel: 01 42 72 47 47. Open: B, L and D, non-stop daily noon–1am. **€**

People-watching is as much a full-time occupation here as it is anywhere else along image-conscious rue Vieille-du-Temple. With its tiny horseshoe-shaped bar, this café is, however, particularly atmospheric and a great favourite with the bourgeois-bohemian crowd. Solid food, rushed but genial service and lots of smoke in the back room.

Regional

L'Alivi

27 rue du Roi-de-Sicile, 4th [B3]. Tel: 01 48 87 90 20. Open: L and D daily. **€€€**
www.restaurant-alivi.com

As soon as you spot the dainty terrace tumbling into a crook of quiet streets, you'll want to sit down at one of its tables. Inside, rust-and-grey floor tiles and high stone walls lend an authentic backdrop, while you tuck into Corsican flavours: herb tart, Corsican charcuterie, chestnut-and-foie gras terrine, coppa-and-leek mousse, sardines and fennel, and olives and veal.

L'Ambassade d'Auvergne

22 rue du Grenier-St-Lazare, 3rd [B1]. Tel: 01 42 72 31 22. Open: L and D daily. **€€–€€€**
www.ambassade-auvergne.com

One of the city's most famous regional institutions, this restaurant offers diners the chance to sink their teeth into the food of the heart of France. Enormous, sturdy tables and dishes with the same character: lentils and sausage, cabbage soup and the famous aligot, a smooth purée of potato, garlic and fresh soft cheese.

Au Bascou

38 rue Réaumur, 3rd [B1]. Tel: 01 42 72 69 25. Open: L and D Mon–Fri; closed Aug and last week in Dec. **€€€**

This small and friendly spot offers one of the best regional experiences in Paris. The menu has an enticing range of Basque dishes, all made with top ingredients, predominantly fish and seafood traditionally caught in the Bay of Biscay (tuna, cod, mussels, shrimp and sardines), plus an exceptional and unusual wine list. Save room for the gâteau basque. The few movie-theatre seats look appealing, but get no points for comfort, so ask to avoid them when you book.

Left: the archetypal Parisian café/bar, Au Petit Fer à Cheval. Bottom: excellent choice of wines at Le Soleil en Cave

Page 35

4 rue du Parc-Royal, 3rd [C2]. Tel: 01 44 54 35 35. Open: L and D Wed–Thur, non-stop Fri–Sun, L only Mon–Tues. **€**

Billed as a restaurant, bar, and salon de thé, this cosy nook, just across from the grassy square Louis-Achille, is above all a crêperie, ideal for lunch or for a rest at teatime. Choose from the vast selection of sweet and savoury crêpes, including the Breton speciality: a salted-butter caramel crêpe.

Contemporary

Café Baci 🍴

36 rue de Turenne, 3rd [D3]. Tel: 01 42 71 36 70. Open: L and D daily **€€–€€€**

A classy, contemporary address that pulls in the beautiful people, just a hop up from place des Vosges. Dim lights, tables arranged for plenty of eye contact with diners at other tables, sweet service, and very good, simple food, attractively presented. Dishes include a delectable baby artichoke salad, pastas, pizzas, grilled meats and Italian desserts such as tiramisu and panna cotta. A great place for a tête-à-tête.

Le Dos de la Baleine

40 rue des Blancs-Manteaux, 4th [B2]. Tel: 01 42 72 38 98. Open: L and D Tues–Fri, D only Sat. **€€–€€€**

The bright yellow exterior gives no clue as to the casual elegance inside, where white tablecloths, quality wine glasses and respectable artworks set the tone. The original food (scallop carpaccio with apple and cabbage, chicken with sorrel sauce and pink peppercorns, asparagus flan and ravioli of apple and cinnamon with mango syrup) is beautifully presented. Reserve.

Did you know?

The Marais is so called because it was once a swamp (*marécage* in French). It was drained and turned into agricultural land – once a major food source for Parisians.

Georges

Centre Georges-Pompidou, 6th floor, rue Rambuteau, 4th [A2]. Tel: 01 44 78 47 99. Open: L and D Wed–Mon, non-stop noon–midnight. **€€€**

With globular, brushed-aluminium pods, bright Pop Art colours, transparent tables, hip DJs and one of the finest restaurant views in the city, Georges is an art installation in its own right. It has been a fashionable destination ever since its opening in 2000, despite having a reputation for discourteous service and inconsequential, rather pricey food.

Maison Rouge

13 rue des Archives, 4th [B2]. Tel: 01 42 71 69 69. Open: L and D Mon–Sat, Br and D Sun. **€€**

Decorated in leather and chrome, with unique lighting, this ultra-hip glasshouse is one of the most fashionable gay venues in town. Food of the moment is served, from steamed bass with spaetzle and lamb with a muesli crust to tiramisu parfait with liquorice, but there are always more mundane pastas, salads and even cheeseburgers on offer. Small portions.

International

404 🍴

69 rue des Gravilliers, 3rd [B1]. Tel: 01 42 74 57 81. Open: L and D daily, Br Sat, Sun. **€€€**

Packed, hip, and atmospheric, with low seating and iron grilles on the windows casting lacy patterns through the dim interior on to the tables. The Moroccan menu features filo-pastry pies, lamb brochettes, an exotic selection of couscous and tagines, as well as a range of harmonious Berber desserts. Respectably good food. Booking essential.

Caves Saint-Gilles – a little corner of Spain in the Marais

L'Aigre Doux

59 rue des Gravilliers, 3rd [B1]. Tel: 01 42 71 44 54. Open: L and D Mon–Fri, D only Sat; closed Aug. **€**

The simple French lunch menu comes at an unbeatable price, but even better are the authentic Iraqi feasts at night, including okra gumbo, kefta (spiced meat-and-sesame balls) with prune sauce, and marinated roasted lamb with cracked wheat. It's a hole in the wall, but with such a humble bill one can't complain.

Les Caves Saint-Gilles

4 rue St-Gilles, 3rd [D2]. Tel: 01 48 87 22 62. Open: B, L and D daily, non-stop 8am–midnight. **€€**

On a quiet street behind place des Vosges, this brightly tiled corner of Spain is a mood-lifter. Newspapers hang at the front near the bar, hams are suspended above the kitchen in the back, and joking waiters stride up and down delivering heaps of paella, assorted tapas, and platters of grilled vegetables or seafood. Desserts include nougats, crema catalana and Spanish ices.

Chez Marianne

2 rue des Hospitalières-St-Gervais, 4th [C3]. Tel: 01 42 72 18 86. Open: L and D daily, non-stop noon–midnight. **€**

An institution in the Jewish quarter, this black-and-white tiled restaurant with grocery attached is a jewel box of rollmops, halva, stuffed fig leaves, tehina, zazki, fried aubergine, baklava and poppyseed bars. Compose your own platter, and, on a summer's day, try to get a place on the sizeable terrace. Take-away falafels can be bought at the counter, if you need a fast but filling lunch.

Chez Ravi

3 rue du Roi-Doré, 3rd [C2]. Tel: 01 42 74 31 22. Open: L and D Mon–Fri, D only Sat. **€**

At night, if you walk down rue de Turenne and look right, you'll spot the outside lights of this Indian restaurant twinkling like gems on a necklace. Inside, blue-and-gold fabrics hang from the ceiling lending an exotic touch. They do

TIP

Falafels in the Jewish quarter are significantly cheaper when ordered to take away instead of to eat in. Some of the best are to be found at **L'As du Fallafel** *(34 rue des Rosiers, 4th, tel: 01 48 87 63 30).*

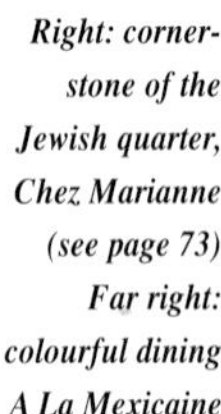
Right: ***corner-stone of the Jewish quarter, Chez Marianne (see page 73)***
Far right: ***colourful dining A La Mexicaine***

tandoori, biryani, daal, and other traditional Indian favourites – all of which are easy on the wallet.

L'Enoteca

25 rue Charles-V, 4th [C4]. Tel: 01 42 78 91 44. Open: L and D daily; closed 1 week in mid-Aug. **€€–€€€**

Good Italian food in casual surroundings on two floors near the Village Saint-Paul. The wine list is good, and the sommelier even better – unlike the maître d' who can be a little pushy. Start with beef carpaccio with rocket salad, move on to spaghetti with clams, or chicken with orange and rosemary, and finish with corleone (an auberge, ricotta, chocolate and orange dessert).

Gli Angeli

5 rue Saint-Gilles, 3rd [D3]. Tel: 01 42 71 05 80. Open: D only daily; closed Aug. **€€**

Some of the best Italian food in Paris is found in this unassuming corner restaurant with rough stone walls, a wide bar, a flirtatious owner and, alas, few free tables. Excellent produce goes into every dish, and there's a cellar of Italian wines that won't disappoint. Booking essential.

Isami

4 quai d'Orléans, 4th [B4]. Tel: 01 40 46 06 97. Open: L and D Tues–Sat, D only Sun; closed Aug. **€€€**

There is something marvellous about eating the freshest seafood imaginable and then stepping out on to a full view of the Seine on the Ile St-Louis. This small Japanese restaurant has a minimalist menu to match the stripped-back décor, but the quality of the sushi and sashimi is way above average. The prices reflect the quality. Book ahead.

A La Mexicaine

68 rue Quincampoix, 3rd [A2]. Tel: 01 48 87 99 34. Open: D only Mon–Fri, L and D Sat–Sun. **€€–€€€**

A La Mexicaine is run by the former cultural attaché from the Mexican embassy and does Mex without the Tex. Kick off with a great margarita in the long, sun-coloured dining room, where ceramic plates dot the walls; then dig into superb guacamole, black-bean soup and tortillas and tacos made in house. Reputedly the best Mexican restaurant in town.

Thanksgiving

20 rue St-Paul, 4th [C3]. Tel: 01 42 77 68 28. Open: L and D Wed–Sat, Br Sat–Sun; closed 3 weeks in Aug. **€€€**

Just around the corner from the tiny grocery store where you can stock up on peanut butter, molasses, marshmallows and other American treats, this little slice of Louisiana serves up genuine Cajun gumbo, pecan pancakes, crawfish pie, a proper Caesar salad and 'mud' pie.

Vegetarian

Piccolo Teatro

6 rue des Ecouffes, 4th [C3]. Tel: 01 42 72 17 79. Open: L and D daily. **€**

Vegetarian restaurants are few and far between in Paris, so this funky eatery with a marked Anglophone clientele has its niche. Gratins of all kinds (spinach, potato and mint or aubergine, tomato, basil and mozzarella), salads, tempeh, fruit juices galore (but also wine and beer), rhubarb charlotte, crumbles and fresh cheese are examples of the healthy yet compelling fare in this small arty dining room.

Le Potager du Marais

22 rue Rambuteau, 3rd [B2]. Tel: 01 42 74 24 66. Open: L and D daily, non-stop. **€**

This pleasant dining room is just one (long) table wide. Try meatless takes on French classics such as cassoulet, or other vegetarian favourites including aubergine ravioli. Finish with yoghurt flavoured with orange-flower water. Homely atmosphere and friendly service.

Bars and Pubs

The Marais is known primarily as the city's gay district, which is not to say that all drinking holes are exclusively gay (although some are). The main concentration of gay bars is found on and between rue des Archives and rue Vieille-du-Temple. As a point of departure, consider the classic **Le Central** *(33 rue Vieille-du-Temple, 4th, tel: 01 48 87 99 33)*, **L'Open Café** *(17 rue des Archives, 4th, tel: 01 42 72 26 18)*, or **Le Cox Café** *(15 rue des Archives, 4th, tel: 01 42 72 08 00)*. For the girls, there's **Les Scandaleuses** *(8 rue des Ecouffes, 4th, tel: 01 48 87 39 26)* or **Bliss Kfé** *(30 rue du Roi-de-Sicile, 4th, tel: 01 42 78 49 36)*.

If you're straight, there are plenty of other spots to choose from. **The Lizard Lounge** *(18 rue du Bourg-Tibourg, 4th, tel: 01 42 72 81 34)* pulls in an English-speaking clientele . The young crowd likes **Les Etages** *(35 rue Vieille-du-Temple, 4th, tel: 01 42 78 72 00)*, a grungy, three-storey bar with happy hour from 3.30pm. Also for a younger crowd is **L'Apparemment Café** *(18 rue des Coutures-St-Gervais, 3rd, tel: 01 48 87 12 22)*, an endless space laid out like a living room, with comfortable furniture, lots to read and parlour games (avoid the food, though). **La Perla** *(26 rue Francois-Miron, 4th, tel: 01 42 77 59 40)* draws a bourgeois-bohemian crowd with its polished atmosphere and good margaritas.

Remember that this whole *quartier* has a high concentration of bars, so meandering the streets, you're guaranteed to stumble across somewhere of appeal. Other venues include: **Chez Ariane** *(168 rue Saint-Martin, 3rd, tel: 01 42 76 93 99)*, ideal for aperitifs and popular for its Sunday jazz concerts; **The Quiet Man** *(5 rue des Haudriettes, 3rd, tel: 01 48 04 02 77)*, an Irish pub in miniature; **Le Web Bar** *(32 rue de Picardie, 3rd, tel: 01 42 72 66 55, www.webbar.fr)*, the chicest internet café in town; **La Belle Hortense** *(31 rue Vieille-du-Temple, 4th, tel: 01 48 04 71 60)*, with a non-smoking reading room; **Bubar** *(3 rue des Tournelles, 4th, tel: 01 40 29 97 72)*, with its excellent wine list; and **Stolly's** *(16 rue Cloche-Percé, 4th, tel: 01 42 76 06 76*), a friendly spot that's popular with the expat crowd.

Out on the Town

From early evening cocktails to early morning clubbing, Paris offers plenty of options for pre- and post-prandial entertainment

You've just had a wonderful Parisian dinner, and you're looking for the perfect spot for a nightcap. Or, perhaps you were so caught up in your evening visit to the Centre Pompidou that you've missed dinner altogether. Maybe you've dined early and are now in the mood for dancing and mingling with the indigenous noctambulant hordes. Or you'd like to hear some mellow after-dinner jazz or some upbeat salsa dancing. Whatever the case, Paris nightlife offers many options for eating late, drinking late, or dancing 'til dawn if you desire.

The Cocktail Hotspots

Parisian trend-setters still love the **Hôtel Costes** *(239 rue Saint-Honoré, 1st, tel: 01 42 44 50 00)*, which serves food until 1am, and has a sleek bar area serving overpriced drinks and playing classic 'lounge music' compilations. For a more subdued evening, **Le Fumoir** *(6 rue de l'Amiral-Coligny, 1st, tel: 01 42 92 00 24)* is a popular choice: cocktails are pricey but well mixed, and finger food is served until midnight. Another hot spot is the **Mezzanine de l'Alcazar** *(62 rue Mazarine, 6th, tel: 01 53 10 19 99)*, which offers a "formule dinatoire" (20 euro for a drink, a dish and coffee) until 10pm, and the right to hang out at your table until late in a sizzling atmosphere.

Most elegant lounge award goes to the **Hemingway Bar**, at the Ritz Hotel *(15 place Vendome, 1st, tel: 01 43 16 30 30)*, where classy attitude and proper attire are required. Ditto at the **China Club** *(50 rue de Charenton, 12th, 01 43 43 82 02)*, a sophisticated cocktail salon that makes the best Bloody Marys in town, with a kitchen open past midnight. And, in the ultra-elite category, the ultimate is **Le Mathis Bar** *(3 rue de Ponthieu, 8th, tel: 01 53 76 01 62)*, an intimate celebrity haunt that opens at 11pm, though you'll need to find a VIP friend before confronting the bouncer.

Cocktails and finger food at Le Fumoir

For a more casual and exotic take on nightlife, try **Andy Whaloo** *(69 rue des Gravilliers, 3rd, tel: 01 42 71 20 38)* to savour Moroccan tapas, great funky decor, mint-and-vodka concoctions and apple-flavoured hookahs.

Terence Conran's Parisian hotspot, L'Alcazar

DJs and Clubs

At **L'Ile Enchantée** *(65 boulevard de la Villette, 11th, tel: 01 42 01 67 99)*, you can order late snacks while listening to DJ sets. If you choose **Café Chérie** *(44 boulevard de la Villette, 10th, tel: 01 42 02 07 87)*, across the street, dive into the crowd, and grab a chilled mojito and a North-African delicacy, cooked daily by the owner's mother, and stored fresh in a self-service machine – ingenious. Students, hipsters and tourists gather every night at the **Nouveau Casino** *(109 rue Oberkampf, 11th, tel: 01 43 57 57 40)*, a celebrated concert hall with a notable taste for rock. At **Favela Chic** *(18 rue du Faubourg-du-Temple, 11th, tel: 01 40 21 38 14)*, Brazilian specialities are served until 10.30pm, at which point everybody starts dancing… on the same benches where they sat to eat. Same thing at **La Flèche d'Or** *(102 bis rue de Bagnolet, 20th, tel: 01 43 72 04 23)*, a big bar with a stage, eclectic live music, and Sunday afternoon dance parties.

For a 'clubby' experience, forget the overrated Bains Douches. The new club to see and be seen is **Le Cabaret** *(2 place du Palais-Royal, 1st, tel: 01 58 62 56 25)*: you can have dinner upstairs, then mingle with the glittery mob below, until sunrise. For a mischievous trek, try the upscale strip-club **Pink Paradise** *(23 rue de Ponthieu, 8th, tel: 01 58 36 19 20)*.

For more traditional dancing, the action is on the boats: head out to the **Batofar** *(Port de la Gare, quai François-Mauriac, 13th, tel: 01 45 83 33 06)*, a popular 'boat club' with a restaurant deck, or to the **Péniche Concorde Atlantique** *(8 quai Anatole-France, 7th, tel: 01 47 05 71 03)*. In summertime, it's a dream spot to begin an evening (admiring the sunset while nibbling appetisers) as well as to finish off the night, with some of the best dance DJs in town.

Cabaret and Jazz

For the full-on glitzy flesh and feathers experience, **Le Lido** *(116bis avenue des Champs-Elysées, 8th, tel: 01 40 76 56 10)* is the slickest of the mainstream Parisian cabarets, and (for a price) you can have dinner with a show. If it's a taste of Pigalle you're after, bypass the Moulin Rouge and head round the corner to the more entertaining **Chez Michou** *(80 rue des Martyrs, 18th, tel: 01 46 06 16 04)*, which has a great line-up of enthusiastic drag acts every night, and above average food.

There are numerous jazz venues in Paris, but the one to go to if you like food with your jazz is the atmospheric cellar club **Le Franc Pinot** *(1 quai de Bourbon, 4th, tel: 01 46 33 60 64)* on the Ile Saint-Louis.

Bastille, République and Canal St-Martin

Off the main tourist tread, this is Paris at its bohemian best. Try out laid-back cafés, exotic eateries and long-established local wine bars

There is no tidy way to describe the jigsaw of neighbourhoods that lock into each other from the Gare de Lyon up to place de la République and beyond to the Canal St-Martin. It's a jumble of grand, tree-lined avenues, grungy alleyways and a few bohemian-chic streets. With little in the way of monumental attractions, apart from the sprawling Père-Lachaise cemetery and place de la Bastille, there can be long hum-drum stretches before you reach the restaurant of your dreams. You might pass a car showroom, a shop full of hammocks, a tearoom bursting with Oriental pastries, an art supply shop, an occult bookstore, a chocolatier with a thatched awning, then a rather alarming little spot with a window packed with dolls' heads and a sign reading, 'We replace broken heads.' Where on earth are you? Before diving into the Métro and racing towards the familiar, remember that parts of town such as these are where you get a real sense of everyday Parisian life. For the most part, these are neighbourhoods 'where the tourists never go', and that means you can relax and delight in the fact that even in a city as well-trodden as Paris, there are still new territories to discover.

Rue Oberkampf

This street is the hippest limb of the 11th *arrondissement*, especially at the upper end, where there's a high concentration of cafés and bars – serious drinkers and dancers of the trendy, international ilk head here at night. A little lower down, below avenue Parmentier, there are neighbourhood food shops, florists, and other speciality shops, including Dionysos *(61 rue Oberkampf, 11th)*, a good Greek grocer and Le Verre Volé *(38 rue Oberkampf)*, a fine wine shop representing small producers. Just off rue Oberkampf is also one of the best Italian grocers in the city, Idea Vino *(88 avenue Parmentier, 11th)*, known especially for Italian wines but also carrying non-perishable edibles. Nearby, rue Jean-Pierre-Timbaud is worth a meander for a number of interesting eateries, such as L'Homme Bleu *(see page 90)* for superb North African food, and plenty of arty-intellectual cafés, notably Les Trois Têtards *(46 rue Jean-Pierre-Timbaud, 11th)* and L'Autre Café *(62 rue Jean-Pierre Timbaud)*, which make almost anyone want to sit down and start writing a novel. On a Tuesday or Friday morning, the bonus in the area is the colourful market on boulevard Richard-Lenoir with fruits, vegetables, fish and tacky lingerie.

***Opposite:** the 1950s-style Café de l'Industrie. **Below:** permanent fixture at the bar of Le Kitch*

Around rue Charonne

Rue Charonne, much closer to Bastille, is another fabulous street. Young designers sell jewellery, handbags, fashions, interiors shops specialising in original modern designs, and there's a tiny glassware shop with goods that range from a €5 shot glass to a 1920s' Murano vase. Perhaps the most sought-after food on the street is the fabulously fresh Vietnamese fare at Paris Hanoï *(see page 90)*. If you're lured deeper into the *quartier*, don't miss the restaurants on rue Paul-Bert and rue Chanzy – there are at least three treasures including Le Bistrot Paul Bert *(see page 84)*. Nearby, rue Faidherbe is leafy and peaceful with some excellent restaurants in a higher price bracket, plus a lovely florist

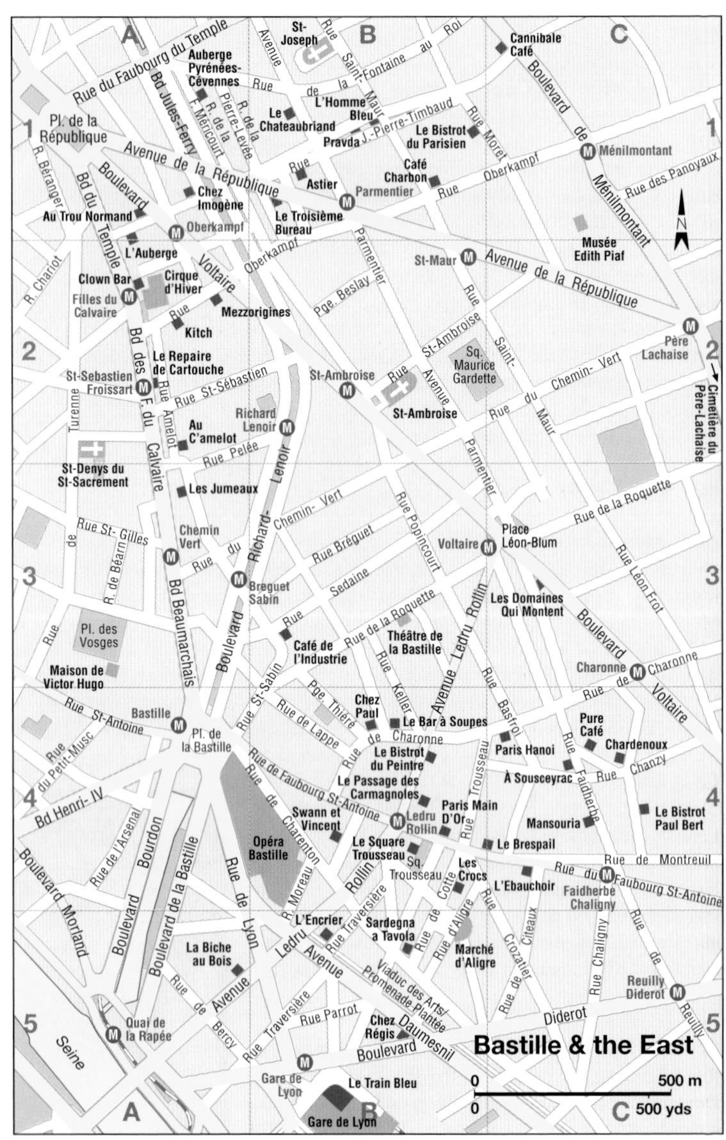

selling hand-painted plates, a tiny antique dealers and, best of all, La Croix & La Manière *(36 rue Faidherbe, 11th)*, an airy workshop with beautiful linens for the home.

FIVE OF THE BEST 

Le Chardenoux: lovely bistro with doors that open on to a quiet street in summer
Mansouria: upscale Moroccan for the city's best couscous and tagine
À Sousceyrac: one of the classiest, old-style bistros in the city
Le Square Trousseau: beauty and the bistro, a movie-set restaurant starring classics and more
Le Train Bleu: glittering belle époque décor that can't be beaten

Viaduc des Arts

The nicest walk this side of town is along avenue Daumesnil, where the Viaduc des Arts houses a strip of artisanal shops, including Atelier du Cuivre *(111 avenue Daumesnil, 12th)* for copper, Baguès *(73 avenue Daumesnil)* for crystal chandeliers, and Atelier Le Tallec *(93–5 avenue Daumesnil)* for exquisite hand-painted porcelain. This makes for a lovely stroll after visiting the Marché d'Aligre/Marché Beauvau *(see page 92)* in the morning. While there, don't miss the curious Graineterie du Marché *(8 place d'Aligre, 12th)*, a tiny shop selling grains for people (beans, peanuts, lentils, pasta), grains for birds (there's a cageful singing out front) and seeds for the garden, along with watering cans.

Once you've visited all these main areas, get lost. Literally. That's the best way to stumble upon the jewels of these neighbourhoods. L'Autre Boulanger *(43 rue de Montreuil, 11th, tel: 01 43 72 86 04)*, for example, is a baker all on his own up a grim street, yet it's one of the most appealing – and best – in the city, with organic sourdough breads baked in a wood-fired oven that makes the shop smell so sweet you want to move in. There's an oil shop amid the camera stores and motorcycle shops of boulevard Beaumarchais: Allicante *(26 boulevard Beaumarchais, 11th)* has a vast selection of award-winning olive oils and all manner of nut, seed and truffle oils. Off in another direction, it's luck indeed if you happen upon the rustic, far-flung wine bar Jacques Mélac *(42 rue Léon-Frot, 11th, tel: 01 43 70 59 27)*. Le Suprême du Marais *(75 rue Amelot, 11th)* is a fairytale charcuterie, but you really have to trail off the main drag to find it. Bières Spéciales *(77 rue St-Maur, 11th)* is a beer-lover's fantasy, with varieties from over 15 countries. The order of the day in these parts is definitely to leave no stone unturned.

Canal St-Martin

The Canal St-Martin begins in the 10th *arrondissement* at square François-Lemaître and leads up to place de la Bataille-de-Stalingrad. Green pedestrian bridges lead from one side to the other, boats glide up and down the high-level water, children's theatre thrives on summery Sundays, and there's a lovely landscaped park at the crook of the canal's elbow, where the paths along the water turn to cobblestone. This is a bohemian strip with a small-town feel and a handful of pleasant places to eat.

Up on the right-hand side of the canal there's really only one restaurant: Le Jemmapes *(82 quai de Jemmapes, 10th, tel: 01 40 40 02 35)*, which is laid back and cheap if you're looking to lunch on a generous salad before visiting the expansive and restful courtyard of the Hôpital St-Louis *(2 place du Docteur-Alfred-Fournier, 10th; closed weekends)*, reminiscent of elegant place des Vosges.

Barmen at Le Bistrot du Peintre

The more fashionable strip of the canal, however, is across the water. At the top end, there's Antoine et Lili *(95 quai de Valmy, 10th, tel: 01 40 37 41 55)*, a kitsch-lover's dream for fashion, decoration and gifts, and lunch in the adjoining doll's-house canteen with stars on the ceiling, red benches, flowery tables, and everything from pasta and sandwiches to lemonade and lollipops. There's even a tarot reader on Wednesday and Friday from 3 to 7pm. Next door, the fashionably feminine Stella Cadente *(93 quai de Valmy, 10th, tel: 01 42 09 27 00)* has a boutique living-room for tea, pastries and pretty bowls of candy. Further down, Chez Prune *(36 rue Beaurepaire, 10th, tel: 01 42 41 30 47)* is the trendiest of the eateries here, with a terrace packed with arty types reading left-wing newspapers. If you can't find space there, a few blocks along, try La Marine *(55 bis quai de Valmy, 10th tel: 01 42 39 69 81)*, styled like a boat, with portholes in the bar.

Some of the area's best food is found slightly off the beaten track on rue de Lancry. The best is at Le Verre Volé *(67 rue de Lancry, 10th tel: 01 48 03 17 34)*, a bistro and wine cellar where you can buy take-away cold champagne to drink along the canal, or, if you've reserved, enjoy a bottle of wine and a meal made from top-notch products in-house. Côté Canal *(56 rue de Lancry, 10th, tel: 01 42 08 38 81)*, an old-time brasserie with a lovely spiral staircase, is a safe bet. The tiny tea-room Couleurs Canal *(56 rue de Lancry, 10th, tel: 01 42 40 60 52)* has lovely food (but no alcohol), all prepared by the owner.

Rue des Vinaigriers is another street worth a stroll for its smattering of art studios and children's clothing shops. Stop for good world food at the miniature Po Mana *(39 rue des Vinaigriers, 10th, tel: 01 40 37 19 19)*, or steal into Le Restaurant de Bourgogne *(26 rue des Vinaigriers, 10th, tel: 01 46 07 07 91)* for an inexpensive neighbourhood lunch.

Brasseries

Le Train Bleu

Gare de Lyon, 12th [B5]. Tel: 01 43 43 09 06. Open: L and D daily. **€€€** *www.le-train-bleu.com*

Go up the main staircase of the station, busy with commuters and pigeons, and suddenly you're in Le Train Bleu's grand belle époque rooms. At the back, there's a bar, Big Ben, with vast leather chairs and heavy wooden tables, where you can talk the afternoon away (and eat a bad sandwich). In the restaurant itself, you can feast on caviar alone (€70 for 30g), or choose from a variety of traditional dishes including foie gras, sole meunière and profiteroles. It's a bit pricey, but the atmosphere can't be beaten.

Bistros

Astier

44 rue Jean-Pierre-Timbaud [B1]. Tel: 01 43 57 16 35. Open: L and D Mon–Fri; closed Aug, Easter and last week in Dec. **€€**

Excellent classic food in a well-known bistro with an interior slightly lacking in charm. Try the escargots, skate and leek terrine, beef with morels, blanquette de veau, or chocolate praline pots. Alternatively, test out the famous cheese and wine lists. Good food but the experience can be tainted by stand-offish serving staff.

L'Auberge

4 rue Jean-Pierre-Timbaud, 11th [A1]. Tel: 01 48 06 15 29. Open: L and D Mon–Fri, D only Sat; closed 3 weeks in Aug. **€–€€**

This family-style dining room in a former dairy offers traditional food that's perfectly respectable and cheap. Choose from goat's cheese crisps with honey, red mullet with pesto, lamb with rosemary, and coconut flan with spice bread. It's surprising to find a sommelier in such a place, but there he is, and on Wednesday nights, for €9, he'll choose an appropriate glass of wine for you for every course.

La Biche au Bois

45 avenue Ledru-Rollin, 12th [A5]. Tel: 01 43 43 34 38. Open: L and D Tues–Fri, D only Mon; closed mid-July–mid-Aug. **€€**

This place still attracts clients who remember what the restaurant was like before war. It hasn't changed much since. Step out of traffic behind the shield of shrubs and you're back in time amid fake flowers with a fan whirring above your head. Coq au vin has been a speciality since 1929, and the fries are still made in-house. Reserve.

Le Bistrot du Parisien

25 rue Moret, 11th [B1]. Tel: 01 43 38 72 38. Open: L and D daily; closed Aug. **€**

It seems as if nothing about this romantic Parisian bistro has

Historic listed restaurant, Le Train Bleu

changed since the beginning of the 20th century. The dinner menu at €24 offers traditional dishes such as magret de canard with green peppercorns, or sole meunière. Round off your meal with delectable tarte Tatin or prunes marinated in Armagnac.

Le Bistrot Paul Bert

18 rue Paul-Bert, 11th [C4]. Tel: 01 43 72 24 01. Open: L and D Tues–Sat. **€–€€**

There are more than 300 wines on this much-loved bistro's list. It's just a small place on an unassuming street and with a few tables outside. Inside are bookshelves, cluttered with books and wines. The food (courgette salad, terrines, apricot tart, pot-au-feu salad with coriander) is cheap and good.

Le Bistrot du Peintre

116 avenue Ledru-Rollin, 11th [B4]. Tel: 01 47 00 34 39. Open: B, L and D, Mon–Sat 8am–12.30am, Br and L Sun 10am–1pm. **€€**

Walking up the broad and leafy avenue, the eye is immediately drawn to this quintessential café/bistro with its delightful terrace. The interior is gorgeous – there's always a place to sit, and you never feel rushed. The typical bistro fare is well made, and service is friendly. A place where you'll want to become a regular.

Did you know?

Ironically, the best *croissants* in France are not crescent-shaped at all. Bakers are obliged by law to shape *croissants* made from margerine into a crescent, while *croissants* made from pure butter must be straight.

***Below and opposite:* Le Bistrot du Peintre**

Le Brespail

Passage Saint-Bernard, 159 rue du Faubourg-Saint-Antoine, 11th [C4]. Tel: 01 43 41 99 13. Open: D only Tues–Sat. **€€**

This is the kind of place that you're unlikely to stumble across by chance: off the main drag, down a paved alleyway, under a vine-covered trellis and behind a wine-coloured exterior. Inside, it's dark and rustic, with stone walls, wooden chairs, a low ceiling and a home-style kitchen in the corner. The menu includes cassoulet, foie gras, blanquette de veau and other Southwestern French classics.

Au C'amelot

50 rue Amelot, 11th [A2]. Tel: 01 43 55 54 04. Open: L and D Tues–Fri, D only Sat; closed Aug. **€€–€€€**

A trendy spot, despite its traditional ambience enhanced by menus scribbled on blackboards in the window. Although the choice isn't vast, the food is wonderfully fresh. Choose from soup and salad entrées, fish specials dictated by the market, duck with cumin and cauliflower, rhubarb nage with sorbet, or soft chocolate cake.

Chardenoux

1 rue Jules-Vallès, 11th [C4]. Tel: 01 43 71 49 52. Open: L and D Mon–Fri, D only Sat; closed Aug. **€€**

The recent change of management has done this glorious century-old bistro proud. The sky-blue ceiling decorated with fluffy clouds and tables covered in crisp white cloths set a romantic scene, and the new chef has a strong commitment to the use of fresh ingredients. Popular dishes range from spice-roasted cod, to boudin noir and apple clafoutis, green peppercorn steak, and salad of artichokes and squid.

Le Châteaubriand

129 avenue Parmentier, 11th [B1]. Tel: 01 43 57 45 95. Open: L and D Tues–Sat. **€**

This English-owned restaurant-cum-wine bar, with sober interior, has a small, daily-changing menu of good-quality dishes. Smoked wild boar with beans, sea-bream with aubergines, chocolate fondant and fruit crumbles are among the dishes on offer. The owner also imports a few British cheeses from Neal's Yard Dairy in London.

Chez Paul

13 rue de Charonne, 11th [B4]. Tel: 01 47 00 34 57. Open: L and D daily. **€€**

Book ahead, especially on summer nights, when the lights at Chez Paul twinkle, the cutlery clinks, and the queue curls around the corner. There are lots of robust meat dishes (although very little fish), traditional starters and desserts – from rabbit rillettes to dandelion greens with bacon, poached eggs, potatoes and herring, to crème brûlée and tarte Tatin. A very pretty place, albeit slightly pricey.

Chez Régis

27 ter boulevard Diderot, 12th [B5]. Tel: 01 43 43 62 84. Open: L and D Mon–Fri; closed 3 weeks in Aug and last week in Dec. **€€**

Go out of the door of the Gare de Lyon and a block or two to the right there's a little red box jutting on to the sidewalk, with green chairs out front. Even the post lady, walking past, recommended it as *Très, très bon!*, and indeed it is, with choices including artichoke heart salad, taboulé with mint, vegetable lasagne, chicken breasts with red tea, and crumble for dessert. It's not worth going out of your way to come here, but it's a good option if you've got a bit of time to kill before your train leaves.

TIP

When walking along the Viaduc des Arts on avenue Daumesnil in the 12th, find the stairs to the rooftop at the end and walk back through lavender and cherry blossoms on the leafy *promenade plantée*. A perfect way to digest lunch.

Clown Bar

Clown Bar

114 rue Amelot, 11th [A2]. Tel: 01 43 55 87 35. Open: L and D Mon–Sat, D only Sun. € No credit cards.

The wine list is excellent and the food very good in this convivial neighbourhood bistro next to the Cirque d'Hiver (Winter Circus). The photographs of clowns and colourful circus images on the walls, plus a ceiling dome full of stars, make for a special atmosphere. Staff are friendly and let you take all the time you like.

Les Crocs

14 rue de Cotte, 12th [B4]. Tel: 01 43 46 63 63. Open: L only Mon–Thur, D Fri–Sat; closed Aug. **€**

Once you tick off your choices on the menu, host-cum-chef Luc jumps into the open kitchen and fixes meat and potato specials in a flash. On Saturday nights, Njulienne, who runs her own Afro-Antillais stand in the Marché d'Aligre, takes over the cooking. Expect marvellous budget feasts of plantain beignets, pastries stuffed with crab, chicken yassa and rum-flamed banana tarts. Reserve.

Les Domaines qui Montent

136 boulevard Voltaire, 11th [C3]. Tel: 01 43 56 89 15. Open: L only Tues–Sat 10am–8pm. **€**

This wine-shop/bistro serves lunch for €13 and you can order any of the 300 bottles they stock, many of which are from small producers, without a corkage fee. There's one special per day, such as paella or daube with olives. Very friendly and knowledgeable staff.

L'Ebauchoir

43–5 rue de Citeaux, 12th [C4]. Tel: 01 43 42 49 31. Open: L and D Tues–Sat. **€€**

This restaurant is all on its own down an unpromising series of streets. When you do reach it, however, it shouldn't disappoint. The friendly staff serve set menus at noon and à la carte at night. Try the avocado with cocktail sauce, gazpacho, tuna with ginger and cardamon, a popular rice pudding, or the macaroons and coffee.

L'Encrier

55 rue Traversière, 12th [B5]. Tel: 01 44 68 08 16. Open: L and D Mon–Fri, D only Sat; closed Aug and last week in Dec. **€**

A comfortable neighbourhood joint near the Marché d'Aligre, with a rustic-style brick wall, slightly scandalous paintings and lamps leaping out above the open kitchen on twisted iron rods. Well-made terrine, swordfish with fennel cream, Roquefort pears, and marquise au chocolat are typical dishes. No reservations.

Le Passage des Carmagnoles

18 passage de la Bonne-Graine, 11th [B4]. Tel: 01 47 00 73 30. Open: L and D Mon–Sat. **€**

Down a lovely cobblestone passage off avenue Ledru-Rollin, this hiding place has a long and luscious wine list, plus pleasurable food to go with it. It's known for its artisanally made andouillette, and the chef's proud of the duck à l'orange and coq-au-vin. Warm wooden interior and relaxed crowd.

Le Repaire de Cartouche

8 boulevard des Filles-du-Calvaire, 11th [A2]. Tel: 01 47 00 25 86. Open: L and D Tues–Sat; closed mid-July–mid-Aug. **€€**

There are two entrances into this rustic, old-world restaurant, which has dark-wood panelling, heavy chairs and Revolutionary scenes upon the walls. The food is upper-end bistro but more creative than the kind of fare usually found in establishments of this type. Sample items from the menu include cauliflower soup with herring caviar cappuccino, roasted cod with fava beans, melon soup with walnut wine, and vanilla cream pots with madeleines. Rewarding.

À Sousceyrac

35 rue Faidherbe, 11th [C4]. Tel: 01 43 71 65 30. Open: L and D Mon–Fri, D only Sat; closed Aug. **€€€**

You really have to be in the know to discover places such as this classy old restaurant – but what a feast when you do. Specialising in food from Southwest France, the whole affair is pure tradition: crisp white tablecloths, a heavy, dark-wooden bar with a zinc top, and of course, the best of old-world cuisine. Dishes include ris de veau with mushrooms, a whole pigeon deboned and stuffed with foie gras, and, in season, a hare royale so special that clients have been known to write ahead to request it. Book ahead.

Le Square Trousseau

1 rue Antoine-Vollon, 12th [B4]. Tel: 01 43 43 06 00. Open: L and D Tues–Sat. **€€**

It's no surprise that this bistro has been used for film sets: inside it's spacious, with Art Deco ceiling lamps, colourful tiles and a glamorous bar with a giant brass coffee-maker behind. In summer, diners squeeze on to the terrace facing a leafy square. Gazpacho, tuna tartare, rosemary lamb and spring vegetables, beef with shallot sauce, chocolate quenelles with mint cream, and raspberry gratin are among the delights available.

Le Troisième Bureau

74 rue de la Folie-Méricourt, 11th [B1]. Tel: 01 43 55 87 65. Open: B, L and D Mon–Sat non-stop 8am–2am, Br Sun noon–midnight; closed 1 week in mid-Aug. **€€**

What a relief – a local place full of locals. You'll spot the barrels outside first (a hint that there's lots of wine inside), and although you won't find the most amazing juices on offer, they are cheap. Brunch on Sunday begins at 11am and features pancakes and maple syrup, and scrambled eggs; the menus for later in the day are also appealing, with dishes including ravioli with cream, artichokes with dill and salmon, poached egg and chorizo, and chicken with Camembert.

Au Trou Normand

9 rue Jean-Pierre-Timbaud, 11th [A1]. Tel: 01 48 05 80 23. Open: L and D Mon–Fri, D only Sat; closed Aug. **€€**

The delightful Square Trousseau

So many bistros resemble each other in Paris that it's difficult to know which to investigate and which to pass by. This tiny box of a place, with chequered tablecloths and white walls, looks no more promising than any other, but when you take your first bite of their artichokes with marinated peppers, tournedos with pears, or ham Parmentier with Cantal, you know you're in safe hands.

Cafés

Le Bar à Soupes

33 rue de Charonne, 11th [B4]. Tel: 01 43 57 53 79. Open: L and D Mon–Sat. **€**
www.lebarasoupes.com

This bright eatery stands out – blinding yellow as it is – on the trendiest street in the *quartier*. Inside, the vibes are calming, with large paintings of fruits and vegetables, good music and only a few small tables. The lunch special includes a glass of wine or coffee, a bowl of soup, and either a cheese or charcuterie plate or dessert.

Café Charbon

109 rue Oberkampf, 11th [B1]. Tel: 01 43 57 55 13. Open: L and D daily, Br Sat–Sun. **€**

This turn-of-the-20th-century café-restaurant is a mainstay on the increasingly trendy rue Oberkampf. It's worth a stop just for the interior, but the lunch and dinner menus offer interesting propositions such as prawn risotto and tuna tartare. Lighter snacks are available too.

Cannibale Café

93 rue Jean-Pierre-Timbaud, 11th [C1]. Tel: 01 49 29 95 59. Open: L and D daily, non-stop noon–midnight. **€**

A laid-back, cheerful and slightly crumbling café-restaurant with trendy music and a young crowd. You can just stop by for a drink, but it's worth staying for a bite, as the food is reasonably priced and prepared with care. Mains include red mullet with tapenade, lamb with tzaziki, and lasagne.

Café de l'Industrie

16 rue Saint-Sabin, 11th [B3]. Tel: 01 47 00 02 94. Open: B, L and D daily, non-stop 10am–1am, Br Sun. **€–€€**

In two facing corner locations, this well-loved neighbourhood haunt has a homely feel despite its 300 seats. Salads, pasta and traditional dishes such as salmon with dill or sausage and potatoes are mediocre

Right and far right: Le Kitch

but served in big portions, at a price that's hard to beat. Good for brunch on Sundays.

Pure Café

14 rue Jean-Macé, 11th [C4]. Tel: 01 43 71 47 22. Open: L and D Mon–Sat. **€€**

An exceptionally pretty café with tables that spill on to the street – perfect for lazy afternoons. The selection includes fish soup with saffron and fennel, lamb with coconut milk and curry polenta, fig tart, rhubarb clafoutis, every drink imaginable, and every possible measure of wine.

Regional

Auberge Pyrénées-Cévennes

106 de la Folie-Méricourt, 11th [A1]. Tel: 01 43 57 33 78. Open: L and D Mon–Fri, D only Sat; closed mid-July–mid-Aug, first week in Jan. **€€€**

There's a reason why this classy spot won a best bistro award: the waiters are friendly, the décor is unique (purple-and-white cloths, terracotta floors, and, oddly, a few stuffed animal heads on the wall), and the hearty food is top-notch. Try lentil caviar or frisée aux lardons to start, followed by cassoulet, pigs' feet, sausage and potatoes, fish quenelles, rum babas or tarte Tatin.

Chez Imogène

25 rue Jean-Pierre-Timbaud, 11th [A1]. Tel: 01 48 07 14 59. Open: L and D Tues–Sat, D only Mon. **€**

A cute and authentic crêperie with a blue façade and Breton blue tiles behind a long wooden bar. There are crêpes of all kinds, both savoury and sweet, plus Breton cider. Enjoy a full lunch menu with wine for just €12.50.

Paris Main d'Or

133 rue du Faubourg-St-Antoine, 11th [B4]. Tel: 01 44 68 04 68. Open: L and D Mon–Sat; closed Aug. **€–€€**

This is an easy place to miss – the dusky interior, viewed with difficulty from the outside, seems nothing extraordinary. But don't be deceived, because you've just found one of the best Corsican restaurants in the city, with superb charcuterie, fish soups, and cumin-roasted pork. Book ahead.

Contemporary

Les Jumeaux

73 rue Amelot, 11th [A3]. Tel: 01 43 14 27 00. Open: L and D Tues–Sat. **€€–€€€**

It's a pleasure to find the best of familiar ingredients used to produce something simple but special. This contemporary gastronomic restaurant, run by twin brothers, pulls this off with class, although the atmosphere can seem a little stiff at times. Tuna with sesame, cod with fava beans and pea ragout, and strawberry gratin, are seasonal fancies, on a menu that changes monthly.

Le Kitch

10 rue Oberkampf, 11th [A2]. Tel: 01 40 21 94 14. Open: non-stop Mon–Fri 11am–2am, evening only Sat–Sun. **€**

The décor lives up to the name: a ceramic bulldog in a yellow shirt sits on the bar, a pot gnome to his right. The chairs are rickety, the bar swathed in fabric, and the food is cheap and cheerful – think Caesar salads, club sandwiches, lasagne and crème brûlée. Popular with a young crowd.

Mezzorigines

18 rue Oberkampf, 11th [A2]. Tel: 01 43 14 05 07. Open: L and D Mon–Sat. **€€**

A trendy crowd (everyone from soccer players to bankers) heads here for modern Mediterranean

Right and below: Pravda

food. The dining room is pleasant, but the toilets are even better: bright China red with gold sinks and stars dangling from the ceiling.

International

La Bague de Kenza

106 rue Saint-Maur, 11th [B1]. Tel: 01 43 14 93 15. Pastry shop open: daily 9am–10pm (2–10pm Fri). Salon de thé open: Tues–Sun 9am–8pm (2–8pm Fri). **€**

Step into this Algerian pastry shop and feast your eyes on sumptuous pyramids of baklava, stuffed dates, and other decadent concoctions of almonds, honey, pistachios and essence of orange blossoms. Or sample them leisurely with mint tea, at the futuristic salon de thé next door.

L'Homme Bleu

55 bis rue Jean-Pierre-Timbaud, 11th [B1]. Tel: 01 48 07 05 63. Open: D only Tues–Sun; closed Aug. **€€**

Exquisitely prepared North African cuisine in a comfortably exotic setting. Choose from a variety of appetisers and couscous or tagines (such as lamb, prunes and almonds, or chicken with olives and candied lemon). Best to reserve.

Mansouria

11 rue Faidherbe, 11th [C4]. Tel: 01 43 71 00 16. Open: L and D Wed–Sat, D only Mon–Tues. **€€€** *www.mansouria.com*

Probably the best Moroccan food in town and definitely in the cushiest surroundings. The windows are mostly screen-covered, letting light through in patchy patterns and lending the inside an air of mystery. Eight menus include varied entrées, a main course and dessert, plus there are several interesting tagines and couscous dishes from which to choose. Dessert is mint tea, pastries, or crêpes with orange-flower cream. Booking recommended.

Paris Hanoi

74 rue de Charonne, 11th [C4]. Tel: 01 47 00 47 59 Open: L and D Mon–Sat. **€**

The hardest thing here is getting one of the 30 seats in this cult canteen, because the food is cheap and famously delicious. Calm décor with a busy open kitchen, where generous servings of soups, raviolis, spring rolls and other Vietnamese fancies are prepared.

Pravda

49 rue Jean-Pierre-Timbaud, 11th [B1]. Tel: 01 48 06 19 76. Open: D only daily, Br Sun. **€€**

For something out of the ordinary, try this place, which is a curious mix. Russian and Mediterranean dishes are served in a trendy modern spot with red scaffolding climbing up behind the bar like ivy. The menu offers marinated salmon with ginger confit, bortsch, pistachio-stuffed rabbit, almond-milk cappuccino, or upside-down rhubarb tart. You can also order mixed platters of fish and vegetables with blinis.

Sardegna a Tavola

1 rue de Cotte, 12th [B5]. Tel: 01 44 75 03 28. Open: L and D Tues–Sat, D only Mon. **€€€**

Outstanding Sardinian food just a hop from the Marché d'Aligre. Dried grapes, laurel and peppers dangle from the ceiling, and horse carpaccio, Sardinian gnocchi, ravioli with ricotta chard and saffron, milk flan with orange-flower water, or nougat are on the menu.

Swann et Vincent

7 rue Saint-Nicolas, 12th [B4]. Tel: 01 43 43 49 40. Open: L and D daily. **€€**

One of a small Italian chain. The décor – colourful floral tiles, massive posters, golden stained-glass lamps – may be contrived but it's pretty nonetheless, and the dishes, written up on a huge blackboard, are perfectly decent, from the aubergine gratin, tomatoes and pepper with mozzarella di buffola, and pasta and veal dishes, to panna cotta and tiramisu.

Bars and Pubs

Generally speaking, nightlife in the 11th and 12th means one of two things: a low-key drink in an unpretentious neighbourhood wine bar or café, or a full-on drinking-and-dancing fest that will go on way into the early hours. There are few exceptions.

If you're young and restless and looking for a drink and a place to twitch your hips, the hottest area in town is around rue Oberkampf. The bar in biggest demand is the belle époque **Café Charbon** *(109 rue Oberkampf, 11th, tel: 01 43 57 55 13)*, and the **Nouveau Casino** club next door *(see page 77)*, but if you can't squeeze in, there are plenty of alternatives up the street. A little nearer the canal, for example, **Favela Chic** *(18 rue du Faubourg-du-Temple, 11th, tel: 01 40 21 38 14)* is popular if you like heady cocktails and dancing on tables.

Closer to touristy Bastille, the cobblestone rue de Lappe has a high concentration of watering holes, mostly slightly grungy. Nearby alternatives abound on rue du Faubourg-St-Antoine, such as **Le Sans Senz** *(49 rue du Faubourg-Saint-Antoine, 12th, tel: 01 44 75 78 78)* and **Barrio Latino** *(46–8 rue du Faubourg-St-Antoine, 12th, tel: 01 55 78 84 75)*, and both clubs serve food.

If you're over 35, rue Charonne is probably preferable for drinks, for example on the terrace of the **Pause Café** *(41 rue de Charonne, 11th, tel: 01 48 06 80 33)* with its fabulous kitsch décor; at **Le Café du Passage** *(12 rue de Charonne, 11th, tel: 01 49 29 97 64)*, which has over 350 wines and 100-plus whiskies on the menu; or in one of the city's best wine bars, the rustic **Jacques Melac** *(42 rue Léon-Frot, 11th, tel: 01 43 70 59 27)*.

In the 12th arrondissement, **Le Baron Rouge** *(1 rue Théophile-Roussel, 12th, tel: 01 43 43 14 32)* is a small down-to-earth wine bar near the Marché d'Aligre, that serves fresh oysters in season and other good food as well as wine. **Le Viaduc Café** *(43 avenue Daumesnil, 12th, tel: 01 44 74 70 70)* has a jazzy atmosphere, vaulted ceilings and a superb terrace in summer. Finally for cocktails, an aperitif, a digestif or even dinner itself, try **Le China Club** *(50 rue de Charenton, 12th, tel: 01 43 43 82 02)*, an elegant venue with a 1930s' feel and piano bar that stays open until 3am in the winter.

Parisian Markets

With the exception of Mondays, you can visit a market – be it covered, street-based or 'roving' – every day of the week in Paris

For the most part, visiting Parisian markets is a morning activity, with stalls opening at 9am and packing up at 1pm. It's best to beat the crowds by arriving early for an unhurried walkabout, either to inspect goods before buying, or simply to appreciate the variety: turbot the size of a bathmat, baguettes stacked high like firewood, paddles of salt cod, golden rows of nut oils, bins of olives, sacks of spices, braids of pink garlic and endless arrangements of salad leaves, aubergines, mushrooms, apples or tomatoes on the vine.

However decorative they look, Parisian markets are, however, living affairs. People jostle and negotiate, queue-jump and ram into your ankles with prams and trolleys. The straightforward way not to get flustered is to play by the rules, most importantly: don't touch goods – that's the vendor's job; and, however disorganised crowds may appear to be in front of stalls, recognise that there is a queue, that it goes in one direction and that you must plant yourself at the correct end of it to be served. Finally, know that every transaction takes time, but if you remain in a relaxed mood, happy to people-watch as you wait, you won't mind.

Marché d'Aligre and street markets

With three distinct sections – although still manageable in size – is the daily market known locally as the **Marché d'Aligre** (place d'Aligre, 12th). It has an indoor part known, officially, as the **Marché Beauvau**, in which the produce is very high-end in quality (and price, especially for fruit and vegetables). There's an excellent stand serving African food, a very reliable fish stand and an Italian speciality shop in the midst of French cheese, poultry and charcuterie. Outside, the produce is cheaper, and the process of buying a noisier experience. A flea-market clutters the centre of the square, but for the most part all you'll find is uninteresting junk, while around the square there are small shops: one roasting coffee beans, one selling wines, one touting baskets and exotic pastas – it's worth spending time at this market and getting to know every corner.

Market streets tend to be less romantic than covered markets because, in essence, they are merely a collection of shops. Still, it is fun to set your purchases down, settle on a terrace with a coffee, and watch the world go by after shopping. They are generally open Tuesday to Saturday, with a long break for lunch, and on Sunday morning.

Arrive early to choose from the best fresh fish on ice

Perhaps the best known and full of character, even if it draws as many tourists as it does residents, is the street market on **Rue Mouffetard** (5th) in the Latin Quarter, which winds its way down one of the oldest streets in Paris towards place St-Médard. Look out for the Italian deli Facchetti and Steff the baker. **Place Monge** (5th) is particularly animated on Sunday morning when it is less touristy than nearby Rue Mouffetard. **Rue Cler** (7th) is an upmarket haunt with good delis, fine hams and cheeses

and an ever-packed café terrace at the Café du Marché. **Rue de Buci** (6th) is a memorably pretty street with a lovely pastry shop, a good florist and an ice-cream shop. **Rue Montorgueil** (2nd), near the old Halles on the right bank, is especially attractive at Christmas when glittering lights criss-cross all the way up the pedestrian street. Here, you'll find the famous pâtisserie, Stohrer, a cluttered spice shop at the lower end and a cheese shop near the top that will vacuum pack cheeses for travellers. It's also worth knowing that just a block away are some of the best kitchen-supply shops in town, such as **A. Simon** *(48–52 rue Montmartre, 2nd)* and **Dehillerin** *(8 rue Coquillière, 1st).*

Roving markets

Among the biggest roving markets are **Breteuil** (starting from place de Breteuil in the 7th on Tuesdays and Saturdays), **Bastille** (flowing from Bastille, in the 11th up boulevard Richard-Lenoir on Thursdays and Sundays) and, the loudest of the pack, **Belleville-Ménilmontant** (exploding from boulevard de Belleville to boulevard de Ménilmontant on the border of the 11th and the 20th on Tuesdays and Fridays).

Above left:* *rue Monge has good specialist stalls. Above: fresh radishes piled high

Each market has a unique character. Breteuil, just below the Eiffel Tower, is the most civilized, with room to manoeuvre, awnings offering shade, and an upmarket clientele. Here you'll find lobsters, snails stuffed with garlic butter, a stand of Lebanese flatbreads baking on the spot, wild strawberries, a foie gras stand and even someone selling fake fur coats. The market at Bastille is enormous, catering to customers of all kinds. There's a man selling newspapers from all over the world on Sundays. Two stands specialise in potatoes and onions, one in mushrooms, one in honey, one in eggs. And flower stalls abound. Belleville-Ménilmontant is in a category of its own. The first thing that hits you is the noise: it's amazingly loud with vendors yelling and buyers gossiping. Almost everyone seems to be wearing a head-dress of some kind. The 'ingredients' are slightly more exotic than those of other markets: more varieties of peppers, many of which are hot; giant watermelons; Chinese cabbage; figs the size of fists; flatbreads made from rye or barley – and more. And, in the midst of all the food are other curiosities: sink plungers next to the stand selling fresh almonds from Tunisia. Mousetraps and hulahoops a conversational distance from vast sacks of rice and bags of herbal teas. And as the crates empty, they are thrown on the awnings and makeshift roofs. From a distance, towards closing time, it looks like a shanty town. This is an exciting, kaleidoscopic market.

And for those looking for a somewhat calmer experience, there's always the modern-day version of a market, **La Grande Epicerie de Paris** at the Bon-Marché on rue de Sèvres in the 6th – the only one open on a Monday.

THE LATIN QUARTER AND SAINT-GERMAIN

Fashion not philosophy rules on the Left Bank, but literary cafés and authentic bistros are still part of its fabric

The Latin Quarter and Saint-Germain-des-Prés, sitting side-by-side, make up the heart of the Left Bank. Once the home of artists and intellectuals, the district has changed over the past few decades, with high fashion replacing high art, and Armani replacing Aristotle as the *lingua franca* of the area. What is generally referred to as the Latin Quarter lies to the east of boulevard St-Michel, which runs from place St-Michel on the banks of the Seine, crossing boulevard Saint-Germain just in front of the ancient Roman baths of Cluny – a reminder that this was once the centre of the original Roman city of Lutétia.

Boulevard St-Michel to rue Monge

The web of pedestrian streets around place St-Michel houses rather too many kebab outlets and low-grade tourist restaurants for its own good. Better to hunt out more attractive propositions within a short walking distance, from the conveniently placed La Lozère *(see page 107)* to quality bistros such as Le Réminet *(see page 104)*, just opposite Notre-Dame. Boulevard St-Michel (or boulevard 'St-Mich', as it is familiarly known) continues past the Sorbonne, and on to the Luxembourg gardens, eventually reaching boulevard du Montparnasse, which runs from northwest to southeast.

The Sorbonne, founded by Robert de Sorbon in 1253, remains one of the world's great seats of learning. Until the time of the French Revolution, all lectures were given in Latin, hence the name 'Latin Quarter'. Parisian student life is now less concentrated than in former days, but in 1968 this was the centre of the student uprisings that shook the country, and place de la Sorbonne remains a thriving centre of student opinion. To enjoy a grown-up intellectual lunch the brasserie Balzar *(see page 100)* still attracts an interesting group of intellectuals, local bourgeoisie and artists in the money. The bookshops that previously dominated the area are gradually being taken over by fashion emporia, but bargain books can still be bought around place St-Michel. The area is home to a bookshop of particular interest to cooks: the Librairie Gourmande *(4 rue Dante, 5th)*.

***Opposite:* Terence Conran's L'Alcazar. *Below:* dessert menu, Chez Fish**

When boulevard St-Michel reaches place Edmond-Rostand the choice is between wandering in the Luxembourg gardens in front of the Senate, where children still play with sand and float boats on the pond (the gardens make a pleasant place for a picnic), or heading off up to the Panthéon *(place du Panthéon, 5th)*, where the great and the good of French life are buried for posterity. From here you can easily reach the picturesque rue Mouffetard, where place de la Contrescarpe has been a favourite

meeting place for bohemians since the early 16th century. The 'Mouffe', as it is popularly known, is also the venue for a great food market. The atmosphere remains impressively Gallic, especially on a Sunday morning, when workers still distribute revolutionary tracts, and stallholders shout out the quality of their produce. The nearby market on place Monge on Wednesdays, Fridays and Sundays is of a more manageable size than the Mouffe, and many local residents buy their food here.

On rue Monge is one of the entrances to the Arènes de Lutèce, no longer the sight of gladiatorial escapades but rather of sedate concerts in summer. For serious plant-gazing head to the calming Jardin des Plantes, formerly the

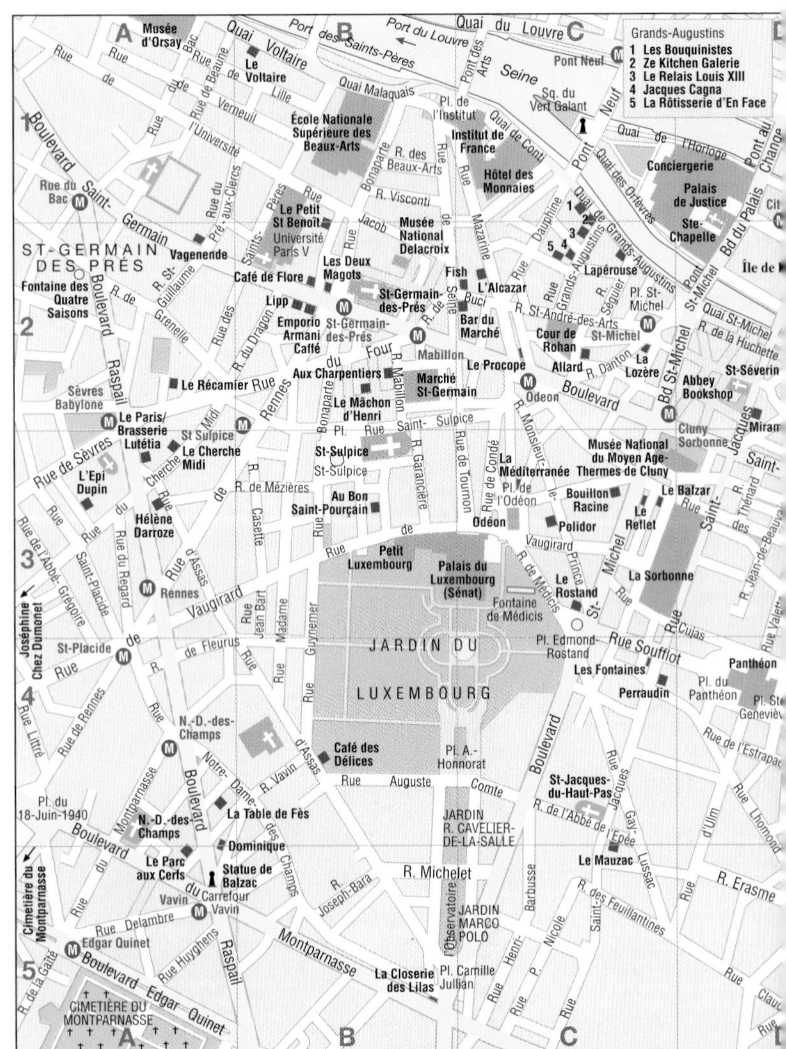

royal botanic gardens, where plants were cultivated to sooth the royal health. It is also the home to the Muséum National d'Histoire Naturelle and a rather bucolic zoo.

Boulevard Saint-Germain

The district's other main artery is boulevard Saint-Germain, running from the Assemblée Nationale and its surrounding ministries to architect Jean Nouvel's elegant Institut du Monde Arabe, with its rooftop restaurant Le Zyriab, which has some of the best views in the capital (but, unfortunately, some of the most disappointing service and food). First stop on the boulevard for food lovers will be the Sunday morning organic market on boulevard Raspail, where the rich new yuppies of the Left Bank delight in the high prices and rural credentials of the products on offer. At this point, you're right on the doorstep of the 7th *arrondissement*, so this is a good place to link up with the sights and restaurants described in the next chapter *(see page 113)*.

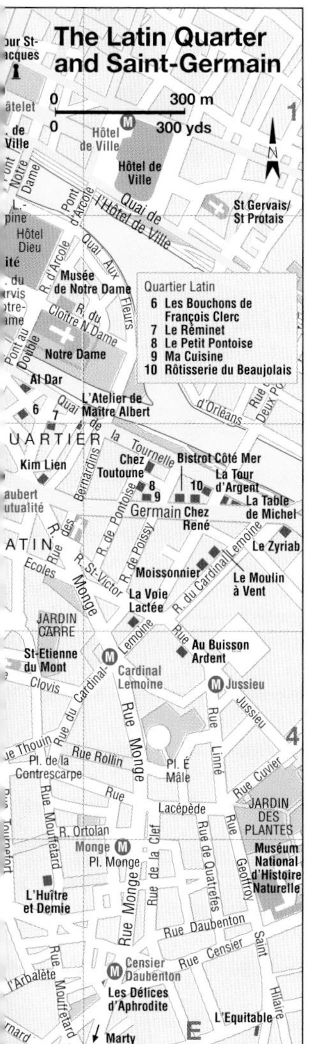

Further down boulevard Saint-Germain-des-Prés is the picturesque church of the same name, the oldest church in Paris, with the surrounding streets the very definition of café society. The crowd has evolved from poets Paul Verlaine and Arthur Rimbaud to writers Jean-Paul Sartre, Simone de Beauvoir and Albert Camus to fashion gurus Karl Lagerfeld and Sonia Rykiel. The changing face of the area is subject to heated debate, and in 1997 an association was formed to preserve the intellectual credibility of the area, led by the chanteuse Juliette Gréco and, amusingly, Rykiel and Lagerfeld, who therefore have the duel role of changing the face of the area and defending its former glories.

Two monuments to the district's literary heyday, the Café de Flore *(see page 105)* and Les Deux Magots *(see page 106)* still provide fascinating, although expensive, venues for people-watching. For a real feel of the charm of Saint-Germain explore the quaint little place Furstenberg (just a stone's throw from the main boule-

Left Bank institution: Les Deux Magots

Five of the Best

Allard: enjoy traditional French food at one of the city's loveliest bistros
Aux Charpentiers: bags of atmosphere adjacent to the Marché Saint-Germain
Balzar: literary brasserie with genuine Latin Quarter style
Chez René: traditional bistro with one of the best cheese boards in town
Le Réminet: family-run bistro opposite Notre-Dame with a talented young chef

vard), where the painter Eugène Delacroix's studio can be visited – or seek out characterful old bistros like Allard or Lipp *(see page 99)*.

On the opposite side of the boulevard from the church, the Marché Saint-Germain shows just how much the district has changed. Despite a tasteful restoration, the old market is now given over exclusively to fashion, surrounded by a very mixed bag of restaurants. It is best to stick to classics such as Aux Charpentiers or the lively Au Bon Saint-Pourçain *(for both, see page 102)* beside the frosty grandeur of St-Sulpice church. Here, you can also find top pâtisserie, Aoki Sadaharu *(35 rue Vaugirard)*, where a Japanese chef produces subtle and imaginative cakes, which are presented like precious Oriental jewels.

Back on boulevard Saint-Germain, the traffic-heavy carrefour (crossroads) de l'Odéon is home to a number of cinemas, and to Le Procope *(13 rue de l'Ancienne Comédie, 6th, tel: 01 40 46 79 00)*, which purports to be the oldest café in the city. Opinions are divided on this, however – for some, the place (now a brasserie) is just a tourist trap serving unmemorable food; for others, it represents three centuries of Parisian history, and offers hearty bourgeois cuisine.

After it crosses boulevard St-Michel, heading east, Saint-Germain becomes less self-consciously fashionable, and the atmosphere benefits from this. The streets around place Maubert, where there is a popular food market, are among the oldest in Paris. The late president Mitterrand lived in rue de Bièvre, near legendary bistro Chez René *(see page 102)*. A stroll down to the river leads to the booksellers that line the magnificent *quais* from here back to place St-Michel.

Haute Cuisine

Hélène Darroze

4 rue d'Assas, 6th [A3]. Tel: 01 42 22 00 11. Open: L and D Tues–Sat; closed in Aug. **€€€€** *upstairs,* **€€€** *downstairs.*

One of the city's top female chefs, Hélène Darroze, originally from the Landes, has brought the best of the southwest to town with a light and whimsical hand. The ground floor is famous mostly for tapas, while, for more formal dining, head upstairs and sample wood-grilled foie gras with caramelised fruits or lamb with couscous, chick peas and mint. Colourful, contemporary setting.

Jacques Cagna

14 rue des Grands-Augustins, 6th [C2]. Tel: 01 43 26 49 39. Open: L and D Tues–Fri, D only Sat and Mon; closed 3 weeks in Aug and last week in Dec. **€€€–€€€€** *www.jacquescagna.com*

The headquarters of what has become a mini empire of Left Bank restaurants. The ancient street and undisguised formality of this restaurant are matched by distinguished haute cuisine, with dishes such as cod in lobster broth.

Lapérouse

51 quai des Grands-Augustins, 6th [C2]. Tel: 01 43 26 68 04. Open: L and D Mon–Fri, D only Sat; closed Aug. **€€€–€€€€**

One of the most romantic restaurants in the city – the kind of place where you make your intentions known – with plush private salons for intimate dinners. The refined classical cooking is as elaborate as the décor. Prices reflect the riverside setting and the historical mystique of the place.

La Méditerranée

2 place de l'Odéon, 6th [C3]. Tel: 01 43 26 02 30. Open: L and D daily. **€€€€**

Opposite the Odéon theatre, this polished restaurant serves fish, fish and more fish. It has had its share of culinary ups and downs, but the decoration, with frescoes by Bérard and Vertès and a carpet designed by Cocteau, make it really special.

Le Paris

Hôtel Lutétia, 45 boulevard Raspail, 6th [A3]. Tel: 01 49 54 46 90. Open: B, L and D Mon–Fri; closed Aug. **€€€€** *www.lutetia-paris.com*

This is the only palace hotel in the Latin Quarter, and its restaurant, decorated by neighbourhood dress designer Sonia Rykiel, has class. Imaginative dishes include sea urchin with quinoa or pear with sesame nougatine and caramel sauce. Unusually for such a gastronomic temple, the chef also offers an appealing vegetarian menu.

Below: Lapérouse. Bottom: artist-designed fish restaurant La Méditerranée

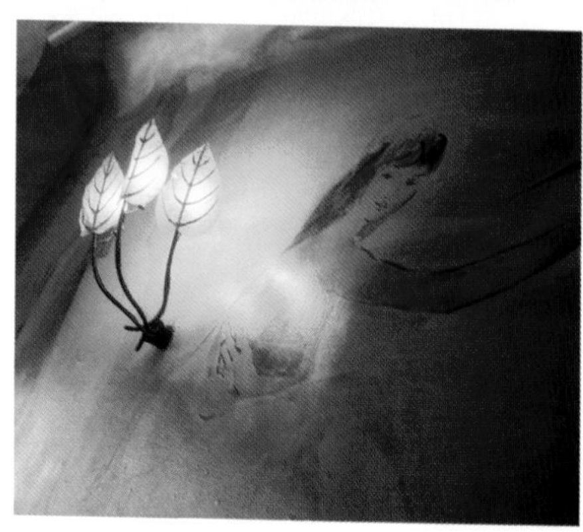

Le Relais Louis XIII

8 rue des Grands-Augustins, 6th [C2]. Tel: 01 43 26 75 96. Open: L and D Tues–Sat, D only Mon; closed 3 weeks in Aug. **€€€€** *www.relaislouis13.com*

One of the most popular classic restaurants in the area with light sophisticated dishes such as asparagus fricassée and saddle of lamb with Provençal vegetables, all prepared to the highest of standards by chef Manuel Martinez. Impressive, historic surroundings and service with flair.

La Tour d'Argent

15–17 quai de la Tournelle, 5th [E3]. Tel: 01 43 54 23 31. Open: L and D Wed–Sun, D only Tues. **€€€€** *www.tourdargent.com*

Right: exquisite presentation at L'Alcazar. Below: the chef at Allard

The famous Parisian restaurant owner, Claude Terrail, former boss at the Tour d'Argent, has now retired, but this hasn't deterred the glitzy clientele who bask in the top-floor view over Notre-Dame. They leave, chastened by the bill, clutching a card identifying the number of the delicious duck they have just consumed. A classic.

Brasseries

L'Alcazar

62 rue Mazarine, 6th [C2]. Tel: 01 53 10 19 99. Open: L and D daily, Br Sun. **€€–€€€** *www.alcazar.fr*

Sir Terence Conran's contribution to the Paris restaurant scene was to transform this former musical hall into a designer brasserie. It's been a hit with Parisians and tourists alike, thanks to the easygoing atmosphere and competitively priced menu, which includes an up-scale interpretation of British fish and chips.

Le Balzar

49 rue des Ecoles, 5th [C3]. Tel: 01 43 54 13 67. Open: L and D daily, non-stop noon–midnight. **€€€** *www.brasseriebalzar.com*

If a brasserie could sum up the atmosphere of an entire city, then Balzar would be high on the Paris list. The classic menu and the comforting 1920s' interior, with mirrors judiciously placed for discreet people-watching, all make for a quintessentially Parisian experience.

Bouillon Racine

3 rue Racine, 6th [C3]. Tel: 01 44 32 15 60. Open: L and D daily. **€€–€€€** *www.bouillon-racine.com*

The Art Nouveau decoration of this former workers' soup kitchen is the main reason to seek out this popular brasserie-style restaurant with a Belgian accent. Sadly, the food and miserable music do not match the setting. Stick to a simple dish – not to mention good beer – and admire the surroundings.

Brasserie Lutétia

Hôtel Lutétia, 45 boulevard Raspail, 6th [A3]. Tel: 01 49 54 46 76. Open: L and D daily, non-stop noon–11pm. **€€€** *www.lutetia-paris.com*

Banks of oysters and fresh seafood form the centrepiece of this popular brasserie attached to the hotel Lutétia, but meat-lovers can enjoy the usual specialities such as choucroute or a juicy steak in a décor that remains a 1960s' aberration.

La Closerie des Lilas

171 boulevard du Montparnasse, 6th [B5]. Tel: 01 40 51 34 50. Open: Br, L and D daily, non-stop 11am–1am. **€€–€€€€**

Spiritual home to Left Bank intellectuals, the Closerie remains one of the most attractive institutions in the city. For dining, choose between the reliable brasserie or the expensive restaurant, which looks the part and still serves great French favourites such as frogs legs and crêpes Suzette. Great bar.

Lipp

151 boulevard Saint-Germain, 6th [B2]. Tel: 01 45 48 53 91. Open: B, L and D daily, non-stop 9am–2am. **€€€** *www.brasserie-lipp.fr*

Brasserie Lipp remains the fashion barometer of Paris. To be offered a table on the first floor is social suicide, but swagger in on the ground floor, nodding to passing celebs, and the unthinkable ascent can be avoided. The rather dull brasserie food is variable, but nobody cares.

Marty

20 avenue des Gobelins, 5th [E5]. Tel: 01 43 31 39 51. Open: L and D daily, non-stop noon–midnight. **€€€** *www.marty-restaurant.com*

The fashionable restoration of this 1920s' brasserie has robbed the place of some of its old ambience, but the surroundings are still plush, and the stylishly presented new menu, with its modern take on French classics, a success.

Vagenende

142 boulevard Saint-Germain, 6th [A2]. Tel: 01 43 26 68 18. Open: L and D daily, non-stop noon–1am. **€€€** *www.vagenende.fr*

A belle époque wonder, Vagenende is the ideal restaurant in which to soak up a sense of the city's past glory. The brasserie-style food is good, without being outstanding. And, although the number of tourists squeezing through the doors can be exasperating, the place still has charm.

Bistros

Allard (🍴)

41 rue St-André-des-Arts, 6th [C2]. Tel: 01 43 26 48 23. Open: L and D Mon–Sat; closed 3 weeks in Aug. **€€–€€€**

The dark Art Nouveau decoration makes this one of the loveliest bistros in Paris, with two intimate, atmospheric rooms evocative of Left Bank life. The traditional food – think duck with olives, roasted lamb, etc – is very good.

L'Atelier de Maître Albert

1 rue Maître-Albert, 5th [D3]. Tel: 01 56 81 30 01. Open: D only Mon–Sat. **€€€**

Down a narrow street parallel to where the late president Mitterrand had his Paris apartment, you'll find this magnificent rôtisserie restaurant with ancient stone walls, a 16th-century fireplace and illustriously prepared, traditional food. A good range of meats roasted on a spit, plus great char-grilled tuna.

TIP

The best-known organic market in Paris is Raspail, open Sunday mornings between the rue du Cherche-Midi and the rue de Rennes in the 6th.

TIP
The minaret of the Paris mosque is a splendid and unexpected 1920s' monument. The complex *(1 place du Puits de l'Ermite, 5th, tel: 01 43 31 38 20)* includes a tiled hammam and tearoom, for mint tea and some sticky Middle Eastern pastries.

Bistrot Côté Mer
16 boulevard Saint-Germain, 5th [E3]. Tel: 01 43 54 59 10. Open: L and D Mon–Sat; closed 3 weeks in Aug. **€€€** *www.bistrotcotemer.com*
Formerly run by top chef Michel Rostang's daughter, Caroline, this popular boulevard Saint-Germain bistro is under new management, but the freshness and precision of the fish cooking remain reliable. Prices reflect the unbeatable position and top-quality ingredients.

Au Bon Saint-Pourçain
10 bis rue Servandoni, 6th [B3]. Tel: 01 43 54 93 63. Open: L and D daily. **€€€** *No credit cards*
A friendly bistro with good traditional cooking – mains such as Coquilles St-Jacques and cassoulet. The patron is possibly too much of a character for some tastes, but he attracts crowds of hungry locals on evenings when only rib-sticking cooking will do.

Les Bouchons de François Clerc
12 rue de l'Hôtel-Colbert, 5th [D2]. Tel: 01 43 54 15 34. Open: L and D Mon–Fri, D only Sat. **€€€** *www.lesbouchonsdefrancoisclerc.com*
François Clerc's trump card is his wine list, not to mention the impressive wine-cellar's stone walls, which lend a rustic ambience to an otherwise rather civilised dining room. Fine wines are sold here at the price you would pay in a shop, with no mark up, and this allows diners the freedom to explore them and find out what's best to accompany dishes such as trotters with truffles, soy-laquered salmon and hot cherry soufflé.

Le Buisson Ardent
25 rue Jussieu, 5th [E4]. Tel: 01 43 54 93 02. Open: L and D Mon–Fri, D only Sat; closed Aug. **€–€€**
Just beside the university, you'll find good-value menus featuring well-prepared dishes such as chicken-leg confit, ravioli and chocolate tart. The frescoes on the walls date from 1925, and the buzzy atmosphere ensures that everyone from university professors to tourists enjoys the experience.

Aux Charpentiers
10 rue Mabillon, 6th [B2]. Tel: 01 43 26 30 05. Open: L and D daily. **€€–€€€**
This long-established bistro just beside the Marché Saint-Germain retains an authentic Left Bank atmosphere. The decoration is inspired by the guild of carpenters, after which the place is named, and the menu offers the sort of homely cuisine (such as a steaming pot-au-feu) that appeals to Left Bank intellectuals.

Chez René
14 boulevard Saint-Germain, 5th [E3]. Tel: 01 43 54 30 23. Open: L and D Tues–Fri, D only Sat. **€€€**
Chez René is a Parisian cliché – a traditional bistro to a tee. The charcuterie, cheese platters and groaning plates of daily specials, such as beef à la mode and coq-au-vin are the real McCoy.

L'Epi Dupin
11 rue Dupin, 6th [A3]. Tel: 01 42 22 64 56. Open: L and D Tues–Fri, D only Mon; closed 3 weeks in Aug. **€€**
One of the great Left Bank success stories, where inspired, market-fresh, modern cooking is served at reasonable prices. Jerusalem artichoke soup, John Dory with saucisson and millefeuille of apple with cinnamon ice cream are typical. Unfortunately, the popularity of this delightfully old-fashioned place makes reservations essential and can lead to hassled service.

The pretty Buisson Ardent

L'Equitable

1 rue des Fossés-St-Marcel, 5th [E5]. Tel: 01 43 31 69 20. Open: L and D Wed–Sun, D only Tues; closed in August. **€€**

An excellent example of the new-style bistros that are springing up all over the city, this place offers reasonably priced cooking that's light and sophisticated without losing touch with tradition. It's not the prettiest restaurant in town, but the chef has real talent. Try the Guinea hen parmentier and end decadently with chocolate mousse.

Les Fontaines

9 rue Soufflot, 5th [C4]. Tel: 01 43 26 42 80. Open: L and D Mon–Sat. **€€€**

Hidden behind a banal café façade is one of the city's best-kept secrets. A bistro, where food is taken seriously, with huge portions of classic dishes such as pigeon roasted with grapes and veal blanquette the order of the day. The food is well cooked, with occasional imaginative flourishes.

Joséphine Chez Dumonet

117 rue du Cherche-Midi, 6th [A3]. Tel: 01 45 48 52 40. Open: L and D Mon–Fri; closed 3 weeks in Aug. **€€€**

When truffles are in season, few can resist the classic bistro preparations that this luxury temple provides. Everything here, from the banquettes to the boeuf bourgignon, is traditional French, and the crowd is fairly formal to match.

Le Mâchon d'Henri

10 rue Guisarde, 6th [B2]. Tel: 01 43 29 08 70. Open: L and D daily. **€€**

In an area with too many touristy restaurants, the Mâchon d'Henri

TIP

The rue Bonaparte was dead on Sundays before the arrival of pâtissier supremo Pierre Hermé at No. 72. The queues for his beautifully constructed cakes and mouthwatering chocolates are unending.

stands apart, serving wholesome traditional bistro food, albeit at a fair price. The elbow-to-elbow tables mean that a degree of social intercourse is inevitable.

Ma Cuisine

26 boulevard Saint-Germain, 5th [E3]. Tel: 01 40 51 08 27. Open: L and D Mon–Sat, L only Sun. **€€**

Despite its position at the far end of the boulevard Saint-Germain, this tiny restaurant is free of style and pretension. Old-fashioned dishes including coq au vin and oeufs à la neige are lovingly prepared by the owner. Good value.

Le Mauzac

7 rue de l'Abbé-de-l'Epée, 5th [C4]. Tel: 01 46 33 75 22. Open: B, L and D Mon–Fri, non-stop 9am–2am; closed 2 weeks in Aug. **€€**

A change of ownership has taken this popular local wine bistro slightly more upmarket than before, but the lovely leafy street near the Luxembourg Gardens in which it's located remains a fine spot to enjoy a simple meal, or just a platter of charcuterie or cheese, with a good glass of wine.

Le Moulin à Vent

20 rue des Fossés-St-Bernard, 5th [E3]. Tel: 01 43 54 99 37. Open: L and D Tues-Fri, D only Sat, closed in Aug and last week in Dec. **€€€**

A long-established traditional restaurant that's popular with bulging businessmen, who tuck into serious snails, steaks and cheese washed down with fine Beaujolais. *Très* French.

Le Parc aux Cerfs

50 rue Vavin, 6th [A5]. Tel: 01 43 54 87 83. Open: L and D daily; closed Aug. **€€–€€€**

This former artist's studio has a delightful interior courtyard, which on a warm summer evening is a real treat. The food is a competent version of modern bistro cooking, with leg of lamb with polenta, red snapper on ratatouille, etc; best sampled at one of the tables outside.

Perraudin

157 rue Saint-Jacques, 5th [C4]. Tel: 01 46 33 15 75. Open: L and D Mon–Fri; closed Aug. **€–€€**

An established haunt of students and intellectuals that is now not quite the bargain it used to be. It still offers a menu for die-hard traditionalists in suitably shabby surroundings with food that your mother might make, such as roast beef and plenty of fruit tarts.

Le Petit Pontoise

9 rue de Pontoise, 5th [E3]. Tel: 01 43 29 25 20. Open: L and D Tues–Sat, L only Sun. **€€**

This intimate spot, which has fast earned a great reputation, offers excellent modern bistro specials, chalked up on the blackboard daily. The boss is currently negotiating to open a branch in London.

Polidor

41 rue Monsieur-le-Prince, 6th [C3]. Tel: 01 43 26 95 34. Open: L and D daily. **€–€€**

This bohemian restaurant is a perennial favourite of students and budget diners. The *plats du jour* have been constant for around 150 years and arrive in hearty helpings. Blood sausage with mash and rice pudding are just the kind of stodgy dishes to expect.

Le Réminet

3 rue des Grands-Degrés, 5th [D3]. Tel: 01 44 07 04 24. Open: L and D Thur–Mon; closed 2 weeks in Jan and 3 weeks in Aug. **€–€€**

The position just beside Notre-Dame could hardly be better for this delightfully run bistro, where Hugues Gournay's cooking is both inventive and tasty. It is also one

TIP

The new style Saint-Germain would not be complete without Armani, and even the most fashion-conscious shopper must eat. The answer is the delicate refined Italian cuisine of the **Armani Caffè** *(149 boulevard Saint-Germain, 6th, tel: 01 45 48 62 15; open: Mon–Sat 11am–11pm).*

Warm welcome and traditional décor at Mauzac

of the few bistros in Paris open on Sunday, which doubles the appeal of the narrow dining room. The mouthwatering dishes include snails, whiting on aubergine caviar, guinea fowl in cream sauce, chestnut cake and a heavenly passion fruit sorbet.

La Rôtisserie d'En Face

2 rue Christine, 6th [C2] Tel: 01 43 26 40 98. Open: L and D Mon–Fri, D only Sat. ***€€€***

This annexe of Jacques Cagna's haute-cuisine empire offers a home-style take on French cooking, but with more sophistication than usual. Leeks with vinaigrette, poached skate with capers, and pineapple crumble are among the delights.

Le Voltaire

27 quai Voltaire, 7th [B1]. Tel: 01 42 61 17 49. Open: L and D Tues–Sat; closed 1 week in Feb, 1 week in May and 3 weeks in Aug. ***€€€€*** *restaurant,* ***€€*** *café.*

A number of regulars consider the riverside Voltaire their favourite Paris address. Classic dishes, including game in season, such as roasted pigeon and saddle of rabbit with thyme, are well prepared and respectfully served. The next-door café offers a well-made croque-monsieur and a lively atmosphere.

Cafés

Le Bar du Marché

75 rue de Seine, 6th [C2]. Tel: 01 43 26 55 15. Open: B and L daily, drinks until 2am, food served 9am–6pm. ***€€***

This lively, atmospheric spot facing the rue de Buci market is good for a cheap and cheerful breakfast, a quick one-dish lunch, or an early evening aperitif. Popular with locals.

Café de Flore

172 boulevard Saint-Germain, 6th [B2], Tel: 01 45 48 55 26. Open: B, L and D, till 1.30am ***€€€***

Did you know?

It was in the war years (1938-1946), that the Café de Flore came into its own. Boris Vian described its appeal: 'Due to the black outs writers didn't go far, so the Flore became like Suez or the Panama, a necessary passage'. Jean-Paul Sartre settled in so well that Paul Boubal, the Flore's convivial manager, had a private phone line installed for him.

Coffee and pastries at Les Deux Magots

No trip to Paris would be complete without a visit to one or both of the Left Bank literary cafés, the Café de Flore or Deux Magots *(see below)*. Don't bother with the food here, but do treat yourself to a café crème and a croissant on the terrace or in the Art Deco interior, and soak up the atmosphere of this former existentialist haunt. Budding philosophers can join discussion groups held in English every Monday.

Les Deux Magots

6 place Saint-Germain-des-Prés, 6th [B2]. Tel: 01 45 48 55 25. Open: daily 7.30–1.30am

Sartre, de Beauvoir and their literary disciples may be long gone, but Les Deux Magots retains something of the charm of their heyday and remains a popular meeting place for rich Left Bank intellectuals. More for a drink and snack than a full meal. Watch the world go by over a steaming cup of their famously good hot chocolate.

Le Reflet

6 rue Chompollion, 5th [C3]. Tel: 01 43 29 97 27. Open: B, L and D daily, food served until midnight. **€**

Steps from the lovely Musée de Cluny, a medieval museum, and opposite an arthouse cinema (films are shown in their original language), this is a laid-back spot for a drink and snack before or after a museum visit or film.

Le Rostand

6 place Edmond-Rostand, 6th [C3]. Tel: 01 43 54 61 58. Open: daily 8am–midnight, food served all day. **€€**

This spacious café with its mahogany bar and polished brass fixtures occupies a lovely spot opposite the Luxembourg Gardens, marred only slightly by the relentless noise of boulevard traffic. The omelettes, salads and other brasserie staples are well made if not the cheapest. It's a popular lunchtime meeting place.

Regional

La Lozère

4 rue Hautefeuille, 6th [C2]. Tel: 01 43 54 26 64. Open: L and D Tues–Sat; closed mid-July–mid-Aug and first week in Jan. ***€€*** *www.lozere-a-paris.com*

Officially, this is the tourist office of the Lozère region, but it's also one of the best-value spots to eat just yards from place St-Michel. Thursday is aligot night, when the luscious mix of potato, cheese, cream and garlic is a winner. Reliably delicious food.

Moissonnier

28 rue des Fossés-St-Bernard, 5th [E3]. Tel: 01 43 29 87 65. Open: L and D Tues–Sat; closed Aug. ***€€–€€€***

This classic Left Bank institution honours the cooking of Lyon. Only the seriously hungry will get further than the famous salad bowls, which make sensational starters, but devotees might follow this with puffy pike quenelles and even find room for rice pudding at the end.

Le Récamier

4 rue Récamier, 7th [A2]. Tel: 01 45 48 86 58. Open: L and D Mon–Sat. ***€€€€***

A favourite of politicians and intellectuals alike, Le Récamier has one of the most appealing, traffic-free terraces in Paris. Add to this the Burgundian cookery, including classic boeuf bourguignon, and you have the recipe for the restaurant's success.

Rôtisserie du Beaujolais

19 quai de la Tournelle, 5th [E3]. Tel: 01 43 54 17 47. Open: L and D Tues–Sun. ***€€€***

The famous Tour d'Argent restaurant owns this popular riverside bistro, so with big brother looking down from just across the street, it is hardly surprising that this rôtisserie's cooking of favourite homely dishes is precise and popular, especially when accompanied by the excellent jugs of Beaujolais. All the classics are on the menu, from coq-au-vin and roasted duck to crème brûlée.

Contemporary

Les Bookinistes

53 quai des Grands-Augustins, 6th [C1]. Tel: 01 43 25 45 94. Open: L and D Mon–Fri, D only Sat. ***€€–€€€*** *www.guysavoy.com*

A Guy Savoy restaurant set on the banks of the Seine, and named after the booksellers opposite. The atmosphere and food are contemporary, in the tempura and tartare fashion.

Le Café des Délices

87 rue d'Assas, 6th [B4]. Tel: 01 43 54 70 00. Open: L and D Mon–Fri; closed 3 weeks in Aug, last week in Dec. ***€€€***

An informal atmosphere and simple décor of stripped wood is the backdrop for one of the city's new success stories. Modern French food is admirably executed, even if crème brûlée au foie gras is never going to be a classic dish.

Fish – La Boissonnerie

69 rue de Seine, 6th [C2]. Tel: 01 43 54 34 69. Open: L and D Tues–Sun; closed Aug. ***€€***

The ancient mosaic above the door originally read 'poissonnerie' (fishmonger), but the tiny adjustment made to the 'p', makes 'boissonnerie' (*boisson* means drink) the name of the game. Here, you can enjoy a glass of fine wine with or without a full meal. The food is Mediterranean with squeaky fresh fish and crisp salads served in a lively Left Bank atmosphere. A fun, friendly and informal venue.

Did you know?

Top chocolate shop **Debauve et Gallais** *(30 rue des Sts-Pères)* supplied Louis XVI with chocolates that were considered good for the health. The shop offers 40 varieties prepared in traditional copper vats and packed in royal blue-and-grey boxes that still look fit for a king.

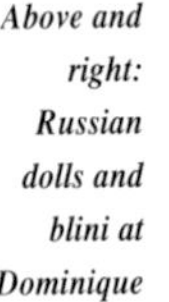

Above and right: Russian dolls and blini at Dominique

Ze Kitchen Galerie
4 rue des Grands-Augustins, 6th [C1]. Tel: 01 44 32 00 32. Open: L and D Mon–Fri. **€€€**
Ze name belies the seriousness of this sleek new modern bistro located just off the riverfront. Cutlery designed by Philippe Starck and colourful modern art back up stylish and innovative preparations of healthy fish tartares, char-grilled meats and pasta – often with an inspired sprinkling of Asian flavours. Desserts are mouth-watering and the service friendly and informed. The three-course lunch menu is good value.

International

Al Dar
8 rue Frédéric-Sauton, 5th [D2] Tel: 01 43 25 17 15. Open: non-stop daily 8am–midnight. **€€**
If you need an evening off from French cuisine then this popular Lebanese restaurant offers a good selection of mezze, accompanied by fine Lebanese wine. The staff are attentive and extremely pleasant.

Le Cherche Midi
22 rue du Cherche-Midi, 6th [A3]. Tel: 01 45 48 27 44. Open: L and D daily. **€€**
A simple Italian trattoria serving an unusually well-prepared menu of Italian classics. Popular with the chic residents of the surrounding area, who are instantly recognised by the effusive boss.

Les Délices d'Aphrodite
4 rue de Candolle, 5th [E5]. Tel: 01 43 31 40 39. Open: L and D Mon–Sat. **€–€€**
A relaxed Greek taverna in the heart of Paris with a long menu including Greek salad, moussaka and meat brochettes. The owners, the Mavrommatis brothers, consider themselves tip-top Hellenic culinary ambassadors.

Dominique

19 rue Bréa, 6th [A4]. Tel: 01 43 27 08 80. Open: D only Tues–Sat; closed late July–Aug. **€€€**
www.dominique-fr.com
This high-end Russian restaurant mixes folklore and Left Bank sophistication in equal measure. For a light meal nibble zakouski at the front of the restaurant, or for a more serious vodka fest settle back into the comfortable red banquettes and enjoy authentic salmon koulibac or beef stroganoff.

Kim Lien

33 place Maubert, 5th [D3]. Tel: 01 43 54 68 13. Open: non-stop Mon–Sat; closed 2 weeks in Aug and last week in Dec. **€€**
With a terrace on place Maubert, nicely protected from the passing cars, Kim Lien is a popular Vietnamese restaurant. Tasty crispy nems and authentic bo-bun please tourists, students and intellectuals alike.

Mirama

17 rue St-Jacques, 5th [D2]. Tel: 01 43 29 66 58. Open: non-stop daily noon–11pm. **€€**
A great little Vietnamese restaurant, always bursting at the seams with a strong local following. The best things on the menu are the simplest, such as the noodle soup or the salt-and-pepper prawns. With a carafe of rosé, a meal here won't break the bank.

La Table de Fès

5 rue Ste-Beuve, 6th [A4]. Tel: 01 45 48 07 22. Open: D only Mon–Sat; closed in August. **€€**
Couscous is one of the French nation's favourite dishes according to a recent survey, and La Table de Fès, with its slightly tatty Oriental décor, has heaps. The owner promotes her cuisine with passion to the many regulars, who say that her pastilla is one of the best in town.

La Table de Michel

13 quai de la Tournelle, 5th [E3]. Tel: 01 44 07 17 57. Open: L and D Tues–Sat, D only Mon; closed Aug. **€€€**
The combination of French culinary know-how and the chef Michel's Italian origins result in an inspired fusion menu. Profiting from a winning position on the Seine, this restaurant must be one of the few places in Europe to have the idea of preparing pasta with foie gras, and the result is rich and intriguing.

Bars and Pubs

Charming as they are, celebrated literary cafés **Les Deux Magots** and **Café de Flore** *(see page 105)* are best enjoyed with a cup of coffee in the daytime. Pride of place for an early evening drink or a late night digestive goes to the elegant **La Closerie des Lilas** *(171 boulevard du Montparnasse, 6th, tel: 01 40 51 34 50)*, where philosophers and writers still gather to debate. **La Palette** *(43 rue de Seine, 6th, tel: 01 43 26 68 15)* remains a favourite haunt of Left Bank artists and designers, with a bustling atmosphere, but for a more sedate glass of rum with a Cuban cigar, try the **Casa del Habano** *(169 boulevard Saint-Germain, 6th, tel: 01 45 49 24 30)*. Up on boulevard du Montparnasse **Le Sélect** *(99 boulevard du Montparnasse, 6th, tel: 01 45 48 38 24)* retains something of its old-fashioned atmosphere. The bar of the **Hôtel Lutétia** *(45 boulevard Raspail, 6th, tel: 01 49 54 46 46)* mixes a mean cocktail, while the swish **AZ Mezzanine bar** *(see page 76)* is one of the city's most fashionable watering holes. Small but sweet, the seductive **Fu Bar** *(5, rue St-Sulpice, 6th, tel: 01 40 51 82 00)* serves martinis to a lively expat crowd.

A Few Words on Wine

Explore Paris's wine shops, seek out its wine bars and use your sommelier's expertise to discover different varieties and vintages

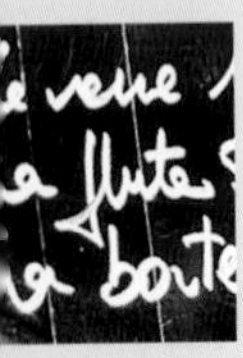

France still makes the best wines in the world. This is not to say that great wines are not made elsewhere (nor that France doesn't produce its share of plonk), but when the best are lined up against the best, France still wins top prize, setting the standard among wine circles across the globe. The best place to taste French wines is in the regions where they are made (even the worst increase in charm when served by a jolly, red-nosed vintner). However, Paris does import the cream of the crop from all corners of the country, so that puts visitors in an ideal position for sampling the widest variety of offerings, from the least expensive (as little as 3 euro for something decent) to the most exorbitant (thousands of euro a bottle).

There are three types of venues in which to find enjoyable wines in Paris: restaurants, wine bars and wine shops. Good restaurants, particularly those with starred ratings, usually have exquisitely edited wine lists with a range of prices and knowledgeable staff to help you narrow down your choice. If you're not an expert, it is worth telling the sommelier your budget, giving him a general idea of what you like, and then handing over the reins. It is, after all, his job to help you find a perfect match for your food. Besides, a good sommelier's choice rarely disappoints, and it is one of the best ways to make new discoveries in a territory that's perhaps not entirely familiar.

Wine Bars

If you're in the mood for tasting several wines, ending the afternoon or beginning an evening in a wine bar is a fun option. There are two sorts of wine bars in Paris: the first is a rustic kind of spot, where simple wines are on offer along with plates of charcuterie or cheese, and sometimes bistro platters. Typically speaking, these places are where you go for a good time, rather than to discover any wines worth remembering. A few down-to-earth wine bars in this category are: **Jacques Melac** *(42 rue Léon Frot, 11th)*, one of the best; **Le Baron Rouge** *(1 rue Théophile Roussel, 12th)*, conveniently located near the Marché d'Aligre; and **Le Rubis** *(10 rue du Marché St-Honoré, 1st)*, especially popular for Beaujolais Nouveau in November.

The second tier of wine bars, aimed more towards serious wine lovers, is a more recent development in Paris. Launched in the early 1980s by Mark Williamson and Tim Johnson, **Willi's Wine Bar** *(13 rue des Petits Champs, 1st)* remains a leading institution. Also worthy of attention are: **Les Juvéniles** *(47 rue de Richelieu, 1st)*; **Le Baratin** *(3 rue Jouye-Rouve, 20th)*; **Les Papilles** *(30 rue Gay-Lussac, 5th)*; **L'Ecluse** *(several locations across the city, including 15 place de la Madeleine, 8th)*, which specialises in Bordeaux wines; and **Le Verre Volé** *(67 rue Lancry, 10th)*. Keep in mind that some of these wine bars also act as wine merchants (*cavistes*), usually selling affordable, hard-to-find wines by up-and-coming producers.

A few of the city's more exclusive wine shops have opened wine bars in house. **Le Grand Filles et Fils** *(12 Galerie Vivienne, 2nd)*, an old-world picture-postcard speciality shop with superb wines (many at excellent value) is one. **Lavinia** *(3–5 boulevard de la Madeleine, 1st)* is the sleekest and most modern example, with the largest selection of international wines in the city. For more glamorous, old-world service – without a wine bar, alas – head for Les **Caves Taillevent** *(199 rue du Faubourg St-Honoré, 1st)*.

Choosing and ordering wine

Despite the French tending to be extremely proud, not to say arrogant, about their wines, there is really not as much pretension around wines as visitors might imagine. They may drink a lot of it (France consumes more per capita than any other country in the world), but outside the wine regions people tend not to wax on about how savvy they are about legs, nose and fermentation. France, therefore, despite its traditions, is a country where the wine novice can feel fairly at ease in his ignorance.

This said, a few tips are worth knowing. The most important is to remember that French wines are traditionally named after regions rather than grape varieties. One buys white Burgundy rather than Chardonnay; St Emilion rather than Merlot. There are exceptions nowadays, particularly in Provence and the Languedoc, where wine-growers have begun making wines with unconventional grape varieties and using New World names on the label: Syrah, for instance. Such wines do not qualify for A.O.C. status (*Appellation d'Origine Contrôlée* – the highest ranking order for wines in France). However, some of the most interesting (and affordable) wines produced in France today come from these renegade wine-makers. In other words, a humble Vin de Pays label on a bottle can be misleading: behind it you may find an excellent wine.

The etiquette surrounding wine is simple and standard. Whenever you order a bottle in a restaurant, the server brings the unopened bottle to your table for approval before opening, then he opens it in front of you and allows you to taste the wine before serving the table. If the wine is corked (has a musty cellar smell) or has some kind of chemical fault (smells medicinal, like vinegar, stale or unpleasant) you can refuse it. One cannot refuse a wine for not liking it, only if it isn't in good health. In high-end establishments, your glass should be kept 'filled' (one-third full). More casual restaurants are a bit more lax. You won't, for example, see the bottle if you simply order *un verre de Chablis* in a bistro. And if you order *un pichet de rouge* (a jug of red), it will come in a small carafe and what you get is what you get. But sometimes, that's all you need.

Wine from Millésime, in the 7th

INVALIDES AND THE 7TH

This chic, aristocratic district is well-endowed with superlative yet surprisingly affordable restaurants, and the Eiffel Tower is never far away

Punctuated at its centre by the Esplanade des Invalides, which blankets the space between the glorious Pont Alexandre-III and the Invalides, and bordered on its western edge by the Champ-de-Mars, the 7th *arrondissement* is one of the most expensive neighbourhoods in town. And since this district is home to the monument that embodies Paris – if not the whole of France – the chances are good that you will find yourself in the area early on in your visit.

But rest assured: just because the neighbourhood is the ultimate in chic, and the Eiffel Tower is the city's biggest tourist draw, it doesn't mean that you will have to pay a premium for clichéd 'tourist' fare. In fact, there are comparatively few restaurants here that fall directly into the 'tourist' category. Interspersed between the ministries and *hôtels particuliers* (private mansions) in the wedge between the Eiffel Tower and the Esplanade are gourmet destinations to suit all price brackets and tastes. The key is to take time to explore the side streets and perhaps resist the temptation to judge a restaurant by an unremarkable façade.

The Stars

The 7th has been a prized residential area since Louis XIV moved his court to Versailles and broke ground for the construction of the Invalides, intended to house 6,000 war veterans, in 1670. The aristocracy lost no time trailing in his wake, constructing sumptuous mansions past Saint-Germain-des-Prés, on the then western border of the city, and along the road that leads to Versailles. Many of the residences built by these wealthy families still stand – not least the Hôtel Matignon *(57 rue de Varenne)*, now the prime minister's residence, and the palatial Hôtel Biron *(77 rue de Varenne)*, now the Musée Rodin. Across the street, the main building of the Invalides (finished in 1676) now houses a military museum. Under the gold-leafed dome of the Eglise du Dôme is Napoléon's Egyptian-style tomb. Many of the other architectural gems scattered throughout the area now serve as ministries and consulates and are difficult to visit.

It is no surprise, then, that between gated and guarded properties are some of the city's most prized and expensive restaurants. First among these is Alain Passard's L'Arpège *(see page 116)*, a three-star gastronomic temple run by one of the only autodidacts in the profession. Though long established, Passard is still considered one of the vanguard for his inventive flair and bold combinations.

***Opposite:* careful preparation at Le 20. *Below:* Italian staple**

Not that everything comes with a three-star price. The biggest gastronomical happening in the neighbourhood lately is the arrival of the much-revered Joël Robuchon, fresh out of semi-retirement. His Atelier *(see page 122)* is an open-plan place with a limited-reservations policy that has customers queuing around the block for hours. Considering the prices of Robuchon's previous restaurants, Atelier is a bargain. The other major star to hop on the high-quality, low-price bandwagon is Christian Constant, virtuoso of the Violon d'Ingres *(see page 116)*, who has taken over an adjacent café to offer a remarkable, and amazingly affordable, culinary experience. Le Divellec *(see page 116)*, one of the city's top fish restaurants, Le Chamarré *(see page 123)* and the provençal Bruno Deligne – Les Olivades *(see page 121)* are other big names to look out for.

The Eiffel Tower itself is the home of one-star Jules Verne *(see page 116)* on its second terrace. While opinions on dining inside a national monument may vary (and it certainly doesn't come cheap), this is still one of the city's best choices for indulging in a gourmet experience with an unbeatable view.

Budget-conscious options

This may be the classiest neighbourhood in Paris, but the quarter's well-heeled are known for having a keen eye for value. Between the Ecole Militaire and the American University, the area draws many students, ensuring plenty of dining options that will not break the bank. New talents are gravitating to the area, flourishing with very reasonably priced fare. Examples that stand out include L'Ami Jean *(see page 120)*, specialising in Basque dishes, and D'Chez Eux *(see page 121)*, for southwestern food. The Bistrot du Breteuil *(see page 117)* and Le Vauban *(see page 119)*, both nestled behind the Invalides, offer excellent-value classic French dishes on prix-fixe menus (wine included). And this is just the tip of the iceberg.

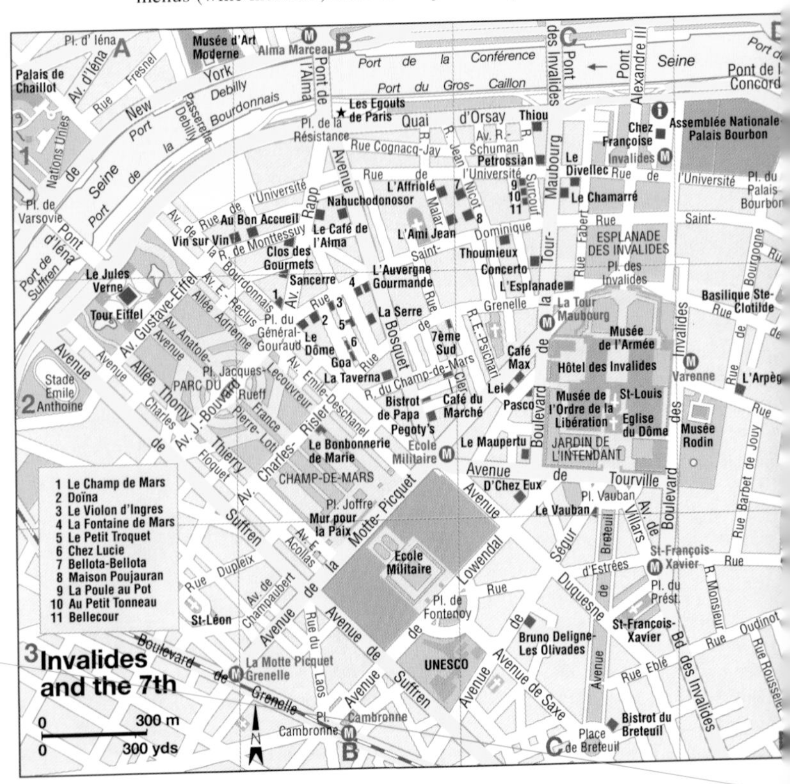

In and around rue Cler

One of the city's great pedestrian market streets, rue Cler also has numerous places from which to watch the locals go about the serious business of food shopping. The largest of these is the Café du Marché *(see page 120)*, known for its huge salads and good brunch fare. (If it is too crowded, try Le Roussillon at the corner of rue Cler and rue de Grenelle; it's less central but cheery and reliable.) On the opposite corner to the Café du Marché is the high-end traiteur Lenôtre, which offers more refined (and expensive) fare. Tarte Julie *(30 rue Cler)* has a few tables and lunch menus for less than €10 (you can also take away).

Backing the colourful fruit, vegetable and flower stands, this convivial street is lined with old-fashioned fromageries, boulangeries and other specialist food shops. People come from far and wide to queue up at Davoli *(34 rue Cler)*, an Italian-style traiteur, which specialises in ham; they also prepare French classics such as pot-au-feu for take-away. Le Lutin Gourmand *(47 rue Cler)* has an irresistible array of very fine chocolates and also offers around 100 types of tea blended on the premises.

Beyond the bustling rue Cler, it's surprising how many specialist food and drinks shops lie tucked behind and between the spartan-looking avenues of this grand district. L'Ambassade du Sud-Ouest *(46 avenue de la Bourdonnais)* is both a restaurant and a food store specialising in the cuisine of Southwest France with jars of Basque pipérade, cassoulet and confit de canard, and a wide assortment of foie gras. Noé L'Antiquaire du Vin *(12 rue Surcouf)* sells rare vintages: some bottles date back more than 100 years. The eponymous owner of Marie-Anne Cantin *(12 rue du Champ-de-Mars)* is renowned as a passionate defender of 'real' cheese, meaning unpasteurised, and the smellier the better. And for something sweet, artisanal chocolatier Michel Chaudon *(149 rue de l'Université)* is famous for his truffles and chocolate sculptures.

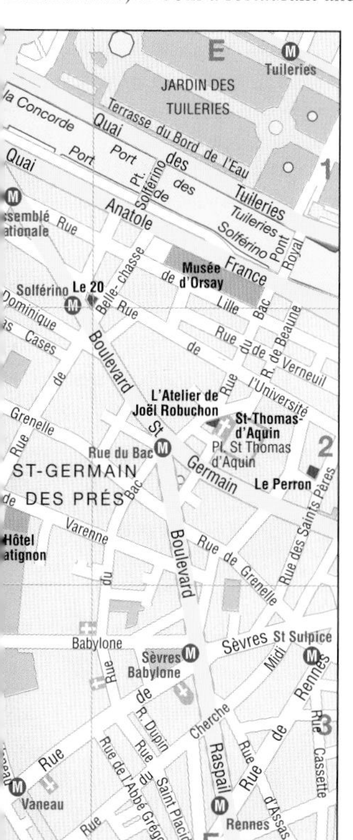

FIVE OF THE BEST

L'Affriolé: for modern French food, vibrant ambience and unbeatable value

L'Arpège: discreet, chic, inventive and worth a splurge

L'Atelier de Joël Robuchon: open-cuisine 'workshop' of the master chef

Bellota-Bellota: delicious tapas and great Spanish wines – good for dinner or drinks

La Fontaine de Mars: hearty fare from the southwest; traditional yet friendly

Did you know?

The Eiffel Tower weighs 10,100 tons in total, 60 tons of which are paint. The monument is repainted every seven years, and the work takes 15–16 months.

Haute Cuisine

L'Arpège

84 rue de Varenne, 7th [D2]. Tel: 01 45 51 47 33 (reservations required). Open: L and D Mon–Fri; closed 3 weeks Aug. **€€€€** *www.arpège-passard.com*

Chef Alain Passard (also an accomplished musician) designed his restaurant to be an acoustically discreet model of contemporary elegance. He has been called 'the poet of terroir' for his imaginative menus and his signature dessert of tomato confite with 12 flavours (he has been known to lay down the challenge that if you can name all the seasonings, the dish is free). Prix-fixe lunch menu.

Le Divellec

107 rue de l'Université, 7th [C1]. Tel: 01 45 51 91 96. Open: L and D Mon–Fri; closed last week in Dec. **€€€€** *www.le-divellec.com*

A temple to fish freshly caught in the Atlantic, set against a décor of nautical chic. The guiding principle is to keep the culinary flourishes light in order to preserve the seafood's natural flavours. Specialities include Breton lobster, oysters à la laitue de mer, and turbot braised with truffles. Windows open on to the Esplanade.

Le Jules Verne

Eiffel Tower South Pillar, 2nd floor (private access lift), 7th [A2]. Tel: 01 45 55 61 44 (reservations only). Open: L and D daily. **€€€€**

Location-wise, this restaurant on the second level of the Eiffel Tower is perfect for a celebration or romantic dinner, though the cooking is not quite as spectacular as the view. Specialities include a tartare duo (beef and langoustine), noix de St-Jacques (scallops) and crêpes with Grand Marnier.

Le Violon d'Ingres

135 rue St-Dominique, 7th [B2]. Tel: 01 45 55 15 05. Open: L and D Tues–Fri, D only Sat and Mon; closed 3 weeks in Aug. **€€€–€€€€** *www.leviolondingres.com*

Culinary star Christian Constant specialises in dishes from his native southwest, such as wood-pigeon *a la plancha*, and sea bass with almonds and capers, which he revises with a light and imaginative touch and serves in plush surroundings. Next door, his traiteur does take-away meals, while a couple of doors down, Café Constant (139 rue St-Dominique, tel: 01 47 53 73 34) offers café fare in a neighbourhood ambience. No reservations, so arrive early.

Try southwestern French specialities at Thoumieux

Brasseries

Le 20

20 rue de Bellechasse, 7th [D1]. Tel: 01 47 05 11 11. Open: L and D Mon–Fri, D only Sat; closed 10 days in Aug and last week in Dec. ***€€–€€€***

A lovely restaurant with red banquettes and caricatures of loyal clients and stars on the wall. The menu and the wine list are well-priced, and the setting is both intimate and lively. A popular locale among low-key fashion types and other creative or literary souls.

Thoumieux

79 rue St-Dominique, 7th [C1]. Tel: 01 47 05 49 75. Open: L and D Mon–Sat, non-stop Sun. ***€€–€€€***

Thoumieux is an authentic Parisian brasserie and a neighbourhood institution. The large dining room lined with red velvet banquettes and mirrors lends itself well to catering for large groups and families. Specialities are southwestern, with a particular affection for the Corrèze region: cassoulet and andouillette in all seasons, as well as excellent escargot and practically any other French classic you could wish for.

Bistros

L'Affriolé

17 rue Malar, 7th [B1]. Tel: 01 44 18 31 33. Open: L and D Tues–Sat; closed 3 weeks in Aug and 2 weeks in Dec. ***€€–€€€***

One of the most appealing bistros in the neighbourhood, with colourful mosaic tables and decorated with traditional *objets de cuisine*. The owner/chef offers a €32 menu that includes starter, main dish, cheese and dessert, and a scaled-back version at lunchtime. The menu is seasonal and changes daily, and dishes are artfully presented with little amuse-bouches (appetisers) such as mini-custards. Reservations recommended.

Bellecour

22 rue de Surcouf, 7th [C1]. Tel: 01 45 51 46 93. Open: L and D Mon–Fri, D only Sat; closed 4 weeks late July–early Aug. ***€€€***

A warm, old-fashioned Lyonnais bistro where you will find traditional recipes from salads to quenelles, and classic fish and game dishes reinvented with an up-to-the-minute twist. The fine wine list features exceptional Burgundies. Reservations recommended.

Bistrot du Breteuil

3 place du Breteuil, 7th [C3]. Tel: 01 45 67 07 27. Open: L and D daily. ***€€***

This civilised bistro, which typically has a packed terrace in summer, has a loyal following among the young and old alike. The €29 menu offers unsurprising but well-prepared classics, and includes an apéritif, three courses, wine and coffee. Service is gracious and friendly.

Great food and friendly dining at Le 20

Le Bistrot de Papa

81 avenue Bosquet, 7th [B2]. Tel: 01 47 05 36 15. Open: L and D daily, non-stop noon–11pm. **€€**

This place offers everything you could hope for in a bistro, from excellent oysters (in season) to delicious quiche. What really puts this place on the map, however, is the French onion soup – a meal in itself.

Café Max

7 avenue de la Motte-Picquet, 7th [C2]. Tel: 01 47 05 57 66. Open: L and D Tues–Sat, D only Mon; closed in Aug. **€**

Although the owner does his best to appear gruff, he is in fact as big-hearted as his Lyonnaise cuisine. This is family fare with salads served in huge bowls and whole terrines with pots of gherkins. Not for the diet-conscious or vegetarians – what you see on the menu (two choices) is what you get. Small, with leather banquettes and bric-à-brac décor.

The archetypal bistro: La Fontaine de Mars

Clos des Gourmets

16 avenue Rapp, 7th [B1]. Tel: 01 45 51 75 61. Open: L and D Tues–Sat. **€€–€€€**

A quiet local address with market-fresh cuisine. One of the more surprising among the prix-fixe categories, as the talented young chef is a disciple of Alain Passard and Guy Savoy. Reservations are recommended.

La Fontaine de Mars

129 rue St-Dominique, 7th [B2]. Tel: 01 47 05 46 44. Open: L and D daily. **€€€**

The menu changes depending on the market, but southwest fare takes pride of place at this 1930s' neighbourhood bistro. In fine weather, the fountain-facing terrace is the ideal setting for a candlelit meal on tables clad with red-and-white chequered tablecloths.

Au Petit Tonneau

20 rue de Surcouf, 7th [C1]. Tel: 01 47 05 09 01. Open: L and D daily; closed 2 weeks in Aug. **€€–€€€**

This unpretentious neighbourhood bistro has been turning out favourites for over 20 years. The chef herself often does the rounds, just to mother the clientele and make sure that they are happy and well-fed – something that they always seem to be.

Le Petit Troquet

28 rue de l'Exposition, 7th [B2]. Tel: 01 47 05 80 39. Open: L and D Tues–Fri, D only Sat and Mon; closed 3 weeks in Aug. **€€**

Le Petit Troquet is no longer a neighbourhood secret, but gladly popularity has not done any damage to its delightful flea-market character or its fresh and inventive

Far left: homemade food at Sancerre. Left: the most famous monument in the 7th

market menu. Fair prices. Reservations recommended.

La Poule au Pot

121 rue de l'Université, 7th [C1]. Tel: 01 47 05 16 36. Open: B, L and D Mon–Fri, D only Sat; closed 3 weeks in Aug. **€€**

A traditional bistro serving dishes such as the one for which it is named: chicken in a pot. Reasonably priced fare.

Sancerre

22 avenue Rapp, 7th [B2]. Tel: 01 45 51 75 91. Open: L and D Mon–Fri, L only Sat; closed 3 weeks in Aug. **€**

In the shadow of the Eiffel Tower, this small, wine bar-cum-restaurant is an ideal place in which to take time out from sightseeing for a light lunch. Simple fare such as sausage, homemade terrines and tarts, omelettes, or goats' cheese salad are the suggested accompaniments for reds, whites and rosés.

La Serre

29 rue de l'Exposition, 7th [B2]. Tel: 01 45 55 20 96. Open: L and D Tues–Sat; closed in Aug. **€**

One peek into the front window says it all: there is a toaster on every table, so you're guaranteed warm bread with your foie gras. Reasonably priced southwestern fare, such as homemade terrines, salads and duck in all its forms.

Le Vauban

7 place Vauban, 7th [C2]. Tel: 01 47 05 52 67. Open: B, L and D Tues–Sun, non-stop 7am–10.30pm. **€€** *www.levauban.com*

This bistro faces the garden of the Invalides and the entry to Napoleon's tomb. The décor is somewhat tacky faux-Italian, but don't let this put you off, as the quality of the food is high. There are reasonable prix-fixe menus for lunch and dinner including apéritif, wine and coffee. House specialities include artichoke hearts with shrimp (appetiser) and an ample steak tartare.

Cafés

La Bonbonnerie de Marie

Avenue Charles-Risler–Allée Adrienne-Lecouvreur, 7th [B2]. Tel: 01 45 55 53 77. Shop open: daily 10am–7pm, outdoor café

TIP

Maison Poujauran *(18–20 rue Jean-Nicot)* is a tiny, quintessential, late 19th-century boulangerie, but behind its old-fashioned pink façade you'll find some of the best baguettes and *sablés* (biscuits) in town (the shop is the official supplier to the Elysée Palace).

open: L only in summer.
€ *(cash only).*
This tiny terrace is home to the only eatery on the Champ-de-Mars. Run by two sisters, its service is cheerful and the fare simple – salade parisienne, plat du jour or crêpes (savoury or sweet). The owner's stylised Eiffel 'toupies' (toy tops) or sculptures are also for purchase. This one's good for children, as adjacent you'll find a take-away crêpe/drinks stand, playground, merry-go-round and marionnette theatre. No reservations.

TIP
Every Thursday and Saturday, the gracious tree-lined avenue de Saxe plays host to the Saxe-Breteuil market. The produce sold by the fruit and vegetable vendors, the charcuterie and cheese specialists, the fishmongers and olive sellers, is as fresh as the rich residents expect.

Le Café du Marché
38 rue Cler, 7th [B2]. Tel: 01 47 05 51 27. Open: Mon–Sat 7am–midnight, Sun 7am–5pm. **€**
The best café on rue Cler, one of the most atmospheric and convivial pedestrian market streets in the city. Come here in the morning and enjoy a café-au-lait and a croissant on the spacious terrace while watching the tumultuous market scene – Parisian street theatre at its best. The kitchen whips up good salads and daily specials at lunchtime, though service can be a bit hurried. Get here early on weekends if you want a good seat.

Le Champs de Mars/ Le Dôme
Place du Général-Gouraud, 7th [B2]. Open: L and D daily. **€–€€**
Near the Champ-de-Mars, these two terraced cafés vie for the passing crowds: of the two, Le Champ de Mars (at the angle of avenue Rapp) is more of a sun-trap and its ambience is slightly less aggressively tourist-orientated, while Le Dôme (opposite, on the corner of rue Saint-Dominique and avenue de la Bourdonnais) has the better view of the Eiffel Tower. Classic, but mediocre bistro fare.

Pegoty's
79 avenue Bosquet, 7th [B2]. Tel: 01 45 55 84 50. Open: L and T daily until 7pm. **€–€€**
Located near the Ecole Militaire, this little oasis serves salads and delicious homemade cakes, as well as proper English tea amid chintzy decorations and comfortable furniture. The smaller room at the back is decorated like a library and is a good place to take refuge in inclement weather. A good pit-stop for shoppers.

Regional

L'Ami Jean
27 rue Malar, 7th [B1]. Tel: 01 47 05 86 89. Open: L and D Tues–Sat; closed 1 week in Aug.
€€–€€€
Unimposing from the outside, rustic and convivial on the inside, L'Ami Jean is one of the capital's top addresses for Basque cuisine. Regional specialities include 'Axoa' or 'Ttoro' (tender veal or beef), and there are also surprisingly refined dishes such as ravioli with lobster. Excellent and well-priced wine list. Reserve.

L'Auvergne Gourmande

127 rue St-Dominique, 7th [B2]. Tel : 01 47 05 60 79. Open: L and D Mon–Sat; closed Aug. **€–€€**

The owners of the Fontaine de Mars *(see page 118)* have expanded next door to showcase favourites from their native Auvergne at a tiny table d'hôte (best to go in parties of 2 or 3). Specials change daily, but centre around beef or pork. For dessert try the fréchun (pears cooked in red wine) or the sultan juste (cross between a cake and a flan, with caramelised apples). No reservations at lunch.

D'Chez Eux

2 avenue de Lowendal, 7th [C2]. Tel: 01 47 05 52 55. Open: L and D Mon–Sat; closed 3 weeks in Aug. **€€–€€€**

Of the several neighbourhood restaurants specialising in southwest cooking, this one is certainly not the cheapest; however, after one look at the entrée trolley, you'll forget about your wallet. Traditional dishes from the Auvergne and further south (ie plenty of duck) are served with a generous hand. At €35 the 'Tradition Gourmande' menu is a good option.

Chez Françoise

Aérogare des Invalides, 7th [C1]. Tel: 01 47 05 49 03. Open: L and D daily. **€€–€€€** *www.chezfrancoise.com*

Don't be dismayed by the fact that this restaurant is below a bus terminal: it is in fact a very Parisian address, with traditional French dishes, a lovely terrace and a wine list for connoisseurs. There are well-priced menus for lunch and dinner and a piano bar every night except Sunday; most Saturdays there is a culinary and/or musical theme (jazz, be-bop, etc).

Le Maupertu

94 boulevard de la Tour-Maubourg, 7th [C2]. Tel: 01 45 51 37 96. Open: L and D Mon–Sat, L only Sun; closed 3 weeks in Aug. **€€–€€€** *www.restaurant-maupertu-paris.com*

A prime address (with terrace) for fresh market cuisine with strong Provençal leanings. Specialities change daily, and the menu is renewed every other month, but favourites include garlic-sautéed chanterelles in season, roasted lamb with herbes de Provence, ratatouille and other sun-drenched dishes.

Bruno Deligne – Les Olivades

41 avenue de Ségur, 7th [C3]. Tel: 01 47 83 70 09. Open: L and D Tues–Fri, D only Sat and Mon; closed in Aug and 2 weeks in Dec. **€€€**

Les Olivades is one of the next best things to being in Provence, with a sunshine-inspired menu seasoned liberally with olive oil. Try the house tapenade, a tasty starter, before digging into a deliciously spicy squid with chorizo, daurade and salmon tartare or a sardine tart. Creative, copious, friendly and good value.

Le Dôme, for Eiffel Tower views

TIP

There are a few expanses of lawn in the area (place des Invalides, Champ de Mars, avenue de Breteuil) where you can stretch out and have a picnic. Make the most of these – elsewhere in Paris walking, let alone sitting, on the grass is usually forbidden.

Pasco

74 boulevard de la Tour-Maubourg, 7th [C2]. Tel: 01 44 18 33 26. Open: L and D daily. **€€–€€€**

www.restaurantpasco.com

Warm and carefully decorated, Pasco specialises in contemporary Provençal dishes with a whimsical twist, such as ceviche of rascasse (scorpion fish) with a hint of bite, vegetable fricassée without the traditional bacon, or mango tarte Tatin. The prix-fixe menus are good value, and wines are reasonably priced too.

Contemporary

L'Atelier de Joël Robuchon

5 rue Montalembert, 7th [E2]. Tel: 01 42 22 56 56. Open: L and D daily. **€€–€€€**

Without question the biggest opening in town in 2003/4 and one that has even had jaded Parisians queuing up for two hours in all weather to sample the warm foie gras brochettes or tapenade with fresh tuna conjured by France's most revered chef. The restaurant is built around an open kitchen, so you can watch the masters at work, and the atmosphere is slick, like that of a bar. It's out with long sophisticated menus, and in with the tapas principal, involving small portions of outstandingly creative dishes (order as many as your appetite or budget will allow). Reservations are accepted for first seatings only (11.30am and 6.30pm) – after that you're on your own. Smoking not permitted.

Au Bon Accueil

14 rue de Monttessuy, 7th [B1]. Tel: 01 47 05 46 11. Open: L and D Mon–Fri. **€€–€€€**

What was once a Provençal bistro has been given a total makeover – the décor is now sleek contemporary, and the menu of classics has been modernised as well. The €29 prix-fixe dinner menu is viewed by

The unbeatable L'Atelier de Joël Robuchon

Local favourite 7ème Sud

many locals as one of the best deals in the neighbourhood, and the wine list is excellent (if expensive). Reservations recommended.

Le Café de l'Alma

5 avenue Rapp, 7th [B1]. Tel: 01 45 51 56 74. Open: B, L and D daily, 7am–midnight. **€€€**

A trendy café and restaurant by the winning team behind La Fontaine de Mars *(see page 118)*. Here, the fare is an enlightened take on cuisine bourgeoise, the ambience discreet and the people beautiful. Luckily, the service remains friendly, unpretentious and consistently good.

Le Chamarré

13 boulevard de la Tour-Maubourg, 7th [C1]. Tel : 01 47 05 50 18. Open: L and D Mon–Fri, D only Sat. **€€€**

Chef Jérôme Bodereau, former sous-chef to Alain Passard at L'Arpège *(see page 116)*, is pushing French cuisine forward with a bold mix of flavours from Mauritius. Curry, lime and rum accents make for a refreshing take on fusion, and with so much of interest on the plate, it's possible to forgive the somewhat run-of-the-mill décor.

L'Esplanade

52 rue Fabert, 7th [C2]. Tel: 01 47 05 38 80. Open: B, L and D daily, non-stop 8am–1am. **€€€**

With a terrace overlooking the park and 'Napoléon III-revisited' décor by Jacques Garcia, this Costes brothers' bar and restaurant is the latest in their constellation of eateries. A bit pricey, but you pay to see and be seen. Typical fashionista food.

Nabuchodonosor

6 avenue Bosquet, 7th [B1]. Tel: 01 45 56 97 26. Open: L and D Mon–Fri, D only Sat; closed 2–3 weeks in Aug. **€€–€€€**
www.nabuchodonosor.net

The intimidating name of this restaurant is the word for a 15-litre bottle of champagne, chosen by the proprietor because he is a bon vivant to the point that these bottles are integrated into the décor. Chef Thierry Garnier caters to meat lovers with an expensive à la carte menu and reasonably priced prix-fixe menus for lunch and dinner.

Vin sur Vin

20 rue de Monttessuy, 7th [A1]. Tel: 01 47 05 14 20. Open: L and D Tues–Fri, D only Sat. Closed Aug and year-end. **€€–€€€**

As the name indicates, this place is all about wine, although chef Pascal Toulza has won a following for the accompaniments to his exceptional list, including Breton langoustines, consommé with foie gras and Lon Vedel Catalon (Catalonian veal). Friendly and intimate.

Right and far right: Thiou, in with the in-crowd

International

7ème Sud

159 rue de Grenelle, 7th [B2]. Tel: 01 44 18 30 30. Open: L and D daily; closed 3 weeks in Aug and last week in Dec. **€€**

This local favourite specialising in Mediterranean flavours draws a young, hip crowd with its laid-back ambience and cool prices. Copious salads and pasta dishes combine flavours from France, Italy and North Africa, with seared tuna a firm favourite. Daily specialities always include a tajine. Good for vegetarians. Reserve at weekends.

Bellota-Bellota

18 rue Jean-Nicot, 7th [C1]. Tel: 01 53 59 96 96. Open: L and D Tues–Fri, Br, L and D Sat non-stop 11am–11pm. **€€–€€€**

A gem of a tapas bar specialising in the rare Iberian ham after which it is named, as well as Spanish cheeses, wine, and seafood from Pontevedra. It's a friendly place, great for grazing or a light, romantic dinner. You can stop in and dine at the bar if you're early; otherwise reserve one of the handful of tables.

Chez Lucie

15 rue Augureau, 7th [B2]. Tel: 01 45 55 08 74. Open: D Mon–Sat; closed 3 weeks in Aug. **€**

A souvenir-studded, good-natured little place offering simple but flamboyant dishes from the French Antilles and Martinique, such as matoutou de crabe, gombo sauce chien, curries or, the house speciality, chicken or lamb colombo.

Doïna

149 rue St-Dominique, 7th [B2]. Tel: 01 45 50 49 57. Open: L and D daily. **€**

It's the very definition of no-frills, but this slightly tacky Romanian restaurant turns out tasty, affordable fare, from the usual poulet-frites or escalope milanaise to Baltic herring, grilled meats and moussaka. Cheap sandwiches too.

Goa

19 rue Augureau, 7th [B2]. Tel: 01 45 55 26 20. Open: L and D Mon–Sat. **€**

A kitsch little corner of southern India in the middle of the 7th, with affordable menus at lunch or dinner featuring curries, tandoori shrimp and the house speciality of Xacuti lamb, garnished with coconut and cloves.

Lei

17 avenue de la Motte-Picquet, 7th [C2]. Tel: 01 47 05 07 37. Open: L and D Tues–Sat; closed 1–2 weeks in Aug and Dec. **€€**

A hot, new arrival in the neighbourhood with open, airy décor and specialities from all over of Italy. The owners are the attractive couple behind the already successful Sasso (14th) and Cailloux (13th), and it looks like they have scored again.

Petrossian

18 boulevard de la Tour-Maubourg, 7th [C1]. Tel: 01 44 11 32 32. Open: L and D Tues–Sat. **€€€–€€€€** *www.petrossian.fr*

An institution since the 1920s, Petrossian is one of Paris's prime addresses for caviar. The kitchen has recently undergone a transformation in an effort to keep up with the times, and the result is a creative and satisfying blend of textures and flavours, and tradition and modernity. Look out for the house speciality: the coupes du Tsar (a large slab of prime fish).

La Taverna

22 rue du Champ-de-Mars, 7th [B2]. Tel: 01 45 51 64 59. Open: L and D Mon–Fri, D only Sat; closed Aug. **€€€**

Chef Gustavo Andreloi and his wife serve warm and simple meals such as vegetable risotto, papardelle, black tagliatelle with palourdes and a lovely tiramisu – all of which belies the somewhat stuffy décor.

Thiou

49 quai d'Orsay, 7th [C1]. Tel: 01 40 62 96 50. Open: L and D Mon–Fri, D only Sat; closed Aug. **€€€**

Known for its exotic Asian-inspired décor and its A-list clientele, Thiou is one of the area's most fashionable addresses. The chef (after whom the restaurant is named) draws a loyal crowd for her French-Thai fusion dishes including le tigre qui pleure (beef) and vegetable-based fare, all of which keep whippet-thin waistlines in check. Just around the corner from Thiou you'll find the red façade of the equally chic Petit Thiou *(3 rue Surcouf, tel: 01 40 62 96 70)*, which serves up a shortlist of the house bestsellers.

Bars and Pubs

It may be anchored by two of the city's most visited monuments, but, aside from a few strategically located brasseries, the western half of the 7th *arrondissement* has not typically been a destination for *l'heure de l'apéro* (cocktail hour). This is changing, however: the Costes Brothers have come to the rescue with the very fashionable **L'Esplanade** *(52 rue Fabert, tel: 01 47 05 38 80; drinks served before 7.30pm or after 10.30pm only, unless you're staying for dinner)*, overlooking the Invalides, and the café-bar-club **Tourville** on place de l'Ecole Militaire *(43 avenue de la Motte Picquet, tel: 01 44 18 05 08; open until 2am; limited menu)*; the latter has the advantage of drawing a beautiful – if young – crowd, plus less pretentious service and many more tables, both inside and out.

To keep pace, the once-dowdy **La Terrasse** *(2 place de l'Ecole Militaire)*, across the street, has spruced up its look as well as its menu, making it an ideal choice if you prefer a less smoky ambience where you can really hear what your drinks partner is saying. The **Comptoir du 7ème** *(39 avenue de la Motte Picquet)* fills up with hip young professionals after business hours, while next door, at No. 37, the sophisticated **Walt** hotel bar *(open daily until 2am)* caters to those seeking a more refined scene.

For a few laid-back drinks and a late-night snack, the **Café Thoumieux** *(4 rue de la Comète; open Mon–Fri noon–2am, Sat 5pm–2am)* is a comfy drinking den popular with the US expat community.

Tearooms

Paris has a deeply rooted tradition of tea connoisseurship, as seen through its superb salons de thé and tea merchants

In a city famous for its cafés, it's hard to imagine that Parisian tearooms would ever compete. But in the past few years, they have boomed almost in defiance, it seems, of the modern world. As the pace of life in Paris speeds up, people are increasingly seeking ways to slow down. Today, countless sipping spots are dotted throughout the city, discreet places, without the bustle and brusqueness of cafés, serving blends of exceptional quality to be consumed without the press of time.

Where to take tea

For taking tea on the town in the afternoon, there is a range of options. The classic is **Mariage Frères** *(30–32 rue du Bourg-Tibourg, 4th, tel: 01 42 72 28 11)*, whose black tea caddies with gold calligraphy look down from their shelves with an air of authority. Behind the wood-pannelled front shop, with its tea-sellers in jacket and tie, the two-storey dining room is lovely for lunch. More elegant, perhaps, is **Ladurée** *(16 rue Royale, 8th, tel: 01 42 60 21 79)*. The opulent, belle époque ground-floor room makes you feel especially spoiled while you nibble on miniature sandwiches and the emblematic macaroons.

Confectionary by Dalloyau, a perfect teatime treat

The beau monde take tea in the Galerie des Gobelins at the **Hôtel Plaza Athénée** *(25 avenue Montaigne, 8th, tel: 01 53 67 66 65)*, where a harpist plays while waiters waltz past with heavy silver trays and dessert trolleys laden with glamorous treats. Other luxury hotels that serve an exquisite tea include the Crillon, the Bristol, the George V and Le Meurice. To feel grander still, take afternoon tea at the little-known **1728** *(8 rue d'Anjou, 8th, tel: 01 40 17 04 77)*. The owner of this gloriously refurbished *hôtel particulier* has selected the Chinese teas herself to be served with exquisite pastries by Pierre Hermé (his patisserie on 72 rue Bonaparte, in the 6th *arrondissement* is well worth a visit).

If you prefer a more homely and relaxed tea experience, **Le Loir dans la Théière** *(3 rue des Rosiers, 4th, tel: 01 42 72 90 61)* is a rickety place with wooden floors, posters on the wall, and family-style desserts served in teapot-sized portions. In the same part of town **Les Enfants Gâtés** *(43 rue des Francs-Bourgeois, 4th, tel: 01 42 77 07 63)* has a similar atmosphere, and a lot more breathing room. **La Fourmi Ailée** *(8 rue du Fouarre, 5th, tel: 01 43 29 40 99)* is another cosy-intellectual nook just a stone's throw from the Seine.

Left and opposite: L'Apar' Thé

If you're willing to go a bit out of your way, the casual but plush **Apar' Thé** *(7 rue Charlot, 3rd, tel: 01 42 78 43 30)* is perhaps the trendiest tearoom in town – the kind of place you want to keep a secret. At **A Priori Thé** *(35–37 Galerie Vivienne, 1st, tel: 01 42 97 48 75)*, if you're lucky enough to get a table outside in the gallery, the setting is hard to beat. And, if you're looking for something exotic, head for **Le Café Maure de la Mosquée de Paris** *(39 rue Geoffroy-Saint-Hilaire, 5th, tel: 01 43 31 38 20)* for refreshing mint tea in a mosque, or to the hushed, sleek Japanese tearoom **Toraya** *(10 rue Saint-Florentin, 1st, tel: 01 42 60 13 00)* with a tantalising display of delicate pastries and an impeccably well-mannered clientele.

Last but by no means least, real tea connoisseurs should not miss an outing to **La Maison des Trois Thés** *(33 rue Gracieuse, 5th, tel: 01 43 36 93 84)*, run by Chinese tea master Yu Hua Tseng. Exclusive artisanal teas, ranging from 10 to 5000 euro a pot, are tasted in Zen-like surroundings that will transport you a million miles from Paris. The blue-green tea, dong ding wulong, with a heady aroma of orchid, magnolia and blackcurrant, is among the specialities. Experience gongfu cha, the ancient ritual of taking tea, in the spacious salon. Be warned, though. Tea is so sacred here that perfume wearers are not admitted.

Tea Merchants

Judging by the number of tea merchants in Paris, tea drinking at home is just as popular. For a first-rate assortment of teas and tea-making accessories, Parisians in the know head for **Betjeman and Bartson** *(23 boulevard Malesherbes, 8th)*, one of the oldest and most exclusive tea merchants in the city. **Mariage Frères** *(branch in the Marais, see above, and at 260 rue du Faubourg-Saint-Honoré, 8th)* stocks some 500 types of tea, accompanied by pots, cups and every other tea-time accessory you could imagine. **La Maison des Trois Thés** *(see above)* also sells fine teas and all the tea paraphernalia you need to make the perfect brew. **AlTea** *(41 rue Charlot, 3rd)* sells organic teas and has a tea room in a garden balcony at the back. One chain of shops, **Le Palais des Thés**, has even opened a tea school at its Marais location *(64 rue Vieille-du-Temple, 3rd)*. For a small fee, students can attend tastings, learn the Japanese Tea Ceremony, or master gongfu cha (Chinese tea art).

Area 8: Montmartre, Pigalle and Batignolles

Montmartre, Pigalle and Batignolles

Away from the overpriced tourist traps, hilly Montmartre has hidden treasures. And for ethnic food, try its adjacent neighbourhoods

Named the 'Mount of Martyrs' after the martyrdom of St-Denis (the first bishop of Paris in the late 3rd century), Montmartre is now a mount of tourism – a top Parisian destination for international visitors, second only to the Eiffel Tower. Its narrow cobblestoned streets, meandering up and down the hill (the 'Butte'), its many stairways and its discreet but numerous islets of green all give the area a unique cachet. And, of course, there's the view. Once you've huffed and puffed to the top (or opted for the little tramway, the 'Funiculaire' – for which you'll probably queue for as long as it takes to get up there anyway), the incredible panorama below the white-domed basilica of the Sacré-Coeur will leave you even more breathless.

At the top of the hill, Place du Tertre abounds in tourist bistros, tatty gift shops and would-be artists. If you're gasping for refreshment, the best options are the landmark bistro La Mère Catherine *(9 place du Tertre, tel: 01 46 06 32 69)* where the term 'bistro' is said to have originated. A wiser course of action when the belly begins to grumble would be to leave the hordes on the place du Tertre and strike out into the back streets of the Butte, that are being recolonised by young bohemians. Away from the tourist hub Montmartre is still full of picturesque narrow villagey streets, ivy-clad cottages, cobbled squares, and atmospheric eateries that won't rip you off or serve you substandard food.

Montmartre to Pigalle

The Abbesses metro station exits on to rue des Abbesses, the focus of Montmartre life, with bustling cafés Le Sancerre and Le Chinon, groceries and wine merchants, and trendy boutiques. The trio of streets east of the station – rue de la Vieuville, rue Yvonne-le-Tac and rue des Trois-Frères – are lined with designer boutiques, offbeat second-hand shops, little galleries supporting local artists and boho bars, especially lively in the evenings. Running parallel to the south of rue des Abbesses, the quiet rue Véron has three good restaurants to choose from which reflect the area's multi-cultural character: Le Mono *(see page 138)* is dedicated to Togolese specialities, Taka *(see page 139)* cooks up delicious Japanese offerings and Le Restaurant *(see page 137)* serves an enticing spicy menu to a fashionable clientele.

***Opposite:* dining at Le Mono. *Below:* blackboard favourites**

Crossing rue des Abbesses, hybrid rue des Martyrs could only exist in Montmartre. Buzzing with life, this is a great strip for food shopping, with fish on ice and bins of fruit tumbling out of shops into the street. Seek out exquisite pâtisseries at both Delmontel *(39 rue des Martyrs, 9th)* and Rousseau et Seurre *(No. 22)*; buy sumptuously aged cheeses at Fromagerie Molard *(No. 48)*; andouillette and pistachio-studded sausages at the Charcuterie Lyonnaise *(No. 58)*; or delectable English specialities at the lovely Rose Bakery *(No. 46)*.

Rue Lepic is another quaint, though slightly grubby, market street that curls up the hill. Don't miss the pâtisserie Les Petits Mitrons *(26 rue Lepic, 18th)* where sublime fruit pies are concocted, and Le Comptoir Colonial *(No. 22)*, offering a cornucopia of oils, spices, syrups and exotic Creole delicacies. Grab a drink at the picturesque Lux Bar *(No. 12)*, or across the street at Les Deux Moulins *(No. 15)*, where Amélie Poulain worked as a waitress in the eponymous movie. Further up the steep rue Lepic sits Moulin de la Galette, one of Montmartre's two remaining windmills, now a restaurant *(see page 134)*.

Pigalle and Nouvelle Athènes

Back down below the Butte, Pigalle, the city's red-light district, is slowly shedding its seedy reputation. Though sex shows and video shops still exist, the brothels and erotic cabarets are being replaced by trendy nightclubs and music venues. Among the cabaret survivors is Chez Michou on rue des Martyrs, home of Parisian drag artists, and, of course, the Moulin Rouge, which has long since cleaned up its act and is now more cheesy than sleazy.

South of boulevard de Rochechouart and boulevard de Clichy, the area known as Nouvelle Athènes is being rediscovered. In the mid-19th century 'New Athens' drew writers, artists and composers, among them Chopin and George Sand, as well as actresses and courtesans. The houses on place St-Georges, the Musée Gustave-Moreau and Musée de la Vie Romantique or the

Le Moulin de la Galette, symbol of Montmartre

Five of the Best

Chez Michel: Brittany-inspired gems by brilliant chef Thierry Breton
Le Restaurant: excellent colonial-style canteen with fusion touches
Le Bistro des Dames: reliable bistro fare and a gorgeous garden
La Famille: trendy new haunt, serving breezy, modern dishes
Sale e Pepe: convivial Italian, with freshness always a top priority

exclusive 'villas' off rue des Martyrs give an idea of its rather grander past. Rue Clauzel is an enclave of bric-a-brac and boho clothes shops, while the lower half of rue des Martyrs has several good bakeries and delis *(see above)*.

Goutte d'Or and Batignolles

If your legs can take it, push your trek east of Montmartre to the Marché Dejean, an African market by the Château-Rouge metro, and explore nearby rue des Poissonniers, where grocery stores sell all sorts of exotic vegetables, fruit and spices that you won't easily find elsewhere. This marks the edge of the gritty African and Arab neighbourhood known as the Goutte d'Or. Long run down with a heavy police presence and dodgy reputation, this area is off the normal tourist route, but has some appealing ethnic restaurants for the adventurous.

If you choose to go in the opposite direction, towards the (much more respectable) 17th *arrondissement*, you'll eventually hit the organic Marché des Batignolles (every Saturday morning, on rue Lemercier). This quiet, residential neighbourhood, which is slowly gaining in popularity and hipness, counts a few little jewels, including the lovely Italian canteen Premiata Drogheria Di Meglio *(90 rue Legendre)* and its more spacious incarnation at 39 rue Truffaut, where you can sit down or take away antipasti, fresh pasta, and delicious cold cuts. Next door, La Maison des Délices sells a stunning selection of teas, jams, coffees and many beautiful and unusual condiments and preserves.

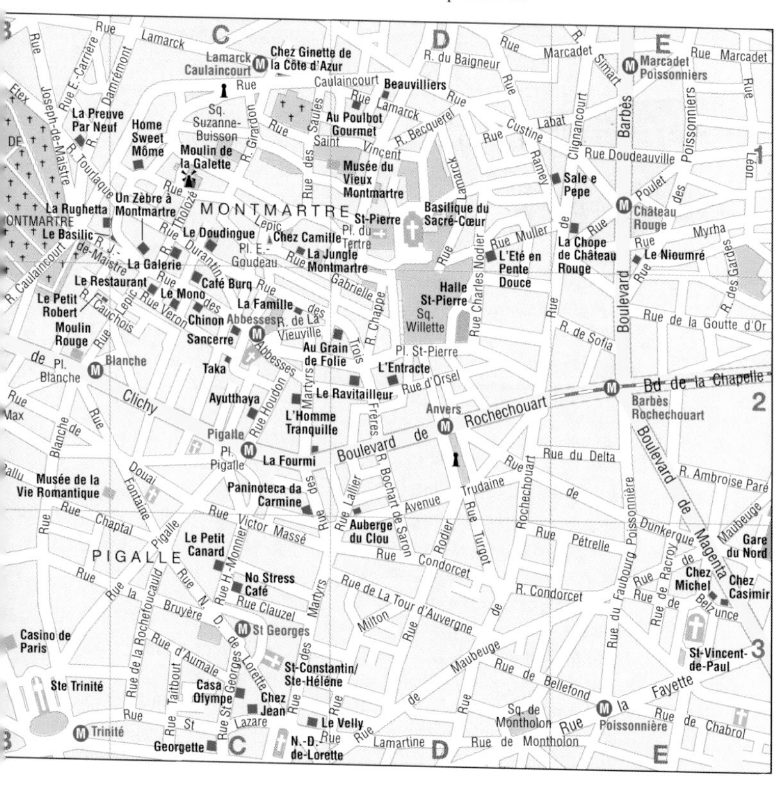

Upmarket, old-fashioned Beauvilliers

Haute Cuisine

Beauvilliers

52 rue Lamarck, 18th [D1]. Tel: 01 42 54 54 42. Open: L and D Tues–Sat, D only Mon. **€€€–€€€€**

Beauvilliers is a grand, old-fashioned restaurant with a dining room suffocating in heavy drapes, Louis-Philippe chairs and lavish bouquets of flowers. It's just the place for celebrations and romantic dinners, especially on the beautiful terrace. Reserve.

Bistros

Aubergine

46 rue des Dames, 17th [A2]. Tel: 01 43 87 67 95. Open: L and D Mon–Fri, D only Sat; closed 1 week in mid-Aug. **€€**

One of the newest spots of the 'trendified' Batignolles neighbourhood, Aubergine bears the colour of its namesake, and has open-brick walls and multicoloured lamp-shades. Sit in one of the comfy couches and dig your fork into salad or steak, and people-watch: the whole arty crowd seems to gather here.

Le Basilic

33 rue Lepic, 18th [C1]. Tel: 01 46 06 78 43. Open: L and D Wed–Sun, D only Tues. **€€**

Located on the photogenic, vine-covered corner of rue Joseph-Lemaistre and rue Lepic (just before the street becomes a steep, sinuous slope), the restaurant in this old inn with exposed beams is rustic and picturesque. It's definitely a Montmartre experience, although the typical French fare is rather average.

Le Bistro des Dames (🍴)

18 rue des Dames, 17th [A2]. Tel: 01 45 22 13 42. Open: L and D Mon–Fri, non-stop Sat–Sun 12.30pm–11.30pm. **€€**

If you sit in the front room, you'll find this bistro comfortable and friendly. Sit in the lovely back garden, however, and things really feel special – you'll enjoy your meal surrounded by trees and festive garlands of lights. The service is competent, and the traditional bistro fare very decent, with highlights including tartares, rocket and parmesan salad and duck aiguillettes in balsamic vinegar.

Chez Casimir

6 rue de Belzunce, 10th [E3]. Tel: 01 48 78 28 80. Open: L and D Mon–Fri, D only on Sat. **€€–€€€**

Hidden behind the pretty St-Vincent-de-Paul church, this offshoot of Chez Michel *(see below)* is a more affordable and laid-back option than its grander relative. The décor is banal, but what really matters is the quality of the produce, which is superb. Dishes include a perfect cauliflower velouté, juicy game hen with blanched fava bean salad and a beautifully caramelised pain perdu (French toast). Nice wine list, too.

Chez Jean

8 rue Saint-Lazare, 9th [C3]. Tel: 01 48 78 62 73. Open: L and D Mon–Fri; closed late-July–Aug. **€€€**

Traditionally decorated with a zinc counter and red banquettes, Chez Jean creates seasonal delights such as cucumber gazpacho with crispy langoustines, foie gras with fennel and pesto curry, suckling pig with carrots in an apricot sauce, and golden angler fish on a bed of chickpeas and citronella milk. For dessert, try the melting chocolate cannelé, a house special.

Chez Michel

10 rue de Belzunce, 10th [E3]. Tel: 01 44 53 06 20. Open: L and D Tues–Fri, D only Sat and Mon, B on reservation; closed 2 weeks in Aug. **€€€**

According to many in the know, this may well be the best restaurant in Paris. Thierry Breton's Brittany home-cooking never ceases to startle, as he unveils a wild rabbit parmentier, crispy dove with carrot onion mousse, boar roast with baby potatoes, and fabulous desserts such as the rice pudding, St-Honoré or the typical – and perfect – far breton. Reserve.

L'Entracte

44 rue d'Orsel, 18th [D2]. Tel: 01 46 06 93 41. Open: L and D Wed–Sat, L only Sun; closed Aug, Christmas and Easter. **€€**

This bistro might look a bit camp, with its red curtains and cluttered furniture, but you'll be seduced by the warmth of owners Carlos and Sonia and their fine home cooking: the French fries are some of the best in the city, the escalope is perfectly done, and every dish is made with the freshest produce around. Booking recommended.

La Galerie

16 rue Tholozé, 18th [C1]. Tel: 01 42 59 25 76. Open: D only Wed–Mon; closed 2 weeks in Aug and at Christmas. **€€–€€€**

This pretty restaurant seems to be booked every night, so don't forget to reserve. Soft candlelight, paintings on the walls and cute bouquets make the setting as romantic as the food is tasty. The menu offers light starters such as a crispy artichoke salad or marinated sardines, and some heartier entrées including aubergine (eggplant) lasagne and spiced pork roast.

Georgette

29 rue St-Georges, 9th [C3]. Tel: 01 42 80 39 13. Open: L and D Wed–Fri, L only Mon–Tues. **€€**

Don't let the kitsch façade dissuade you. Once you're through the door, the clean surroundings and warm smells are as seductive as the outside is off-putting. Georgette's menu is reliable, with staple dishes including organic purslaine and goats' cheese salad, stuffed courgette (zucchini) flowers, and caramelised andouillette.

Au Grain de Folie

24 rue La Vieuville, 18th [D2]. Tel: 01 42 58 15 57. Open: L and D Mon–Sat, non-stop Sun 12.30pm–11pm. **€**

TIP

To escape the crowds head for the charming **Musée de la Vie Romantique** *(16 rue Chaptal, 01 48 74 95 38).* The museum is dedicated to the lives of the writers, musicians and artists who lived in this area of the 9th known as New Athens. The tearoom and garden provide a lovely, secluded haven.

Self-named 'a vegetarian place for non-vegetarians', this is a quaint spot for a healthy bite on your way to the Butte. It feels like the cluttered kitchen of an (organic) French farm. Sit at a gingham-covered table, among the cooking utensils and pot plants, and enjoy a bowl of homemade soup, a crispy vegetable platter, or a slice of salty tart.

Le Morosophe

83 rue Legendre, 17th [A1]. Tel: 01 53 06 82 82. Open: L and D Mon–Sat. **€€–€€€**

In an inviting, dark-wood-panelled ambience, Le Morosophe (which means, in Rabelaisian lexicon, 'wisdom in madness') puts the accent on all things classically French. Come here to re-discover terrines, ravioles (tiny cheese raviolis from Royans), or the €15 daily special: pot-au-feu, choucroute garnie, petit salé or boeuf bourguignon, depending on the day.

Le Moulin de la Galette

83 rue Lepic, 18th [C1]. Tel: 01 46 06 84 77. Open: L and D Tues–Sat, L only Sun. **€€–€€€**

In a quaint Montmartre location (an historical windmill), this candlelit restaurant combines ambiance with an attractive menu – think chilled vegetable soup with brocciu (Corsican cheese), piquillos stuffed with codfish, and duck with fruit and bacon on a skewer. Booking is necessary – in summer, ask to sit on the lovely, shaded patio.

Did you know?

Montmartre was once dotted with windmills, originally built for grinding wheat and pressing grapes. Today, only two of the 30 windmills remain: the Moulin du Radet and the Moulin de la Galette on rue Lepic, now a restaurant *(see right)*.

Au Grain de Folie – a rare vegetarian restaurant

Le Perroquet Vert

7 rue Cavalotti, 18th [B1]. Tel: 01 45 22 49 16. Open: L and D Tues–Fri, D only Mon and Sat. **€€–€€€**

Ghosts of Picasso, Jean Gabin and Edith Piaf still haunt this half-timbered house a few blocks away from place de Clichy. Although the décor is comfortably old-fashioned, the food has been modernised and lightened, with dishes including sardine pissaladière, langoustines with mango, red berries duck, hog fish and grilled fennel.

Au Poulbot Gourmet

39 rue Lamarck, 18th [D1]. Tel: 01 46 06 86 00. Open: L and D Mon–Sat, L only Sun Oct–May; closed 2 weeks in Aug. **€€–€€€**

At Poulbot, the food is seasonal, and oscillates between classic and modern, with dishes such as snail curry, skate galantine, veal tongue, and rouget filets on a bed of risotto.

La Preuve Par Neuf

5 rue Damrémont, 18th [B1]. Tel: 01 42 62 64 69. Open: L and D daily. **€€**

Hidden behind the Montmartre cemetery, and worth a detour, is this friendly eatery, which offers an excellent, well-priced menu. Daring creations are mixed with classics and include asparagus gazpacho with baby scallops and redcurrants, anchovy toasts with apple julienne, herb lamb chops, and steak with roquefort sauce. Nice quiet pavement terrace for sunny days.

Le Velly

52 rue Lamartine, 9th [C3]. Tel: 01 48 78 60 05. Open: L and D Mon–Sat; closed 3 weeks in Aug. **€€–€€€**

Food preparation at Home Sweet Môme

In his 1930s-style bistro, Alain Brigant's cuisine has been celebrated for over four years. The menu is improvised every day, depending on market finds. Choose from beef with herbs, grilled codfish with mash, or a melon minestrone with fromage frais. Desserts are delicious, and the bread is homemade.

Cafés

3 Pièces Cuisine

25 rue de Cheroy, 17th [A2]. Tel: 01 44 90 85 10. Open: B, L and D daily 8am–2am, Br Sat–Sun. **€**
This fashionable café/brasserie set in a former laundry is the perfect place (for under-30s) to relax with a cocktail before dinner. It's all about the atmosphere, really. The small but adequate menu includes safe bets such as chicken breast in cream sauce or grilled steak.

Café Burq

6 rue Burq, 18th [C2]. Tel: 01 42 52 81 27. Open: D only Mon–Sat 7pm–midnight. **€€**
If you want to observe Montmartre hipsters in action, come to Café Burq. Formerly a wine bar, it has been revamped into a trendy café, with pop lights, slate tiles, retro chairs and a satisfying menu that includes roasted camembert, terrines and little Spanish specialities. It can be rowdy in the evenings, particularly on DJ nights.

Chez Ginette de la Côte d'Azur

101 rue Caulaincourt, 18th [C1]. Tel: 01 46 06 01 49. Open: non-stop daily noon–midnight. **€€**
With its bamboo-framed terrace, colourful lanterns, and wooden, poster-filled interior, Ginette is a sexy French café that always draws a crowd – young and old locals mixed with international patrons. The food is decent but overpriced, the waiters are moody, but the atmosphere pleasant.

L'Eté en Pente Douce

23 rue Muller, 18th [D1]. Tel: 01 42 64 02 67. Open: L and D daily. **€** *www.parisresto.com*
In summer, this airy, cobblestoned terrace, at the foot of the endless staircase leading to the Sacré-Coeur, is a picturesque spot for a drink. The cosy veranda is also a haven on wintery days. Pity the food is so mediocre, because this is one of the loveliest settings in the city. Better stick with a pot of tea and a slice of tart.

La Fourmi

74 rue des Martyrs, 18th [C2]. Tel: 01 42 64 70 35. Open: daily until 2am, food served noon–11pm. **€**

TIP

Stop by the chaotic mess hall of the **Marché St-Pierre** *(2 rue Charles-Nodier, closed Mon)*, for tablecloths, napkins, aprons and all imaginable fabrics, sold by the metre at knock-down prices.

Drinks and games at Amélie Poulain's Deux Tabacs

This designer café on a busy Pigalle corner buzzes with trendy shoppers by day and clubbers by night. Come here more for the scene than the food.

Home Sweet Môme

61 rue Lepic, 18th [C1]. Tel: 01 42 57 88 93. Open: L and D Tues–Sun 11am–7pm, 11am–midnight Jun–Sept. **€–€€**
www.petitappetit.net

Deliriously colourful, with Christmas lights and eclectic knick-knacks, this tearoom-turned-restaurant also includes a corner where you can buy flowery flip-flops and fuzzy rabbits. The terrace is set with garden furniture and funky umbrellas. Sandwiches, salads and charcuterie plates are available all day, while a more elaborate menu is served for brunch, lunch and dinner.

No Stress Café

2 place Gustave-Toudouze, 9th [C3]. Tel: 01 48 78 00 27. Open: L and D Tues–Sat, Br Sun, non-stop daily in summer; closed 2 weeks in early Jan. **€**

In summer, the outdoor green-and-mauve tables of this hip café are crowded with a mix of Parisian youth and foreign visitors in the know. It's a lovely spot for lunch or a light evening bite, offering a selection of tapas, salmon tartare, chicken satay and basic burgers and fries.

Le Sancerre

35 rue des Abbesses, 18th [C2]. Tel: 01 42 58 47 05. Open: daily 7am–2am. **€**

This is a must-visit café on rue des Abbesses, drawing an eclectic, young, arty crowd. Salads are appetising and generous, the wines are good, and pavement chairs allow you to enjoy the scene.

Un Zèbre à Montmartre

38 rue Lepic, 18th [C1]. Tel: 01 42 23 97 80. Open: L and D daily non-stop 11.30am–11.30pm. **€€**

There isn't actually a zebra at this Montmartre hotspot, but décor is certainly theatrical – think flamboyant curtains, purple couches and tile-covered tables. There's an uneventful but decent menu of poached egg salad, croque-monsieur and grilled salmon, etc.

Regional

Casa Olympe

48 rue St-Georges, 9th [C3]. Tel: 01 42 85 26 01. Open: L and D Mon–Fri; closed 1 week in May, 3 weeks in Aug and 1 week in Dec. **€€–€€€**

Curry-coloured walls and Murano chandeliers lend warmth to this friendly bistro. Chef Olympe Versini's celebrated menu includes marinated tuna, boudin crisps with mixed greens, tarragon sorbet and the house speciality: oven-roasted lamb shoulder, served with potatoes, tomatoes and whole garlic. Fabulous desserts. A local favourite.

TIP

On weekends, the **Puces de Saint-Ouen** *(Porte de Clignancourt)*, north of Montmartre, is the largest flea market in Paris, with over 2,500 dealers grouped in over a dozen individual markets, most of them opening off rue des Rosiers. Great for furniture and antique kitchenware – with plenty of opportunities for snacking between rummaging.

Le Petit Canard

19 rue Henri-Monnier, 9th [C3]. Tel: 01 49 70 07 95. Open: L and D Mon–Fri, D only Sat. **€€**

In this friendly restaurant owned by – and catering to – duck lovers, you can dig into the bird in question in every imaginable incarnation, from confit to magret to sausage. If you're spoilt for choice, simply go for the 'Gros Canard' tasting plate, offering a portion of each.

Le Petit Robert

10 rue Cauchois, 18th [B2]. Tel: 01 46 06 04 46. Open: D only Tues–Sat. **€€**

A favourite among residents in the know, this quaint restaurant serves southern-inspired dishes (Basque and otherwise), such as a salad of oranges and red onions, fresh anchovies, jellied museau de boeuf, stuffed cabbage, and chicken with preserved lemons. Eclectic art pieces and good jazz music add to the overall homely feel.

Contemporary

Auberge du Clou

30 avenue de Trudaine, 9th [D2]. Tel: 01 48 78 22 48. Open: L and D Tues–Sun. **€€–€€€** *www.aubergeduclou.com*

Located on a quiet, tree-lined avenue just down from chaotic place Pigalle, this elegantly refurbished inn attracts many diners (including celebrities) with its eclectic, global menu. Choose between the lamb tartare, coriander shrimp beignets, spicy langoustines with pineapple (Caracas) or stuffed duck with grilled figs (Jakarta). The wacky desserts include lotus and jack fruit ice cream with tea syrup.

La Famille 🍴

41 rue des Trois-Frères, 18th [C2]. Tel: 01 42 52 11 12. Open: D only Tues–Sat, Br Sun. **€€**

A recent addition to the Montmartre restaurant scene, La Famille has immediately become one of the hippest. The interior is tastefully simple (powdery white walls and graceful, suspended lampshades) – a clean canvas on which to show off exciting creations such as raw shrimps served with passion fruit, pan-fried tuna with grilled polenta, and pink grapefruit sorbet.

Le Restaurant 🍴

32 rue Véron, 18th [C2]. Tel: 01 42 23 06 22. Open: L and D daily, Br Sun. **€€**

Sophisticated minimalist dining at La Famille

Hip, vibrant and exotic – the plainly named Le Restaurant

TIP

Down the northern side of the Butte, past the vineyard on rue des Saules (planted in memory of the area's winemaking past) towards the Mairie du XVIIIe (the town hall of the 18th *arrondissement*) is a busy residential area. The shopping hub here is rue du Poteau, where you'll find several good food shops including the excellent **Fromagerie de Montmartre** (9 rue du Poteau, 18th) and Greek, Auvergnat and Italian delis.

A no-nonsense name for a colonial-style address serving a spiced-up, sweet-and-sour prix-fixe menu (€20 for two courses). Diners, showbiz folk among them, pour in for seasonal dishes by chef Yves Peledeau and the friendly brouhaha. Reservations recommended.

La Table de Lucullus

129 rue Legendre, 17th [A1]. Tel: 01 40 25 02 68. Open: L and D Tues–Sat. **€€€–€€€€**

The décor here is modest, but young chef Nicolas Vagnon is anything but. Scribbled on huge blackboards, his ambitious menu, mostly involving wild fish, aims at pure tastes. The fresh catch of the day can be served raw, sautéed, grilled or poached, and the wines are impeccable. Sadly, service can be slow. No-smoking policy and reservations essential.

International

Ayutthaya

5 rue Houdon, 18th [C2]. Tel: 01 42 64 19 53. Open: L and D Tues–Sun. **€–€€**

Although the décor here is as unfussy as the space is cramped, it's one of the best addresses for Thai specialities. The long menu includes lip-smacking ginger chicken, and fish steamed in a lotus leaf. Service is friendly but slow.

Le Mono

40 rue Véron, 18th [C2]. Tel: 01 46 06 99 20. Open: D only Thur–Tues; closed Aug. **€**

If you read what's posted on the walls, you'll learn the whole story of the Akakpo family, who moved from Togo in the 1960s and have been running this restaurant ever since. Decorated like a straw hut, it is dedicated to Togolese specialities, such as akboudessi (fish and exotic vegetables) or g'bekui (beef, fish and shrimp in a spinach sauce). The good mood is contagious, and the food is a bargain.

Naoko

11 rue Biot, 17th [A2]. Tel: 01 40 08 08 78. Open: L and D Mon–Sat. **€€**

Stylishly adorned with aquariums and origami, Naoko offers an authentic Japanese experience. Beyond the ultra-fresh sushi and maki, everything that chef Mishishita concocts behind the wide, open counter, is delicious, from tofu fritters and tuna tartare with plums to spicy seaweed cornets.

Le Nioumré

7 rue des Poissonniers, 18th [E1]. Tel: 01 42 51 24 94. Open: L and D Tues–Sun, non-stop noon–midnight. **€**

In the heart of the Goutte d'Or, this Senegalese family restaurant does first-rate African standards from mafé (rice and lamb with peanuts) and kandja soup to yassa (chicken in an onion and lemon sauce). Service is rather slow, but you can always sip a bissap (ginger juice) and eavesdrop on the happy chatter of local diners while waiting.

Paninoteca da Carmine

61 rue des Martyrs, 9th [C2]. Tel: 01 48 78 28 01. Open: L and D Tues–Fri, non-stop Sat Sept–May, non-stop daily Jun–Aug; closed last week in Dec. **€**

Despite its deceptive hole-in-the-wall look, this Italian kitchen does excellent food. The heavy-accented owner has a genuine talent for pizzas (try the Marinara, with fresh tomato, garlic, parsley and arugula), fresh pasta and scrumptious antipasti. Take-away available.

La Rughetta

41 rue Lepic, 18th [B1]. Tel: 01 42 23 41 70. Open: L and D daily. **€€**

A classy Italian joint, loved for its oven-crisp pizzas and fresh pasta dishes. The seductive carte des vins is heavy on wine from regional vineyards, and the dessert menu has every Italian speciality you could want from tiramisu to panna cotta and biancaneve (meringue with vanilla ice-cream and caramel).

Sale E Pepe

30 rue Ramey, 18th [E1]. Tel: 01 46 06 08 01. Open: L and D Tues–Sat. **€€**

On summer nights, regulars swarm to this Italian joint, hoping for an outdoor table. You'll join the throng once you've tasted the super-fresh fare served. A winning €20 menu includes an appetiser, pasta dish, crisp pizza and dessert. For groups, food is served in big, family bowls. No smoking.

Taka

1 rue Véron, 18th [C2]. Tel: 01 42 23 74 16. Open: D only Tues–Sat. **€€€**

Hidden on a corner below rue des Abbesses, this Japanese eatery is where to enjoy the creations of Mister Taka, whose sashimis, yakitoris and shabu-shabu take sushi to a new level of art. It's small and always busy, so it's best to reserve.

Bars and Pubs

If your idea of having a drink is to sit at a terrace and people-watch, then rue des Abbesses is where you should head – this stretch and the area around it are lined with cafés such as the **Chinon** *(No. 49)*, **Sancerre** *(No. 35)* or **Progrès** *(7 rue des Trois-Frères)*. Numerous French TV stars, singers, artists and other 'Bobos' (Bohemian Bourgeois) live here, so sightings are almost always guaranteed.

If you're more in the mood for an intimate drink with friends, a better option is **Chez Camille** *(8 rue Ravignan, 18th , tel: 01 46 06 05 78)*, a lively little bar with a bright yellow façade, perfect for an *apéro* (apéritif). Despite its grubby look, **La Chope de Château-Rouge** *(40 rue de Clignancourt, 18th, tel: 01 46 06 20 10)* is a neighbourhood favourite, not only for its genuinely boisterous atmosphere, but also because there's free couscous for everyone on weekend nights.

For a trendy drink, visit **Le Ravitailleur** *(50 rue d'Orsel, 18th, tel: 01 46 06 20 64)*, a new cocktail lounge with a shimmering counter built out of the wing of an aeroplane. Filled with comfy pillows and decorated with beautiful tiles, **Le Doudingue** *(24 rue Durantin, 18th, tel: 01 42 54 88 08)* is a good choice for a quiet nightcap in good company. And if you're looking for a hot spot in which to end the night, head out to **La Jungle Montmartre** *(32 rue Gabrielle, 18th, tel: 01 46 06 75 69)*, an African restaurant and bar that serves up homemade ginger rum and plays excellent dance music until 2am.

L'Oisive Thé

Butte-aux-Cailles and Chinatown

Paris is a city where a few steps down a side street can bring you to another world, and the 13th *arrondissement* is no exception. Hidden just south of place d'Italie is the tranquil villagey *quartier* of the Butte-aux-Cailles, where quiet streets dotted with old street lamps and lined with leafy trees are animated by students chatting on the terraces of the cafés and restaurants. Though a few trendy restaurants have opened here, it's still an unassuming area and delightful to visit. Chinatown is a close neighbour, roughly bordered by avenue d'Italie and avenue d'Ivry, and running south to the edge of the city. It's home to the colourful Chinese, Vietnamese and Thai community, and a kitsch paradise for jade figurines, exotic fruits, rice bowls, fine teas and tea sets, and good-quality Chinese dresses.

Map on Inside Front Cover

L'Avant-Goût

26 rue Bobillot, 13th. Tel: 01 53 80 24 00. Open: L and D Tues–Fri. **€–€€**

Great value for money, L'Avant-Goût offers simple yet inventive cuisine in a compelling, up-to-the-minute atmosphere. This is probably the neighbourhood's best restaurant, and everyone knows it, so book ahead. There's also a take-away menu, which includes pot-au-feu in a giant casserole.

Les Cailloux

58 rue des Cinq-Diamants, 13th. Tel: 01 45 80 15 08. Open: L and D Tues–Sat; closed 3 weeks in Aug and 2 weeks in Dec. **€€**

Fresh pasta is the speciality at Les Cailloux, where a two-course lunch menu with a glass of wine is only €12.50. Start with rocket and fennel salad or parma ham, before moving on to penne with asparagus, or salmon carpaccio with courgettes. The dinner menu includes grilled meats and heartier dishes than those available at lunch.

Chez Nathalie

45 rue Vandrezanne, 13th. Tel: 01 45 80 20 42. Open: L and D daily. **€€**

It's the attention to detail in this pretty little restaurant that makes dining here a treat. Starters include a particularly good goat's cheese salad with herbs and an aubergine terrine with red peppers; mains vary in richness from chateaubriand with gratin dauphinois to broiled monkfish with saffron sauce and steamed vegetables. Desserts including 'very chocolate cake' with salty caramel sauce will make you swoon.

Chez Paul

22 rue de la Butte-aux-Cailles, 13th. Tel: 01 45 89 22 11. Open: L and D daily. **€€**

This friendly, elegant bistro, once a favourite haunt of late photographer Robert Doisneau, proudly serves up traditional fare of foie gras, roast suckling pig with sage and daily specials fresh from the market, such as seabass and pike-perch. There's also a wonderful selection of French apéritifs. Reservations are recommended – request a table on the terrace in fine weather.

Mei Kwai Lou

1 rue du Moulinet, 13th. Tel: 01 45 80 09 95. Open: L and D Mon–Sat; closed two weeks in Aug. **€**

A spotless haven, offering fantastic value for money just two steps from the busy avenue d'Italie. There's a fixed lunch menu for

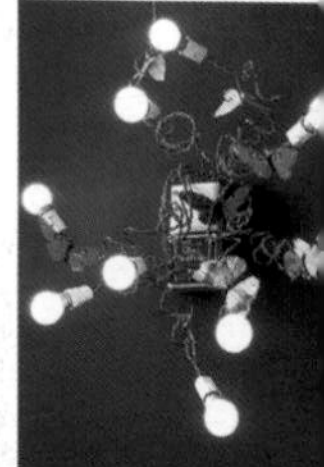

***Top:* Lighting Chez Nathalie. *Above:* menu du jour. *Opposite:* L'Oisive-Thé, Butte-aux-Cailles**

less than €10, and a dinner menu at under €15, and you can choose from the typical array of pork, chicken and seafood dishes – plus the more exotic quail with five flavours, steamed sting-ray with ginger, and frogs' legs in Chinese spices.

Paradis Thai

132 rue Tolbiac, 13th. Tel: 01 45 83 22 26. Open: L and D daily. **€€**

Right and below: the welcoming, exotic Paradis Thai

The exotic yet understated mood in this, one of the more elegant restaurants in the neighbourhood, is set by the enormous, backlit elephant in the entrance. The discreet décor offsets beautifully presented Thai and Vietnamese specialities, and the varied menu considerately indicates the level of spiciness for each dish. Take-away orders are also available.

Paris – Vietnam

98 avenue de Choisy, 13th. Tel: 01 44 23 73 97. Open: L and D Wed–Mon, non-stop 10am–11pm. **€**

For true lovers of kitsch, this restaurant is a temple – think red Chinese lanterns, strings of coloured lights, gold buddha statues and illuminated photos of Vietnamese dishes, in what may be the tackiest place in Paris. The food, however, is fresh, delicious and served with a flourish.

Sinorama

118 avenue de Choisy, 13th. Tel: 01 53 82 09 51. Open: L and D daily. **€**

Offering delicious food and bustling with a mostly Chinese clientele, Sinorama is exactly the kind of restaurant one hopes to find in Chinatown. Try the stuffed crab's legs, crispy chef's chicken or tasty beef with bamboo shoots. There's lots of choice, as the menu runs to several pages, with every dish translated into English; some staff speak English too. No reservations.

Le Temps des Cerises

18 rue de la Butte-aux-Cerises, 13th. Tel: 01 45 89 69 48. Open: L and D daily. **€–€€**

The main attractions here are the old-fashioned décor, lovely relaxed atmosphere and friendly staff. The food is fairly standard, classic, value French fare.

Belleville and Ménilmontant

Belleville refers to the area north of the Belleville metro station, along – and to the east of – rue de Belleville, which snakes its way uphill. Ménilmontant is directly south and includes part of trendy rue Oberkampf *(see page 79)*. Home to many of the city's immigrants, both *quartiers* form an ethnic pastiche of cultures, with Arabs, Chinese, Jews, Thais – you name it – all jumbled together. It's not unusual to find a Muslim butcher shop, Chinese DVD store and a Turkish sandwich kiosk on the same corner. The food, of course, is as diverse as the residents. Take a breather at the top of rue de Belleville, near the Pyrénées metro station, and look downhill for an exceptional view of the Eiffel Tower.

Le Baratin

3 rue Jouye-Rouve, 20th. Tel: 01 43 49 39 70. Open: L and D Tues–Sat; closed 1 week in Jan and 2 weeks in Aug. **€**

You can't get more Parisian than this cosy bar à vin tucked away off rue de Belleville, where the daily menu reflects the best of the morning's markets. Mains vary from canette (baby duck) to grilled salmon or steak. The fixed-price lunch menu is only €12.50; dinner is à la carte, and good wines are available at decent prices. Reservations recommended.

La Boulangerie

15 rue des Panoyaux, 20th. Tel: 01 43 58 45 45. Open: L and D Mon–Fri, D only Sat; closed 2 weeks in August. **€**

www.restaulaboulangerie.com

A favourite with the locals, La Boulangerie is a comfortable, friendly restaurant where the evening menu is less than €20 during the week. Traditional French dishes are prepared with care and offered with a good choice of wines, including a selection of 'prestige wines'.

Le Coin de Verre

38 rue de Sambre-et-Meuse, 10th. Tel: 01 42 45 31 82. Open: D Mon–Sat **€€**

Hosts Michel and Hugues make you feel as if you're in their living room with a gaggle of their crazy friends. The stone walls and a fire in the hearth behind the curtained door create an exceptionally cosy ambience. There's only a small selection of dishes, such as pork and lentils, perhaps a fish option, and always a cheese plate, but plenty of inexpensive wines.

Krung Thep

93 rue Julien-Lacroix, 20th. Tel: 01 43 66 83 74. Open: D only daily; closed 1 week in Aug and 1 week in Dec. **€€**

Krung Thep's unassuming exterior conceals an extraordinary restaurant of traditional Thai cuisine. Patrons clamber up on seats behind ornately decorated, raised tables, to choose from an extensive menu – a task made easier by a photo album of the dishes. It's lots of fun, and the staff are friendly too. Reservations strongly recommended.

Rital et Courts

1–3 rue des Envierges, 20th. Tel: 01 47 97 08 40. Open: L and D Tues–Sun, non-stop 10am–midnight in summer. **€**

A stylish bistro-trattoria in a stellar location serving up reasonably priced antipasti, pasta and meat dishes. Lunch menus start at €10, and evening menus range from €15–23. Short films are shown on television screens in the afternoon and at midnight. The terrace

TIP

Enter **Tang Frères** (48 avenue d'Ivry, 13th, tel: 01 45 70 80 00; open Tues–Sun 9am–7.30pm), a sprawling Chinese grocery store, and you'll think you've stumbled into a busy Shanghai marketplace. Check out aisle upon aisle of exotic goods, including fruits, herbs and teas, all on sale for reasonable prices.

Algerian delicacies

TIP

To stock up on all things Egyptian, head for **Le Caire** *(63 rue de Belleville, 19th, open Tues–Sun 10am–10pm)*, a tiny grocery store packed to the rafters with spices, nuts, cheeses, teas, fresh pastries, barrels of olives, even small take-away packs of freshly made specialities such as tapenade and delicious marinated artichokes.

backs on to the top of the Parc de Belleville, offering one of the best views in Paris.

Le Sainte Marthe

32 rue Ste-Marthe, 10th. Tel: 01 44 84 36 96. Open: D daily, 5pm–2am. **€**

The interior here – all red velvet and low lighting – is alluring, but the terrace looking out over the lovely square Ste-Marthe is even better. The food sounds quite nice – dishes include rabbit, salads and an apple-and-black pudding tart – but it turns out to be quite carelessly made. This place is best for drinks, really – happy hour stretches from 6pm until 10pm. Cheerful clientele.

Les Trois Marmites

8 rue Julien-Lacroix, 20th. Tel: 01 40 33 05 65. Open: D only Tues–Sun. **€**

A delightful little restaurant that serves dinner only, for a fixed-price menu at €16. There are only a few dishes – such as sweet pepper feuilleté, grilled seabass with steamed vegetables or pork with spiced honey and mash – but they're done well. Reservations recommended at the weekend.

Le Zéphyr

1 rue du Jourdain, 20th. Tel: 01 46 36 65 81. Open: B, L and D daily, 8am–2am; closed 2 weeks in Aug. **€€**

This is a gorgeous Art Deco brasserie, offering tasty, inventive cuisine. A fixed-price dinner menu is available for €26, but à la carte choices are intriguing if the budget can stretch to them; starters include tuna tartare and oliviade, and foie gras with green tomato compote, while mains range from pork with grapefruit caramel and pineapple risotto, to salmon and spinach ravioli. Reservations recommended at the weekend.

THE 14TH ARRONDISSEMENT

This area was at the height of its fame around the turn of the 20th century, when it experienced an influx of foreign writers and artists, and many of the restaurants frequented by Ernest Hemingway and other novelists still remain on the wide boulevard du Montparnasse. East of – and behind – the modern Montparnasse tower lie the tranquil Montparnasse cemetery and also the pedestrian rue Daguerre area, which has a villagey (although slightly trendy) feel about it. Secret gardens and tiny cobblestoned streets lined with small private houses are characteristic of the 14th, and there are several good restaurants to discover here.

Apollo

3 place Denfert-Rochereau, 14th. Tel: 01 45 38 76 77. Open: L and D daily. **€–€€**

A trendy bar and restaurant, in an otherwise conservative area of town. Located in part of the Denfert-Rochereau RER station, the now-hip 1970s' décor and enormous terrace create a good setting for what could loosely be described as modern French food.

Aquarius

40 rue de Gergovie, 14th. Tel: 01 45 41 36 88. Open: L and D Mon–Sat. **€**

Paris is not known for its vegetarian restaurants but this one is good, always full, and has a nice, homely atmosphere. The Celtic chef and his Brazilian team put out a variety of fresh and inventive dishes; desserts (apple crumble, chocolate cake, etc) are always excellent.

L'Assiette

181 rue du Château, 14th. Tel: 01 43 22 64 86. Open: L and D Wed–Sun; closed in Aug and at Christmas. **€–€€**

Lulu, the cigar-smoking owner, is a local star. Her strong personality, ultra-simple cooking and obsession with impeccably sourced ingredients have made this a Mecca for gourmets in the know. Dishes lean towards the southwest and include foie gras, roast lamb, sausage from the Landes region and homemade caramel ice cream. Everything is cooked to perfection.

La Cagouille

10 place Constantin-Brancusi, 14th. Tel: 01 43 22 09 01. Open: L and D daily. **€–€€** *www.la-cagouille.fr*

A fish-only place with specialities including Marennes d'Oléron oysters, black sea bream grilled with cumin, and red mullet in olive oil. Service is attentive, the wine list extensive, and desserts are good. In warm weather, take a seat at the pleasant outdoor seating – it makes up slightly for the somewhat plain interior.

La Coupole

102 boulevard du Montparnasse, 14th. Tel: 01 43 20 14 20. Open: B, L and D daily, non-stop 8am–1am. **€–€€** *www.coupoleparis.com*

The tables never stop turning at this famous, atmospheric 1927

Classic brasserie, the vast La Coupole

brasserie, which seats 400 people. The code's relaxed – you can dress up or wear jeans – and you can dance downstairs to a theme that changes nightly. Alternatively, simply tuck into the typical brasserie fare from seafood to choucroute.

Le Dôme

108 boulevard du Montparnasse, 14th. Tel: 01 43 35 25 81 Open: L and D daily, Tues–Sat mid-July–Aug. **€€**

Another Montparnasse classic from the 1930s, more upscale (and expensive) than in Hemingway's day. Fish is the speciality of the house, and they make a very good bouillabaisse. There's a nice wine list, too, especially the whites.

Enzo

72 rue Daguerre, 14th. Tel: 01 43 21 66 66. Open: L and D Mon–Fri, L only Sat; closed Aug. **€**

Poker-faced Vincenzo Camerino has been feeding the locals for 20 years. Decorated with black-and-white photographs from Italian movies, the tiny restaurant is liveliest at lunchtime, when consistently good paper-thin pizzas, salads, pastas and carpaccios are served.

Try the excellent bouillabaisse at Le Dôme

Les Petites Sorcières

12 rue Liancourt, 14th. Tel: 01 43 21 95 68. Open: L and D Tues–Fri, D only Mon and Sat. **€**

A husband-and-wife team (the husband was formerly at Joël Robuchon's) serve simple classic food with a creative touch in friendly, kitsch surroundings. It's especially good for lunch, with dishes including lentil soup, chicken fricassée and apple tart.

Le 14 juillet il y a toujours des lampions

99 rue Didot, 14th. Tel: 01 40 44 91 19. Open: L and D daily. **€**

This small, friendly restaurant is usually noisy, packed and smoky, but the generous helpings of good, rustic food at a low price are a big draw. The short menu changes frequently, and there's a good range, from pumpkin soup to fish in butter sauce and chocolate mousse.

Sasso

36 rue Raymond-Losserand, 14th. Tel: 01 42 18 00 38. Open: L and D Tues–Sat; closed 2 weeks in Aug and last week in Dec. **€**

A popular recent addition to the neighbourhood, Sasso does good Italian food including grilled vegetables, plenty of pasta and a plat du jour, all for a very fair price. There's also a respectable wine selection.

Le Severo

8 rue des Plantes 14th. Tel: 01 45 40 40 91. Open: L and D Mon–Fri, L only Sat; closed 3 weeks in Aug. **€€**

Warm and welcoming little bistro with a chalkboard list of daily specials, made largely with produce from the Aubrac region in the heart of France. The meat dishes are good, the wine list exceptional.

Above: Je Thé…Me

THE 15TH ARRONDISSEMENT

Paris' largest neighbourhood, this southern area has the Seine River running down its western flank and is delineated by the elevated metro on its northern side. Like the 14th, the 15th was home to many artists in the 1920s and 1930s, and there are now a great number of restaurants here from which to choose.

Chen

15 rue du Théâtre, 15th. Tel: 01 45 79 34 34. Open: L and D Mon–Sat; closed in August. **€€–€€€**

Considered one of Paris's 'Grandes Tables', Chen is located in an incredibly drab building just off the Seine, but the cuisine is excellent quality and a perfect balance between Chinese and French sophistication. A half Peking duck served in three courses and lobster with Szechwan spices are just two of the delicacies served here. Proprietor Mr Chen died recently, but his wife continues to run the restaurant.

C'est Mon Plaisir

8 rue Falguière, 15th. Tel: 01 42 73 07 02. Open: L and D daily. **€**

A lovely, small restaurant serving southern French food with a creative touch. Terrine from Gordes, roast lamb with thyme flowers, or sea bream cooked with mango and lime go perfectly with one of the inexpensive, but carefully selected, local wines.

De la Garde

83 avenue de Ségur, 15th. Tel: 01 40 65 99 10. Open: L and D Mon–Fri, L only Sat, closed 3 weeks in Aug. **€€–€€€**

Bargain prices for exquisite food a cut above the usual modern bistro fare. The kitchen sends out unusual yet earthy dishes with a hint of decadence such as foie gras ravioli, roast skate with rosemary butter and some lip-smacking desserts.

La Dinée

85 rue Leblanc, 15th. Tel: 01 45 54 20 49. Open: L and D Mon–Fri; closed 3 weeks in Aug. **€€**

Talented chef Christophe Chabanel mans the stoves at this elegant neighbourhood bistro putting his very individual stamp on French bistro fare. The prix fixe menus are very reasonably priced for such quality cuisine.

Je Thé… Me

4 rue d'Alleray, 15th. Tel: 01 48 42 48 30. Open: L and D Tues–Sat; closed in Aug. **€**

This restaurant is located in a converted 19th-century grocery store

Chef at Je Thé...Me

on a pretty street with several artists' ateliers nearby. The décor is delightful, and the food (crawfish fricassée, fillet of duck breast with rock salt, or fish stew, etc) is consistently good.

Le Gastroquet

10 rue Desnouettes, 15th. Tel: 01 48 28 60 91. Open: L and D Tues–Fri, D only Mon, closed in Aug. **€€€**

Friendly, if slightly formal, bistro, with a loyal following of local gourmands. Mussel soup, confit de canard, coquilles St-Jacques and other comfortingly familiar dishes are executed with skill, care and the occasional inventive twist.

Le Numide

75 rue Vasco-de-Gama, 15th. Tel: 01 45 32 13 13. Open: L and Mon–Fri, D only Sat; closed Aug. **€**

Come here for Berber and North African food at its best. The owners are welcoming and helpful, and the well-priced food is delicious, particularly the artichoke, fava bean and lamb tagine and the lamb couscous flavoured with oranges and cinnamon.

La Plage

Port de Javel-Haut, 15th. Tel: 01 40 59 41 00. Open: L and D daily. **€€**

During the warm months, this restaurant along the Seine is a good place to watch both river traffic and Parisians. The terrace overlooking the water makes up for a slightly snobbish atmosphere and rather average food. The à la carte menu includes simple main dishes such as saddle of rabbit with vegetables.

Stéphane Martin

67 rue des Entrepreneurs, 15th. Tel: 01 45 9 03 31. Open: L and D Tues–Sat. Closed 3 weeks in Aug. **€€€**

Stéphane Martin's perfectly prepared modern bistro fare, made from fresh seasonal ingredients, coupled with the charming service ensure that his bistro is always full with Parisians in the know. Worth going out of your way for. Reservations advised.

Le Troquet

21 rue François-Bonvin,15th. Tel: 01 45 66 89 00. Open: L and D Tues–Sat; closed 3 weeks in August and last week in December. **€–€€**

A treasure of a bistro, owned by a top chef who concocts divine dishes from the Pyrénées/Basque region at very fair prices. Pleasant staff and good wines sourced from small vineyards.

The 16th Arrondissement

The 16th is a neighbourhood that the hip love to hate, but when it comes to dining, it shouldn't be ignored. Home to several of Paris' *grandes tables* (great dining institutions), it also has a few off-the-beaten track restaurants – and some excellent places for ethnic cuisine.

59 Poincaré/La Terrasse du Parc

59 Poincaré*: 59 avenue Raymond-Poincaré, 16th. Tel: 01 47 27 59 59. Open: L and D Tues–Fri, D only Sat Sept–Apr.* ***La Terrasse du Parc****: 57–9 avenue Raymond-Poincaré, 16th. Tel: 01 44 05 66 10. Open: L and D daily May–mid-July, Tues–Sat mid-July–Sept.* **€€–€€€€**

Alain Ducasse oversees a team that runs one flawless kitchen and both locations, using the first during the winter and La Terrasse in the summer. Fillet of roast duck with tender potatoes, rump steak in a ginger-and-lime sauce and lobster with white beans are brought to the table by a pleasant and efficient staff.

Astrance

4 rue Beethoven, 16th. Tel: 01 40 50 84 40. Open: L and D Tues–Sun. **€€€**

Chef Pascal Barbot is one of the most famous young chefs working in Paris today, producing a worldly, imaginative, state-of-the-art cuisine with a streak of good humour. Specialities include crab and avocado salad with citrus zests and almond oil, toasted bread soup, and pepper and citronella sorbet. It's well worth taking the time to savour the tasting menu. Book a month in advance.

Brasserie de la Poste

54 rue de Longchamp, 16th. Tel: 01 47 55 01 31. Open: L and D daily. **€€**

For a dinner before an outing that will take you late into the night, this small brasserie with friendly staff and very good traditional cooking is ideal. There are nice salads, a gorgeous beef braised with carrots and an array of truly delicious desserts. A great neighbourhood address.

La Cantine Russe

26 avenue de New-York, 16th. Tel: 01 47 20 65 17. Open: L and D Tues–Sat; closed Aug. **€**

Set in the Russian Conservatory (est. 1923), this modestly priced restaurant is a hangout for the Russian community, music students and showbiz types.

Fakhr El Dine

30 rue de Longchamp, 16th. Tel: 01 47 27 90 00. Open: L and D

The vibrant brasserie La Gare (see page 150)

daily, non-stop noon–midnight. **€–€€** *www.fakhreldine.com*
This chic Lebanese restaurant is a fixture in the 16th. Come here for good mezze and grilled meats, plus a nice selection of wines.

La Gare

19 chaussée de la Muette, 16th. Tel: 01 42 15 15 31. Open: L and D daily. **€**
This old train station has been successfully converted into a brasserie and attracts a decidedly bourgeois-bohemian clientele. The upstairs bar is in dark wood and has a terrace overlooking the train tracks; downstairs, the restaurant seats 200 and has another terrace. The food is good French-fusion.

Converted station, La Gare

Kambodgia

15 rue Bassano, 16th. Tel: 01 47 23 31 80. Open: L and D Mon–Fri, D only Sat; closed 3 weeks in Aug. **€–€€**
The French owners are very attentive to the excellent Southeast Asian cuisine served in this dark restaurant best suited to dinner. Coconut and lemongrass soup, honey-coated chicken with lemon, pork in a caramel-and-coconut sauce and ginger-flavoured fish served in a banana leaf are just a few mouth-watering examples.

Le Kiosque

1 place de Mexico, 16th. Tel: 01 47 27 96 98. Open: L and D daily. **€**
The former journalist who owns this attractive restaurant focuses on a different French region each week. Attracts a media-heavy crowd.

Restaurant du Musée du Vin

Rue des Eaux, 5–7 square Charles-Dickens, 16th. Tel: 01 45 25 63 26. Open: L only Tues–Sun; closed last week in Dec. **€** *www.museeduvinparis.com*
Built into one of the many Parisian quarries, the Wine Museum has a small restaurant that is only open for lunch. The wine list is like an encyclopaedia, the menu offers traditional French food, and the cheese platters are impressive.

Le Pré Catelan

Route de Suresnes, Bois de Boulogne, 16th. Tel: 01 44 14 41 14. Open: L and D Tues–Sat; closed 2 weeks late Feb. **€€–€€€€**
The location of this Michelin-starred establishment in the middle of the Bois de Boulogne is one of a kind. In summer, the terrace is lovely, while enormous bouquets of flowers decorate the Art Nouveau dining room in winter. Chef Frédéric Anton joyfully uses ceps and truffles and pays special attention to his luscious desserts. Haute cuisine.

6 New York

6 avenue de New-York, 16th. Tel: 01 40 70 03 30. Open: L and D Mon–Fri, D only Sat; closed 3 weeks in Aug. **€€€**
At this trendy annexe of Apicius, one of Paris' *grandes tables*, chef Jérôme Gangneux serves roast poultry with girolles in a foie gras sauce or creamy risotto with fresh peas, coppa and langoustines. The French toast made with brioche and dulce de leche makes for a lip-smacking dessert.

Le 70

Parc des Princes, 24 rue du Commandant-Guilbaud, 16th. Tel: 01 45 27 05 70. Open: L only Mon–Fri; closed 3 weeks in Aug. **€–€€** *www.le-70-restaurant.com*
Gourmet soccer fans will be in seventh heaven at Le 70, which is located on the grounds of the soccer stadium and features photographs depicting soccer highlights. The talented chef does beef braised with carrots and cumin, veal served with cannelloni, apple sorbet and other culinary delights.

The 17th Arrondissement

The 17th *arrondissement* is a wealthy and, for the most part, conservative district, characterised by wide, tree-lined boulevards, and home to the chic Parc Monceau. The small pocket of streets north of avenue de Villiers is a traditionally working class, now hip and young area known as Batignolles. For restaurants in this area *see pages 128–139*.

Le Bistrot d'à Côté

16 avenue de Villiers, 17th. Tel: 01 47 63 25 61. Open: L and D Mon–Fri, D only Sat. **€** *www.michelrostang.com*

Red and white chequered curtains and well-prepared bistro classics make dining at this, Michel Rostang's annexe, a pleasant, typically French experience. There's a large and varied menu, and swift and friendly service.

Caves Pétrissans

30 bis avenue Niel, 17th. Tel: 01 42 27 52 03. Open: L and D Mon–Fri; closed Aug. **€**

As if preserved in a belle époque timewarp, this 1900 bistro serves wine and more wine, and simple French cooking. Outdoor seating.

L'Entredgeu

83 rue Laugier, 17th. Tel: 01 40 54 97 24. Open: L and D Tues–Sat; closed Aug. **€**

Seemingly situated in the middle of nowhere, l'Entredgeu follows the trend of small bistros offering great food on fixed-price menus. Portions are generous and satisfying – hence it's always packed.

Guy Savoy

18 rue Troyon, 17th. Tel: 01 43 80 36 22. Open: L and D Tues–Fri, D only Sat; closed 3 weeks in Aug. **€€€€** *www.guysavoy.com*

On a small street off place de l'Etoile, this is Guy Savoy's flagship, three-star restaurant. Relaxed elegance and sublime haute cuisine – artichoke and truffle soup or poached and grilled pigeon served with a beetroot millefeuille. Perfect for a long, leisurely lunch or a civilised dinner far from the madding crowd.

Le Troyon

4 rue Troyon, 17th. Tel: 01 40 68 99 40. Open: L and D Mon–Fri. **€€€€**

Young chef Jean-Marc Notelet turns out glorious food at this soothingly minimalist restaurant decked out in beige and wood. The €35 prix fixe menu is good value and the wine list offers inexpensive but superb wines. Excellent service.

Divine French desserts

What to Eat Where

The personality of each neighbourhood is reflected in the type of eating places on offer. On the right bank (from west to east) the areas around the Champs-Elysées, the Louvre and Palais Royal have a high concentration of glamorous fine dining establishments, both traditional and avant-garde, run by high profile, often Michelin-starred chefs. The core of the 8th *arrondissement*, known as the 'Golden Triangle', is a particularly thriving restaurant district, with popular new places. The streets, and the delightful passageways and squares, between the Opéra and Bourse (the Stock Exchange) contain some of the finest bistros in Paris. Just east of the Palais Royal, the commercial centre of Les Halles is a soulless gastronomic desert and should be avoided, though a small network of narrow streets around it are dotted with traditional brasseries that give a sharp reminder of old Paris. The Marais offers a vibrant restaurant scene and overflows with corner cafés, terraced restaurants and trendy bars. A focus for arty media types and the city's gay community, it's the place to come more for a relaxed and casual meal than fine dining. Further east still, the old working class districts of the Bastille and République draw a more bohemian crowd. Though age-old neighbourhood haunts are falling victim to the relentless gentrification process, you can still come across some real, characterful finds, old and new, tucked away down back streets. Further north, up in Montmartre, you should avoid eating in the tourist hub of place du Tertre, but to the south, around place des Abbesses, you will find some lovely restaurants, in particular in rue des Abbesses, rue Véron and rue Lepic.

Over on the Left Bank, the Latin Quarter and Saint-Germain areas have a lot of overpriced restaurants serving uninspiring food, but among the tourist traps are some classy bistros and brasseries, not to mention the iconic pavement cafés, so much a part of Paris's literary history. The aristocratic 7th *arrondissement*, may be home to the Eiffel Tower, but there are surprisingly few touristy places. Between the mansions and ministries are gourmet destinations to suit all price brackets and tastes.

Cafés, bistros and brasseries

Cafés occupy every street corner of Paris and range from the tiny, tatty neighbourhood haunt to the spacious and refined with *belle époque* interior and acres of seating inside and out. As a rule, cafés are good for casual lunches on the go, offering French-style sandwiches (a lot of baguette and a little filling), omelettes, toasted cheese and ham sandwiches (croque-monsieur, or – with an egg on top – croque-madame) and other snacks. The daily specials, or plats du jour, are not the bargain they once were, but in most cases they are still a comparatively cheap deal. A café breakfast of milky coffee or hot chocolate with a croissant, pain au chocolat or freshly baked baguette served with little pots of unsalted butter and jam, is one of the greatest pleasures the city has to offer, particularly if it's on a terrace in fine weather. Unless you like your tea luke warm and exceedingly weak, it's best avoided in cafés. For a decent cuppa, seek out one of the city's many fine tea rooms *(see pages 126–7)*.

Brasseries offer more substantial meals than cafés. They are usually large, bustling places with an extensive menu, and serve food throughout the day and well into the night. Many serve Alsatian specialities, such as choucroute and steins of beer; others specialise in shellfish.

Where brasseries are spacious and clamorous, bistros are more intimate, serving traditional French fare, usually at modest prices. A number of bistros have a regional bent, proudly boasting their provincial specialities. In Auvergnat bistros, think blue cheese, potatoes, walnuts, and superb beef; with Southwestern bistros, it's foie gras and duck; Basque flavours include hot pepper, salt cod and ham; and Provençal bistros guarantee ratatouille, lamb and bouillabaisse.

Ethnic cuisine

North African restaurants are probably the best represented in the French capital, offering emblematic dishes like couscous and tagine (braised meat, often with preserved lemons and dried fruits). Japanese restaurants of the fast-food variety have all but taken over the 1st *arrondissement*, in and around the rue des Petits Champs. For cheap Vietnamese, head for the Porte d'Italie neighbourhood, not far from the student stomping grounds in the Latin Quarter. For Indian food, explore the 10th *arrondissement* around the Gare du Nord. African food is found in Belleville. And good Lebanese food is dotted all over.

Opening Hours

Most restaurants serve lunch between midday and 2.30pm, but they are at their busiest between 1 and 2pm. In the evening, restaurants open around 8pm, but the French tend not to go out to eat before 8.45pm, and much later in trendier places. Despite these hours, most kitchens close early, so a 10pm dinner reservation would be stretching it, although more popular restaurants may have two sittings, at 8pm and 10pm. If you want a meal outside these eating times, try a brasserie or a café, the majority of which serve at almost any hour. Opening times do vary though, so it's always best to call before setting out.

Reservations

You rarely have to book for lunch, but dinner is another matter. The more fashionable places can be booked up weeks, or even months, in advance. So to avoid disappointment it's best to reserve, especially for weekends.

The Menu

Good-value, fixed-price menus are common in fine restaurants and in simple eating places alike, but better restaurants tend to offer them only at lunch. If you plan on ordering the fixed menu in the evening, read it carefully to make sure that the words déjeuner seulement (lunch only) are not included. The more upmarket restaurants offer a menu dégustation (tasting menu) and usually everyone at the table must order it to make it worthwhile, as it involves serving numerous courses and is difficult to orchestrate when some people at the table have ordered a simple three-course meal. French wine is, of course, the perfect accompaniment to French food *(see pages 110-111)*.

Alternatively, or additionally, you can order mineral water, sparkling or not (gazeuse or non gazeuse). Beer is drunk only with sandwiches, with simple meals such as steak frites, as a thirst quencher, or with Alsatian meals in brasseries. Cider served in an earthenware bowl is the traditional accompaniment to savoury crêpes, the Breton speciality. Coffee is never served with milk after a meal in France, unless specifically requested. This said, decaffeinated coffee (café décaféiné, déca for short) is available everywhere. A wide range of digestifs (after-dinner drinks) are available in even the most ordinary of cafés, from the roughest of brandies to the smoothest of cognacs.

Prices

Eating out in Paris is no longer the bargain it was; with the introduction of the euro in 2002, many restaurateurs hiked up their prices. A three-course meal with wine for one in an ordinary bistro is around €30, while the same thing in a fashionable bistro can come to €50; a similar meal in an haute cuisine restaurant can cost around €200. The best value at the upmarket places is provided by a set lunch (le menu du jour or prix fixe), at around €120. The prices given here *(see page 3)* are intended as guidelines only.

If you're just having a drink, remember that the price varies according to where you are sitting; it's cheapest to sit or stand at the bar, more at a table, and the most expensive to sit outside (that said, it's usually worth paying the few extra euro for the view and people-watching potential).

Service charge and tipping

A service charge of 12–15 percent is by law included in the price given at restaurants, bars and cafés, so you don't have to tip. However, it is polite when paying for drinks to round up the total, and to leave €1–5 after a meal, depending on the service.

Credit Cards

Most restaurants take credit cards, but there are a few cafés and bistros which do not, so check first.

Dress

As the world knows, Parisians dress with style; if you are going to an upmarket restaurant, you too should make an effort to look good, or you may not get a table. For men, this usually means jacket and tie.

Waiters

Waiting staff in Paris have a reputation for being brusque and intimidating. But while they may be surly, they are professionals and most take their job seriously. If you have a little French, don't be afraid to ask their advice on the menu, particularly the plat du jour (dish of the day) and the wine list. *(See also the Menu Reader on pages 12–15.)*

Public Transport

Paris is a relatively compact city, and the best way to appreciate it is on foot. That said, the métro (underground) system is clean and efficient. Stations are clearly marked on the individual maps in this book, and with the help of the métro map at the back, you can work out your route. The métro operates from 5.30am until around 12.30am. The lines are identified by numbers, colours and the names of their terminals, so Line 1 running east is shown as Château de Vincennes, and going west as La Défense. To change lines, look for the orange *correspondance* signs. The métro runs in conjunction with the RER – suburban express trains.

The métro and the buses use the same tickets – you can buy a book or *carnet* of 10 from bus or métro stations and some *tabacs* (tobacconists), which offers a considerable saving. Other options are the Paris Visite card, valid for one, two, three or five consecutive days or, for shorter stays, the Mobilis card, which allows an unlimited number of trips for a day on the métro, bus, suburban SNCF, RER and the night buses.

Buses tend to be slow because of the traffic, but they do allow you to see the city. Tickets can be bought from the driver or at métro stations, as buses take the same tickets as the trains. Remember to punch your ticket (but not your travel card) into the *composteur*. Most buses run from 6.30am to 8.30pm, although some routes continue until 12.30am. For more information on public transport, contact www.ratp.fr.

Taxis

Hailing a taxi in Paris is not as easy as in London or New York; you may have to order one (ask at your hotel) or find a taxi rank. Official taxis have a light on the roof; if the taxi is free, it will be white, and if the taxi is occupied, the light shines orange.

Food Shops

Bakeries/Boulangeries

L'Autre Boulanger *(43 rue de Montreuil, 11th)* Don't be fooled by the grim location; this boulangerie sells the most delicious organic bread, cooked in its own wood-fired oven.

Gosselin *(123–5 rue St-Honoré, 1st)*

Julien *(75 rue St-Honoré, 1st)*

Two of the best boulangeries in Paris.

Maison Poujauran *(18–20 rue Jean-Nicot, 7th)* A tiny and very pretty bakery dating back to the late 19th century selling some of the best baguettes and biscuits (sablés) in Paris.

Rose Bakery *(46 rue des Martyrs, 9th)* You can try English cakes and specialities here.

Cheese/Fromageries

Marie-Anne Cantin *(12 rue du Champ-de-Mars, 7th)* The eponymous owner is a passionate defender of 'real' (ie. unpasteurised) cheeses.

Fromagerie Molard *(48 rue des Martyrs, 9th)* A fine and varied selection of perfectly aged cheeses.

Fromagerie de Montmartre *(9 rue du Poteau, 18th)* Vintage cheese shop in a food-obsessed street.

Delicatessens/Traiteurs

L'Ambassade du Sud-Ouest *(46 avenue de la Bourdonnais, 7th)* This restaurant and food shop specialises in the cuisine of southwest France, offering cassoulet, confit de canard, Basque pipérade, foie gras...

Charcuterie Lyonnaise *(58 rue des Martyrs, 9th)* An astounding variety of sausages and saucisson, including one flavoured with pistachio.

Davoli *(34 rue Cler, 7th)* An Italian-style traiteur specialising in ham; they also prepare French classics like pot-au-feu to take away.

Fauchon *(26–30 place de la Madeleine, 8th)* One of France's best-known and best-loved delis, with a ready-made food section, cheese, fish and exotic fruit counters, an Italian deli, fine wines, chocolates and more.

La Fermerie *(24 rue Surcouf, 7th)* French regional specialities such as rabbit with summer vegetables sold in jars; you can try before you buy.

Frascati *(14 rue de Turenne, 4th)* An Italian delicatessen selling ready-made meals and all things Italian.

La Grande Epicerie de Paris *(38 rue de Sèvres, 7th)* All your finest food fantasies, at the Bon-Marché store.

Hédiard *(21 place de la Madeleine, 8th)* Dating from 1880, Hédiard was the first to introduce exotic foods to the Parisians. It specialises in rare teas and coffees, unusual spices, jams, candied fruits and imported produce, all beautifully packaged.

Pasta Linea *(9 rue de Turenne, 4th)* Heavenly pasta dishes to eat in or take away, plus the best dried pasta.

Le Suprême du Marais *(75 rue Amelot, 11th)* A vast array of charcuterie, as well as excellent pâtés.

Cakes/Pâtisseries

Aoki Sadaharu *(35 rue Vaugirard, 6th)* This Japanese pastry chef makes subtle and imaginative cakes resembling precious jewels.

Delmontel *(39 rue des Martyrs, 9th)* A favourite with the locals of Montmartre.

Finkelsztajn *(27 rue des Rosiers, 4th)* Poppy-seed cakes, halva, apple strudel and delicious rye bread are available at this Jewish pâtisserie and grocers; they also do good falafels. Also at 24 rue des Ecouffes.

Les Petits Mitrons *(26 rue Lepic, 18th)* Wonderful French pastries, in particular its sublime tartes aux fruits.

Pierre Hermé *(72 rue Bonaparte, 6th)* Elaborate cakes and chocolates made by a superstar pâtissier.

Stohrer *(51 rue Montorgueil, 2nd)* One of the oldest and most famous pâtisseries in Paris.

La Tour des Délices *(Passage Jouffroy, 9th)* Mouthwatering cakes in a 19th-century shopping arcade.

Chocolate/Chocolatiers

Debauve & Gallais *(33 rue Vivienne, 2nd, and 30 rue des Saints-Pères, 7th)* Exclusive chocolate from a company dating back to the time of Louis XVI.
Le Lutin Gourmand *(47 rue Cler, 7th)* Fine chocolates and 100 types of tea blended on the premises.
Maison du Chocolat *(8 boulevard de la Madeleine, 1st)* One of five branches in the city offering delicious creations.
A la Mère de Famille *(35 rue du Faubourg-Montmartre, 9th)* Chocolate and sweet shop founded in 1761, famous for its fabulous vintage décor and old-fashioned bonbons
Michel Chaudon *(149 rue de l'Université, 7th)* The eponymous chocolatier is famous for his truffles.

Ice Cream/Glaces

Berthillon *(31 rue St-Louis-en-l'Ile, 4th)* Legendary ice-cream makers; look for the queues onto the street.

Wine shops/Vin

Les Caves Taillevent *(199 rue du Faubourg St-Honoré, 8th)* A vast stock and range of prices; daily tastings.
Idea Vino *(88 avenue Parmentier, 11th)* An Italian wine shop which sells non-perishable food from Italy too.
Lavinia *(3–5 boulevard de la Madeleine, 1st)* Wines from all over the world, and knowledgeable staff. Also sells books on wine (many in English) and has a restaurant.
Legrand Filles et Fils *(1 rue de la Banque, 2nd)* An old-fashioned shop selling fine wines, tea, coffee, bonbons, glasses and wine-related gadgets.
Noé L'Antiquaire du Vin *(12 rue Surcouf, 7th)* The place to go for rare vintages, some over 100 years old.
Le Verre Volé *(38 rue Oberkampf, 11th)* Fine wine shop representing small producers.

Specialist Shops

Allicante *(26 boulevard Beaumarchais, 11th)* Oil in all its glory, including award-winning olive oil, nut, seed and truffle oils, and even oil extracted from apricot, peach and avocado stones.
Bières Spéciales *(77 rue Saint-Maur, 11th)* A wide selection of beers from over 15 countries.
Boutique Maille *(6 place de la Madeleine, 8th)* This is heaven for lovers of mustard, selling full range of Maille's condiments.
Le Comptoir Colonial *(22 rue Lepic, 18th)* Filled with exotic Creole delicacies; a delight to the senses.
Dionysus *(61 rue Oberkampf, 11th)* A good Greek grocers.
Goumanyat *(3 rue Dupuis, 3rd)* A beautiful upmarket spice shop, specialising in saffron.
Graineterie du Marché *(8 place d'Aligre, 12th)* A tiny shop selling pulses and grains of all kinds – beans, lentils, peanuts, and even birdseed.
Izraël *(30 rue François-Miron, 4th)* An Aladdin's cave, stuffed with interesting pickles, oils, preserved lemons, nougat and spices from all over the world.
La Maison de la Truffe *(19 place de la Madeleine, 8th)* A temple to the exclusive – and expensive – truffle; oils, sauces and the real thing when in season (Nov–Mar). Also has a small restaurant.
Maison du Miel *(24 rue Vignon, 9th)* A wide range of honey from sources all over the world, plus bee-related products such as royal jelly.
Mariage Frères *(30 rue du Bourg-Tibourg, 4th)* Some 500 types of tea, as well as every imaginable accessory to make the perfect cuppa.
Thanksgiving *(13 rue Charles V, 4th)* Providing a little taste of home to American expats and tourists, this shop sells everything from measuring cups to mini marshmallows.

A–Z of Restaurants

Bistros

Brasseries

Cafés

Contemporary

Haute Cuisine

Regional

Vegetarian

International

A–Z of Bars and Pubs